Nationalism and Society

Nationalism and Society
Germany 1800–1945

Michael Hughes
Lecturer in History, University College of Wales,
Aberystwyth

Edward Arnold
A division of Hodder & Stoughton
LONDON   BALTIMORE   MELBOURNE   AUCKLAND

© 1988 Michael Hughes

First published in Great Britain 1988

British Library Cataloguing Publication Data

Hughes, Michael
  Nationalism and society: Germany 1800−1945
  1. Germany − Politics and government − 19th century
  2. Germany − Politics and government − 20th century
  I. Title
  943.08   DD204

ISBN 0 7131 6522 7

Typeset in Linotron Palatino by Setrite Typesetters Limited.
Printed and bound in Great Britain for Edward Arnold, the
educational, academic and medical publishing division of
Hodder and Stoughton Limited, 41 Bedford, Square, London
WC1B 3DQ by Richard Clay Ltd, Bungay, Suffolk

Contents

Abbreviations   vi

Foreword   vii

1   Introduction   1

2   Nationalism: Sentiment and Action   8

3   Germany before 1815: Rebirth of a Nation?   30

4   Germany 1815−1850: The Rise and Fall of
    Liberal Nationalism   55

5   The Partition of the Nation 1850−1871   101

6   The Fractured Nation: Germany 1871−1914   130

7   The Lost Children: German Nationalism in
    Austria 1866−1914   164

8   The Nation Betrayed: The First World War
    and the Revolution of 1918   175

9   The Cold Civil War: German Nationalism in
    the Weimar Republic   189

10 National Socialism: The Apotheosis of
    Nationalism?   206

11 Nationalism in the Germanies since 1945   219

Index   235

Maps

1   The German Confederation in 1815   56
2   The Unification of Germany 1867−71   126
3   Germany Divided post-1945   218

Abbreviations

Am.H.R.	American Historical Review
Cent.Eur.H.	Central European History
Ec.H.R.	Economic History Review
Eur.Stud.Rev.	European Studies Review
Eur.Stud.Q.	European Studies Quarterly
HJ	Historical Journal
J.Cont. H.	Journal of Contemporary History
J.Hist. Id.	Journal of the History of Ideas
JMH	Journal of Modern History
P. and P.	Past and Present
Pol. Sc. Q.	Political Science Quarterly

Foreword

I acknowledge with grateful thanks the great help given me by the staff of the library of the German Historical Institute, London, and the Hugh Owen Library, Aberystwyth. I also acknowledge the generosity of the University College of Wales in allowing me study leave in the third term of the 1986–7 session to complete the manuscript. Without the help and encouragement of my wife and son and my friends Dr and Mrs J. Marek and Dr and Mrs J. Hoare it would not have been finished so quickly. It is dedicated to the memory of William.

Michael Hughes
September 1987

1

Introduction

This is a study of nationalism in the nineteenth and twentieth centuries, based on the German experience. The aim is to supplement the many excellent general histories available[1] by offering an interpretation centred on the theme of nationalism. It also seeks to offer an interpretation of modern German history which is not rooted in the nationalistic legends coined by Treitschke and others after the unification of 1871. The so-called 'German problem' has become the object of considerable research in recent decades, a by-product of investigation of events in Germany in the years between 1933 and 1945, probably the most intensively studied 12 years in history. Attempts to finds the roots of National Socialism have led historians backwards into the *Kaiserreich* established by Bismarck in 1871 and there is now a massive literature on the period 1871 to 1918. The periods 1815 to 1848 and 1850 to 1866 have received less attention. There has been a major historical debate on the question of continuity in German history since the publication in 1946 of Friedrich Meinecke's *The German Catastrophe*, an English translation of which appeared in 1950.[2] It is still continuing and has produced some very ill-tempered exchanges in historical journals and at international historical conferences. The approach adopted by historians has sometimes been coloured by their own political views and opinions are so polarized as to justify the description of the debate as 'stultified by controversy'. At the risk of accusations of 'myopic antiquarianism' or 'woolly-minded empiricism', this work will try to offer a more objective view.

The 'German question' or 'German problem' is complex, involving as it does diplomatic, constitutional and social issues. It is a European as well as a German issue. As traditionally interpreted, it centres on the question of German unification in the nineteenth century, the attempt to find a suitable political framework for

[1]H. Holborn, *A History of Modern Germany*: II 1648–1840, III 1840–1945 (1965); W. Carr, *A History of Germany 1815–1985* (3rd edn, 1987); E. Sagarra, *An Introduction to Nineteenth-Century Germany* (1981); G.A. Craig, *Germany 1866–1945* (Oxford, 1978) and *The Germans* (1984); J.C.G. Röhl, *From Bismarck to Hitler. The Problem of Continuity in German History* (1970); A.J. Ryder, *Twentieth Century Germany: From Bismarck to Brandt* (1973); W. Conze, *The Shaping of the German Nation. A Historical Analysis* (1979); F. Hertz, *The German Public Mind in the Nineteenth Century* (ed. F. Eyck) (1975).
[2]F. Meinecke, *Die deutsche Kastrophe* (Wiesbaden, 1946).

some 70 million people, the largest nationality in Western Europe, who are said to have needed or wanted some measure of political unity but who, for centuries, had lived in separate states. Thanks to their long possession of real political power, the states enjoyed a legitimacy the nation lacked.

The aim is to investigate the role of an idea, in this case the concept of the nation, in forming political behaviour. An attempt will be made to show how the political behaviour of groups in German society came to be influenced by ideas deriving from the concept of the German nation, first in terms of the creation of a single political entity including the nation and later of attempts to realize visions of an ideal Germany in a political framework. The effects of nationalism on German politics and society and on Germany's relations with her neighbours will be examined. The second is important because the 'German problem' always had an important European dimension: since the sixteenth century the Continent had become used to a weak 'Germanic space' at its centre. Any alteration of this situation would change the European balance of power.[3]

This study is not a *histoire des mentalités* but a chronological account of events in Germany from about 1800 to the present tracing the emergence of nationalism as a movement, or a collection of movements, and its impact on the politics of German states. It will seek to challenge the traditional view that nationalism was one of the great formative influences of the modern age, a spontaneous mass movement which arose in the aftermath of the French Revolution and continued to play a major role in the politics of the nineteenth century. The early nineteenth century was *not*, as some historians would have us believe, the age of nationalism.[4] Rather nationalism was characteristic of the increased leisure and improved material life-styles, enjoyed at least by the middle classes, and the age of mass politics in the later nineteenth century. This account posits that, at least until the last quarter of the century, nationalism was a minority movement, deeply divided and with only a marginal impact on German political life. There was never in Germany a single nationalist movement; there were always several different strands. These divisions continued even when mass nationalism emerged after 1871, partly as a result of economic and social changes and partly as a result of deliberate government policies. Radically

[3]'The force that three times turned Europe upside down was German nationalism': MacGregor Knox's introduction in Carole Fink *et al* (eds.), *German Nationalism and the European Response* (Norman, Oklahoma, 1985), p.4.
[4]For example L.W. Cowie and R. Wolfson, *Years of Nationalism. European History 1815–1890* (1985).

different views of what form the ideal Germany should take prevailed among the German people and this contributed to the serious polarization of the nation, which was, ironically, one of the consequences of the supposed national unification of 1871.

Some definition of nationalism is required and will be attempted in Chapter 2, though this book is in no sense intended as a theoretical treatise and offers no new definitions of a phenomenon so Protean in its manifestations as to defy precise definition. The word is often used as a convenient shorthand term for an extremely complex and variable phenomenon which can exist in a great variety of different forms in a single society, as was the case in Germany during the period we shall be looking at. Although it will be necessary to show how the sentiment of community central to nationalism developed, nationalism will not be examined as an intellectual movement and there will be no detailed analysis of the writings of nationalist authors. In connection with nationalism the use of the term 'intellectual' is anyway questionable. Original concepts put forward by philosophers in the course of their intellectual investigations have been taken over and refashioned by nationalists, often being perverted out of all recognition in the process. Nationalism has proved an easy and undemanding basis for a political system. Like religious faiths, which it resembles in some respects, it provides ready-made answers to problems and many nationalist publicists and politicians have been depressingly second-rate.[5] Nationalism has the great advantage that it enables people to identify with supposedly higher and more spiritual things without making any great demands on their intellect. There is a considerable danger not only of predating the emergence of nationalism as a significant movement but also of overestimating the influence exercised by nationalist propagandists and politicians. The problem with too many investigations of the emergence of nationalism is that they rely on the pronouncements of nationalist writers. It is very difficult to find reliable evidence on the impact of their ideas on the mass of 'ordinary' people but there has been a tendency to exaggerate it in the past.

It will be argued that in the course of the nineteenth century the fundamental nature of German nationalism changed or rather that

---

[5]R.S. Peters, 'Hegel and the Nation State', in D. Thomson (ed.), *Political Ideas* (1966), p. 132: 'Unfortunately, too, it was the expanded version of [Hegel's] ... ideas, rather than their solid centres that, historically speaking, exerted the most influence'. Nationalist enthusiasm can elbow aside obvious realities. The Italian international jurist Pasquale Mancini claimed in 1851 that the nation not the state was the basis of international law. This was not so then and has never been the case since. M.S. Korowicz, *Introduction to International Law* (The Hague, 1964), p. 283.

one form of it was displaced, as the most important manifestation, by another. As a recognizable phenomenon it emerged at the time of the French Revolution. It was a product of the same developments around the turn of the eighteenth to the nineteenth century which eventually produced, among other things, modern democracy: the decline of 'feudalism', the emergence of the bourgeoisie and the politicization of the masses. At first the two movements, nationalism and democratization, seemed to be progressing together hand in hand. In its predominant form in early-nineteenth-century Germany nationalism was associated with political Liberalism and was liberating in its intentions. It was deeply optimistic, even Utopian, and envisaged a society of individuals enjoying the classic Liberal freedoms and an international community of free nations without restraints on their liberty. As a result of the triumph of Liberal nationalism, all the ills which afflicted mankind — war, ignorance, disease and poverty — would disappear. It first became clear that there was an incompatibility between the achievement of individual freedom and the attainment of German national goals in the course of the revolutions of 1848.

The failure of the revolution of 1848—9 and the manner in which Germany was 'unified' in 1871 produced an identity crisis, as the German state which emerged was a '*Reich* without a nation' (*Reich ohne Nation*). It was unable to produce a sense of unity and collective identity among its citizens and, as a result, it was never accepted as legitimate by many Germans. The 'unification' of 1871 was achieved as a result of international politics; nationalism, in any form, played an extremely marginal role. The description of the creation of the *Reich* as the 'unification' of Germany is inaccurate: it was in fact a division of the German nation. Ironically, the creation of the *Reich* did lead to the emergence of mass nationalisms but it did nothing to promote the unity of the German people. Almost from its beginning, the *Reich* was seen by some as a fragile and precarious structure and its brief existence saw the deep division and polarization of the German *Volk*. Nationalist movements were able to mobilize large numbers of people but were unable to integrate them because of divergent social interests. Soon the new German government discovered that nationalism was a useful instrument of political control and manipulation. The masses were to be involved and their political consciousness increased but not in the cause of their own liberation. Nationalism worked in the cause of national unity and power, not the freedom of the individual. Once national unity became the highest goal, everything else became subordinate to this. The nation was seen as having rights superior to those of individuals and as possessing a freedom of action and a freedom from moral restraints more complete than those claimed by the dynastic states of the eighteenth century. *Raison d'état national* was more absolute than the traditional form. The nation was seen as being able to do whatever it thought necessary in its own interests. It could not be subjected to restraints of morality as it was held to represent the highest morality: 'my country, right or wrong'. Such views were widespread and enjoyed great intellectual respectability in Germany after 1871, though they were not allowed to exist without challenge from opponents of this extreme nationalism. There *were* democratic nationalists in Germany but they suffered defeat after defeat.

By the accession of William II in 1888 various forms of the movement were active in German political life and by the end of the century the most vigorous form of German nationalism was a force of the political Right, mobilized and manipulated against 'international' forces like Liberalism, Socialism and democracy. The idealism that was always an element in nationalism began to become dominant in the late nineteenth century, with growing rejection of the real world and a search for a perfect Germany. A deficient appreciation of realities was to be a major problem among sections of the German intelligentsia and political élites.

A different form of nationalism was also adopted by groups who were profoundly dissatisfied with the Germany in which they lived and who refused to see it as true expression of the essence of the nation. They put forward a new vision of an ideal Germany, derived partly from Romantic notions long circulating in intellectual circles. The nation was no longer seen, as earlier, as a free association of people united by history, blood or language but as a spiritual entity, possessed of a mystical force of its own and greater than the sum total of the individuals of which it was composed. The individual could no longer choose whether or not he was a member of the nation but had become the prisoner of a relentless biological determinism. The nation was a community of blood and much more: full members of it had to share a common vision of the future.

Briefly, in August 1914 the German nation experienced unprecedented unity. The shattering of this unity and Germany's defeat restored the pre-war divisions in an even more acute form. One result was the emergence of Adolf Hitler, promising a National Revolution which would restore permanent unity to a German nation racially and spiritually cleansed and more truly German. The disastrous failure of this vision appears to have destroyed German nationalism.

It might be argued that such a development, the mutation of nationalism into something dangerous, is inherent in it, however liberating its original dynamic: whatever its origins, nationalism inevitably leads to some kind of imperialism or fascism, threatening peace between states and freedom within states.[6] This is open to serious question, if only because nationalism is so variable a phenomenon. In addition, German nationalism differed in many important respects from other nationalisms in Europe.

A factor which makes a study of German nationalism difficult from the outset is that the Germans have systematically distorted their own history, particularly since 1871. They are certainly not unique in this respect but German history seems particularly prone to persistent myths. The Borussian legend, created after the unification of 1871, has been very resilient and echoes of it can still be found in some English-language accounts of German history, though it has been largely eliminated from German historiography. The legend posits that it was Prussia's destiny to lead and unify Germany, at least from the seventeenth century on. The whole of German history from the reign of the Great Elector to 1871 could be portrayed as the inexorable rise of Prussia to fulfil this mission and everything else could be written off as irrelevant. Even when it was demonstrated that Prussia did not have a German mission, it was held that, in pursuing its own narrow state interests, Prussia had unconsciously served all-German interests.

The Borussian myth was itself a variant of the German equivalent of the Whig theory of history, which sees German history in terms of state-building, applied first to individual states, especially Prussia, and then to the creation of a German nation-state. The absence, or virtual absence, for centuries of a single German state and the persistence of loyalty to the 'narrow fatherland' (*enges Vaterland* or *Heimat*), the individual state like Prussia or Bavaria or a smaller region, alongside the greater but more remote German fatherland, were also important factors in the development of this approach to Germany's past.

Another myth is the nationalist legend, which places excessive emphasis on the power of ideas in bringing about change in society, in this case in the power of the idea of the nation to cause the unification of Germany, and the power of intellectual élites to determine the course of events. The nationalist myth also holds that the creation of the *Reich* in 1871 was progressive and desirable, the logical culmination of previous developments, especially

---

[6]Hans Kohn, *The Idea of Nationalism* (New York, 1945), pp. 575–6; O. Pflanze, 'Characteristics of Nationalism in Europe 1848–1871', *Review of Politics* 28(1966), pp. 129–43. A view of nationalism as an incurable disease can also be found in Tom Nairn, *The Break-Up of Britain* (2nd edn, 1981), p. 359; H. Glaser, *The Cultural Roots of National Socialism* (1978); and the anarchist view of nationalism, R. Rocker, *Nationalism and Culture* (Stillwater, 1978). The view that German nationalism changed in this way has recently been restated: G.L. Mosse, 'Friendship and Nationhood: About the Promise and Failure of German Nationalism', *J. Cont.H.* 17 (1982), pp. 351–67.

the supposed growth of German nationalism. One aim of this work is to demonstrate that this view is erroneous. The *Reich* was not the product of German nationalism but was designed to frustrate it.

Traditionally there has been excessive emphasis on the role of personalities in modern German history, especially Bismarck and William II in the nineteenth century. Both were struggling to work an unworkable system, the product of a society strapped into an outdated political and social framework while in the full flood of industrialization. Bismarck's 'achievement' in particular needs fundamental reassessment. His opportunistic exploitation of nationalism was deeply damaging to Germany and in 1890 he handed over to his successors a country with serious problems. Germany suffered from the difficulties of chronic partial modernization, which were to afflict it until the middle of the twentieth century. After 1871 the gap between the German government and German society widened steadily. Nationalism was to act as another dangerous ingredient in a very unpleasant brew.

The concept of 'Germany' changed during the period to be examined. As will be shown, the idea of a nation contains a large element of self-definition. At its widest 'Germany' is taken to mean the area inhabited by people who spoke German dialects and whose governments conducted administration in High German. This excludes those like the Swiss Germans, whose communities had consciously excluded themselves from the German nation, or those, like the Transylvanian 'Saxons', who lived in isolated pockets distant from the German heartland. It includes areas with non-German populations ruled by German governments, like the Polish provinces of eastern Prussia. Until 1806 the Germans had a political framework in the form of the Holy Roman Empire. After the collapse of the Empire a united Germany, in reality, only existed under the Confederation (*Bund*) from 1815 to 1849 and 1850 to 1866 and in Hitler's Greater Germany (*Grossdeutschland*) from 1938 to 1945. From 1806 to 1815, from 1849 to 1850 and from 1866 to 1938 there was no 'Germany' in the form of a single political framework including the whole nation and this has been the situation since 1945.[7] The German nation now seems to be irreversibly divided into separate states and there is no evidence of any great desire among the majority of Germans to change this. If German nationalism has been a powerful force, it has also been remarkably unsuccessful.

---

[7]This division has not always caused problems for the Germans: *Meyers Grosses Konversations-Lexikon* (Leipzig, 1888), a kind of popular encyclopedia, stated in volume 14, under *Nation*, that, just as a single state can be made up of people of different nationalities, so one nationality can be divided into several states: 'For many nations, for example the Germans, are strong enough to provide material for several states.'

2

Nationalism: Sentiment and Action

It would perhaps be advisable at this point to attempt to define nationalism before considering its development in Germany. There is a vast literature on the topic and wide divergence of opinion as to its nature.[1] So far no satisfactory comprehensive explanatory theory has been put forward and indeed it is hard to see how a phenomenon which has changed so much over time and which has appeared in so many different forms can be reduced to defined criteria. The focus of attention has changed over the years. Many early studies concentrated on the idea of nationalism and the development of the concept of the nation in the writings of nationalist publicists.[2] Since 1945 there has been considerable sociological research into nationalism and nation-state building as political/social movements.[3] Some of the products of these new approaches are marked by an egregious abstruseness of language; nationalism theory has become something of a quagmire, deep and muddy, frequently not worth the struggle.

All commentators seem agreed that the nation is a concept of unity, which can be based on a large range of different criteria, among which a common language or culture is the most frequently

[1]H.A. Winkler and T. Schnabel (eds.), *Bibliographie zum Nationalismus* (Göttingen, 1979). A bibliography in English: K.W. Deutsch and R.L. Merritt (eds.), *Nationalism and National Development. An Interdisciplinary Bibliography* (Cambridge, Mass., 1970). Recommended starting places for a study of nationalism: H. Seton-Watson, *Nations and States. An Enquiry into the Origins of Nations and the Politics of Nationalism* (1982); E. Kedourie, *Nationalism* (1961); Royal Institute of International Affairs, *Nationalism* (report of a working party chaired by E.H. Carr) (1939); L.L. Snyder (ed.), *The Dynamics of Nationalism. Readings in its Meaning and Development* (collected extracts) (Princeton, 1964); E. Gellner, *Nations and Nationalism* (Oxford, 1983); H. Kohn, *The Mind of Germany. The Education of a Nation* (1962); F. Meinecke, *Cosmopolitanism and the National State* (Princeton, 1970); F. Hertz, *Nationality in History and Politics. A Psychology and Sociology of National Sentiment and Nationalism* (1944); R. Weltsch, 'Hans Kohn on Nationalism', *Orbis* 10 (1967), pp. 1310–26; K. Minogue *Nationalism* (1967); R.M. Berdahl, 'New Thoughts on German Nationalism', *Am.H.R.* 77 (1972), pp. 65–80.
[2]C.J. Hayes, *The Historical Evolution of Modern Nationalism* (repr. New York, 1968) and *Essays on Nationalism* (New York, 1926); H. Kohn, *The Idea of Nationalism* (New York, 1945), *The Age of Nationalism* (New York, 1962) and *Nationalism: Its Meaning and History* (Princeton, 1965); L.L. Snyder, *German Nationalism. The Tragedy of a People* (Harrisburg, 1952), *Varieties of Nationalism* (Hinsdale, Ill., 1976) and *Roots of German Nationalism* (Bloomington, 1978); B.C. Shafer, *Nationalism. Myth and Reality* (New York, 1955).
[3]K.W. Deutsch, *Nationalism and Social Communication* (Cambridge, Mass., 2nd edn, 1966); C. Tilly (ed.), *The Formation of National States in Western Europe* (Princeton, 1973); L. Tivey (ed.), *The Nation State* (Oxford, 1981); J. Breuilly, *Nationalism and the State* (Manchester, 1982); Anthony Smith, *Theories of Nationalism* (1971) and *The Ethnic Origins of Nations* (1986).

mentioned. Other criteria could be added: common adherence to a constitution or an ideology, common subjection to a dynasty, a shared historical experience, for example in nations like Australia, Canada or the USA, or religion, such as in Israel or Pakistan. The nation would seem to need four essential ingredients: it must possess a defined territory or desire one, there must be criteria by which members of the nation are distinguished from non-members, there must be a consciousness of membership of a community with some realistic basis of unity and there must be a desire to be independent and self-determined. In addition there is usually a consciousness of some special value or mission which all members of the nation share.

Broadly, there are two views about the origins of national sentiment. One starts from the premise that the sentiment of nationality is essentially spontaneous, unforced and, in some sense, voluntary. According to this school of thought there must be some basis of common sentiment shared by the members of the nation, a national consciousness rooted so far back in the past as to be as good as natural. Nations are not artificial but organic. Only the nation, it is argued, develops naturally from the growth of the human community and must have some basis in reality. Governments can help to foster it by propaganda, the education system, compulsory military service or the media but these alone are not enough. Nations therefore form the only legitimate basis for political organization; all others are doomed to failure because they are fundamentally unnatural.[4] For Mazzini (1805−72), one of the fathers of modern idealistic nationalism, the nation fulfilled the need for something between the individual, who was too small, and the whole of humanity, which was too large.[5] Among the dozens of definitions offered since 1800, the following two will illustrate this view. Professor Pasquale Mancini, in his inaugural lecture on 'Nationality as the Basis of International Law' at Turin in 1851 defined it as

> a natural community of people with a common territory and common origins, customs and language, united for a common life and common social awareness.

[4]Kedouri, *Nationalism*; W.J. Mommsen, 'Power Politics, Imperialism and National Emancipation 1870−1914', in T.W. Moody (ed.), *Nationality and the Pursuit of National Independence* (Belfast, 1978): 'The process of national emancipation must be considered the dominant feature of nineteenth-century European history.' Benedict Anderson in *Imagined Communities* (1983), p. 12: 'nation-ness is the most universally legitimate value in the political life of our time.' In spite of its sub-title, *Reflections on the Origins and Spread of Nationalism*, Anderson's work is, in reality, a study of the concept of the nation and it has nothing to say about Germany.
[5]D.E.D. Beales, 'Mazzini and revolutionary Nationalism', in D. Thompson (ed.), *Political Ideas* (1966), pp. 143−53.

In 1984 Professor Bernard Willms of the University of Bochum wrote:

> The idea of the nation is the establishment of the identity of the individual in an objective relationship to a concrete historical—political totality, which the individual recognizes and accepts as his own.[6]

The French theologian and orientalist Ernest Renan, lecturing in the Sorbonne in March 1882, answered the question 'What is a nation?' to the effect that it is a daily plebiscite.[7] In other words, he maintained, the nation is essentially democratic and self-defining and cannot be artificially created.

Others take a different view, seeing the sentiment of nationality as essentially artificial. They argue that it was not the product of instincts and experiences but began in the minds of a few who gradually won mass support for it by propaganda and education. For example, Eric Hobsbawm in *The Invention of Tradition*[8] writes of 'mass-produced tradition' and defines nationalism as a dual phenomenon, a 'civic religion', designed to glue together the mass society of the industrial age, and a device adopted by governments to deal with social changes which threaten to disrupt the existing order.[9] Many exponents of this view start out from the Marxist concept of ideologies, including nationalism, that they are a creation of the groups which dominate production, that nationalism is a typical bourgeois ideology, an essentially temporary phase in the development of the bourgeois economic and social system. It is designed to create larger 'national' markets for capitalism, which, by its spread, would eventually dissolve the nations. Marx foresaw a world economy, a world society and even a world culture and opposed national self-determination where it threatened to break up large markets, for example in the Austro-Hungarian empire. Nationalism was a sure sign of backwardness and would be made unnecessary by social liberation. It was, furthermore, irrelevant to the proletariat, whose future lay in internationalism. This reflects a significant failure of Socialist thinking to come to terms with

---

[6]P.S. Mancini, *Diritto Internazionale* (Naples, 1873), p. 37ff. B. Willms, 'Überlegungen zur Zukunft der Deutschen Nation', in Willms *et al.* (eds), *Nation und Selbstbestimmung in Politik und Recht* (Berlin, 1984), pp. 85—108.

[7]It must be remembered that Renan was here arguing that Alsace-Lorraine should properly belong to France because its population, although partly German-speaking, wished to be French. The full meaning, or lack of meaning, of this famous quotation is better revealed in Renan's whole sentence: 'It is a daily plebiscite, just as the existence of the individual is a permanent affirmation of life.'

[8]E. Hobsbawm, 'Inventing Traditions', in E. Hobsbawm and T. Ranger, *The Invention of Tradition* (Cambridge, 1983), pp. 1—14.

[9]The ideas are explored in Breuilly's work, p. 352ff. (see note 3 above) and T. Nairn, *The Break-Up of Britain* (1981), especially chap. 9.

nationalism in the nineteenth century, which was to have important results in Germany and Austria.[10] A rather more subtle version of this is found in the Italian Communist Gramsci's notion of 'hegemony', put forward in his *Prison Notebooks*.[11] This posits that dominant groups rule with the consent of the dominated through the creation of a consensus based on a system of benefits, values and key symbols, in which the nation can play a powerful role. National solidarity can be employed as a means of disguising the oppressive class nature of the state by creating imaginary unity.[12] Gramsci shares the view of national sentiment as essentially artificial.

A lot of learned ink has been used in attempts to reduce the apparently infinite variety in which nationalism has manifested itself, and continues to do so, by defining typologies of national sentiment and nationalism, by putting them into categories or by delineating phases in their development. C.J. Hayes divided nationalism into humanitarian, Jacobin, traditional, Liberal and integral or total (i.e. fascist) forms. There are simplified variants of this, reducing the types to three, Liberal, traditional/monarchical and totalitarian/integral. Some commentators have sought to draw a clear distinction between the Western/ French or self-determined/ subjective model and the Eastern/German or predetermined/ objective model of the nation. Others have extended this by designating three chronological phases, Western European, Central European and Eastern European, all different in character. The Western version is associated with Liberalism and arose in already existing states like France, the Central arose in areas with cultural unity but no political unity like Germany and Italy and the Eastern among peoples oppressed by other nationalities.[13] The French concept of the nation was defined by the abbé Siéyès in *Q'est-ce que le Tiers État* (1789) as 'a body of associates living under one common law and represented by the same legislature', in other words it involves the voluntary subordination of the individual to a common body of laws. The American and French Revolutions spawned ideas of national rights arising from this, in particular the idea that the desire of the nation is superior to all other rights,

[10]E. Cahm and C. Fisera (eds.), *Socialism and Nationalism in Contemporary Europe 1848–1945* (3 vols., Nottingham, 1978), I: general articles; C. Herod, *The Nation in the History of Marxian Thought* (The Hague, 1976).
[11]*Selections from the Prison Notebooks of Antonio Gramsci*, ed. Q. Hoare and G.N. Smith (1971); J. Joll, *Antonio Gramsci* (1977).
[12]G. Hurd (ed.), *National Fictions* (British Film Institute, 1984); Stuart Hall, 'Culture, the Media and the Ideological Effect', in J. Curran *et al* (eds.), *Mass Communication and Society* (1977).
[13]J. Plamenatz, 'Two Types of Nationalism', in E. Kamenka (ed.), *Nationalism. The Nature and Evolution of an Idea* (1976), pp. 22–36.

first put forward in the debate on the future of Avignon in 1791. The wish of the inhabitants of the city of Avignon to become part of France was held to override international law, in this case the pope's ownership of Avignon.[14]

In contrast to this view, that membership of the French nation was open to anyone accepting French law, the 'German' concept saw a man's nationality as predetermined by his culture or blood, regardless of his own wishes. But the distinction is oversimple. It ignores the cultural element in French nationalism at the time of the Revolution (for example the encouragement of cultural uniformity through attacks on minority languages within France) and the underlying assumption in the German model that the union of all people of German blood in a single state would produce common institutions. German nationalism, and probably all nationalisms, contain both subjective and objective elements. As the nineteenth century progressed, the so-called German model was to emerge in Germany as a dominant form of nationalism, that is the search for German unity for its own sake, as a means of expressing the unique essence of the German *Volk*. The Western model, German unity as a means of achieving constitutional objectives, was to recede into the background. Some historians see this supposed distinction between French and German nationalism mirrored in the so-called 'War against the West',[15] the intellectual rejection by some German nationalists of western ideas and models and the search for a specifically 'German way' in ideas, politics and social organization. One unusual feature of German national sentiment was that it existed in a cultural form long before it found political expression. Later we shall be considering the argument of some historians that it became political too late and that an emphasis on culture, language and blood therefore played an excessively important role in it. Many nationalists in the nineteenth century, including Liberal nationalists, saw Germany as a delayed or retarded nation and it is argued that this produced in the later nineteenth century a kind of collective sense of inferiority and a constant need to catch up and overtake other nations.[16]

The Czech political scientist M. Hroch distinguishes A, B and C phases in the development of nationalism.[17] In the first it is

---

[14]A. Kemiläinen, *L'affaire d'Avignon (1789–91) from the viewpoint of nationalism* (Helsinki, 1971).
[15]Kohn, *The Mind of Germany*, chap. 4 for the 'War against the West'.
[16]The phrase 'belated nation' was, apparently, first used in H. Plessner, *Die verspätete Nation* (1935, repr. Frankfurt, 1982). The sub-title of the work is interesting: *On the political seducibility of the bourgeois spirit.*
[17]M. Hroch, *Die Vorkämpfer der nationalen Bewegung bei den kleinen Völkern Europas* (Prague, 1968).

confined to a small section of the intelligentsia, the 'awakeners to nationhood', who study the language, literature and history of the nation. In the second phase, groups emerge within the élites devoted to the pursuit of national goals, who create a fermentation of national self-awareness and attract the beginnings of a mass following. This is the *Volkswerden*, the 'becoming of the nation'. In the C phase nationalism emerges as an organized mass movement involving all levels of society in the pursuit of national aims. Germany does not fit into this pattern.[18]

Some commentators have put forward the idea that nationalism is 'genuine' or good when it is a liberal or emancipatory movement and that it is perverted and becomes bad when it turns into imperialism or is used to promote socially conservative aims, as was increasingly the case in Germany after 1880.[19] This notion of 'healthy' and 'unhealthy' nationalism would seem difficult to sustain. The view that nationalism is always the product of progressive changes caused by the modernization of societies is put forward, among others, by K.W. Deutsch, one of the pioneers of the sociological approach to nationalism.[20] Deutsch begins from the premise that the nation is a communication community. He distinguishes national awareness and nationalism. The first is the result of the progressive development of communication within a large community, by which it becomes integrated and begins to view itself as a distinct body. A point arises at a certain stage in this process, 'nation-building', when growing literacy, movement from the countryside into towns and social mobility reach a level at which intensive communication is possible in a large community. When such a group proceeds to seek to create a domain or state, within which it will govern itself, nationalism has emerged. According to Deutsch and his followers nationalism develops when society has achieved partial modernization and itself speeds up the process of change by involving more members of the society in politics, widening their horizons and providing new goals to aim for. Modern nationalism, according to this view, is therefore a product of and a cause of political emancipation. He defines four stages in the process of modernization which a political and social system must encompass. The first two are defined as *penetration*, the

---

[18]There are other typologies in E.H. Carr, *Nationalism and After* (1945) and L. Wirth, 'Types of Nationalism', *American Journal of Sociology* 41 (1936), pp. 723–37.
[19]The English language summary in Otto Dann (ed.), *Nationalismus und sozialer Wandel* (Hamburg, 1978) talks of 'nationalism in its genuine phase' though elsewhere in the book Dann claims to be dealing with nationalism in a purely neutral way without the pejorative associations sometimes attached to it. W.J. Mommsen (see note 4 above) writes of 'legitimate national policies', meaning the pursuit of democracy, as distinct from power politics and imperialism.
[20]See note 3 above.

development of common administrative and legal structures controlling a territory and population, and *identity creation*, the development of a common political culture by 'political socialization',
by which the state becomes legitimized in the eyes of its subjects.
In these two stages nation-building is achieved. To complete
modernization, the processes of *participation* and *distribution* have
to be accomplished, the democratization of decision-making and a
fair sharing out of the resources of the society. If all four processes
are not satisfactorily carried through, crises of development will
occur. A variant of this has been put forward by Stein Rokkan,
who isolates four crisis points in the modernization process.[21]
Before nation-building can proceed, a state must overcome the
penetration crisis, achieving the end of political feudalism and the
victory of the centralizing state over local powers, and the standardization crisis, the modernization of the social infrastructure and of
political institutions, the transition from a society of Estates to a
society of classes. When these have been achieved, the crises of
participation and redistribution are faced, the admission of new
social groups to political power and the fight for better economic
and social conditions for the lower classes. Because Germany was
unable to overcome the last two crises, it is argued, it remained
partially modernized and nationalism became a divisive rather
than integrative force.

A variant of this, a social—psychological explanation, has been
offered, among others, by Daniel Katz, who argues that nationalism
provides an alternative value system, when traditional authorities,
convictions and values have lost their legitimacy as a result of
change in a society, and reduces the insecurity and tension arising
from the decay of traditional communities by building a new
collective identity around which a society can unite. Nationalism
allows the individual to submerge himself in a greater whole and,
through identification with the nation and its symbols, to fulfil
emotional and even sexual needs vicariously. For those with frustrated and empty lives or with personality disorders nationalism is
especially appealing and, by implication, there would be no need
for it if everyone enjoyed rich and fulfilled lives as individuals.[22]

It could be objected, among other things, that all this seems to
be based on a teleological approach which assumes that the
democratic national welfare state is the ultimate stage of progress.

[21]Stein Rokkan, 'Dimensions of State Formation and Nation Building. A Possible Paradigm
for Research on Variations within Europe', in Tilly, *The Formation of National States*, pp.
562—600.
[22]D. Katz, 'The Psychology of Nationalism', in J.P. Guildford (ed.), *Fields of Psychology* (New
York, 1949), pp. 163—81 and 'Nationalism and a Strategy of International Conflict Resolution',
in H.C. Kelmann (ed.), *International Behaviour* (New York, 1965).

It also seems to accept that nationalism is only legitimate if it is emancipatory when, obviously, it can also be a conservative ideology mobilized to prevent 'participation' and 'distribution'.

All such attempts to establish a typology of nationalism fail because they start from the premise that nationalism is a single phenomenon and do not recognize that each nation's nationalism is unique and has distinctive features and that it can exist simultaneously in many different manifestations in a single society, as was the case in Germany in the period to be examined. It must also be remembered that German nationalism was not one but several different movements and that the German's picture of himself and his place in the world was very complex. Allegiance to the concept of Germanness has in the past had to take its place in a complex web of other allegiances, to family, class, occupational group, locality, region, state and Church, which acted as the dominant factors in forming political attitudes and behaviour. In this connection, one must beware of equating political action with the modern democratic system, voting, parliaments, political parties and so on. There was a lively if usually unpublicized political debate within bureaucracies in eighteenth-century Germany between 'progressive' and 'conservative' groups. At a lower level were the politics of the Estates, the village and the town and, ultimately, the politics of the riot. All this existed before organized democratic institutions emerged. As will be shown, it was only in the later nineteenth century that Germans began to answer the fundamental questions involved in all politics—'Who are my friends? Who are my enemies? What can be changed and how? What changes can be prevented and how?—in national terms. Only then did national sentiment come to occupy a prominent place in the hierarchy of loyalties in the minds of most Germans and there were still deep disagreements as to who were the enemies of the *Volk* and great differences between the visions of Germany held by different groups within the German nation.

Otto Dann's definition of nationalism as

> the political and ideological movement of a population or population group which understands itself to be a nation and which, mobilized by processes of modernization, seeks to achieve political self-determination or autonomy within its own territory, to defend its autonomy against other peoples or, respectively, to increase its territory at the cost of other peoples[23]

seems to recognize better the chameleon nature of the phenomenon and the basic irrelevance of the factor or factors which symbolize

[23]Dann, *Nationalismus und sozialer Wandel*, p. 14.

the integration of a nationality, language or whatever. National cohesion is not dependent on cultural homogeneity. A study of Germany in the nineteenth and twentieth centuries shows that nationalism can be liberal or conservative or anything. Like all ideologies, it is a mixture of conviction and self-interest. It is available, like religion, for anyone who chooses to use it, to support or oppose change, to justify increasing popular participation in decision-making or the continuation in power of traditional élites, as the basis for international peace or unrestrained imperialism. The nation is a mixture of objective/historical and subjective/self-defining factors. Both views, the artificial and the organic, objective and subjective, are applicable to Germany, as will be shown. National sentiment existed as an idea in the minds of a small minority, which gradually extended its appeal. A spontaneously growing sentiment of unity can also be shown to have existed among the Germans. Germany manifested both nationalism from below, a spontaneous movement arising in a society without government participation, and official nationalism or nationalism from above. In addition, mass nationalism appeared spontaneously in a xenophobic negative form. Nineteenth-century Germany saw several such outbreaks, when foreign governments were seen as trying to seize German soil, but they were usually short-lived.

Nationalism was available for use as a life-buoy for governments in trouble, as a means of integrating different social groups with divergent aims and of convincing them that their common interests with their fellow members of the nation were more important than their class or group aspirations or that these aspirations could best be achieved through the pursuit of greater national goals. This form of conservative nationalism also existed in Germany: in the early nineteenth century governments made use of the national idea to serve their narrow state ends and later in the century the German government was to devote considerable effort to creating Hobsbawm's 'mass-produced tradition'.[24]

For the purpose of this study it will be assumed that patriotism or xenophobia can exist as purely passive national sentiments not necessarily determining men's political behaviour. Nationalism, in contrast, is active, a movement, in which there are two essential ingredients: sentiment and action. The distinction is more explicitly expressed in German than in English with the words *Nationalismus* and *Vaterlandsliebe* (love of the fatherland). National sentiment can exist without nationalism in the form of an awareness of

---

[24]Hobsbawn, 'Inventing Traditions' and 'Reflections on Nationalism', in T.J. Nossiter (ed.), *Imagination and Precision in the Social Sciences* (1972), pp. 385–406.

difference or distinctiveness which does not lead to political action. An example of this can be seen in modern Wales, where political nationalism has a derisory following in spite of a strong feeling of distinctiveness in the population. Nationalism is not an inevitable product of the sentiment of nationality nor is it based on a single system of values which the nation, however defined, is held to embody and which integrates its members. Different nationalisms can exist within a single nation.

Nationalism must contain an element of aspiration. Like Peter Pan it never grows up: if it does, it disappears. Nationalism involves dissatisfaction with the existing situation and the desire to change it by the achievement of national goals. It envisages an attainable ideal centred on the nation, seeking for example to achieve 'national self-determination', whatever that is, to make the nation and the state coterminous, to achieve a tangible demonstration of the supposed innate superiority of the nation or to exclude foreign influences from the nation. The most common aspiration is the creation of a nation-state but this is not essential, in spite of the statement by Johann Kaspar Bluntschli, a leading Liberal jurist, Swiss-born but active in Germany, in 1866: 'Every nation has the vocation and right to form a state. Just as mankind is divided into a number of nations, so the world should be divided into the same number of states. Every nation is a state, every state a nation.'[25] Only in the later nineteenth century did 'nation' and 'state' become virtually synonymous. The nation still has no status in international law. The rights of individuals and states are internationally recognized but 'national rights' are not. The United Nations Human Rights Declaration of 1966 states that all peoples, not nations, have a right to self-determination but this can only operate if they have a state or state-like organ to act for them.

Sometimes national goals can be concrete but they can also be vague and undefined, but none the less powerful for that. A quasi-religious or Utopian element is an essential ingredient of nationalist movements. Like religions and other ideologies it is innately optimistic and posits the availability of a perfect world on earth. It appeals to the inborn need in human beings for idealism and a belief in immortality provided by a religion or a substitute religion.[26]

[25]J.K. Bluntschli, *Allgemeine Staatslehre* (6th edn, 1866). The idea of the ethnically homogeneous nation state as a norm has been challenged: W.H. McNeill, *Polyethnicity and National Unity in World History* (Toronto, 1986).
[26]'Patriotic sentiment was transformed into a pseudo religion. Men wanted to appropriate a piece of eternity which the nation provided': G.L. Mosse, 'Friendship and Nationhood', *J.Cont.H.* 17 (1982), p. 359. A.J. Hoover, *The Gospel of Nationalism. German Patriotic Preaching from Napoleon to Versailles* (Stuttgart, 1986), an investigation of the role of the clergy in the development of nationalism in Germany.

This is true of all manifestations of nationalism from Mazzinian idealism to National Socialism. It is the purpose of this study to try to show how and why in the case of Germany the sentiment of nationality became the motor of political behaviour and, in the process, nationalism.

One ingredient of nationalism, the development of the sentiment or idea of Germanness, will be considered first. Consciousness of Germanness existed long before the nineteenth century, though claims by the 'historian' Kurt Pastenaci during the Third Reich, to have found evidence of a distinct German nation in the Stone Age, were exaggerated.[27] A distinct German language was developing in the eighth century and the spread of the Church and the growth of the Frankish state speeded up the process by which the different Germanic tribal groups (*Stämme*) came together. In about AD 830 Bishop Frechulf of Lisieux in his *World Chronicle* speculated about the origins of the Franks, Goths and other Germanic nations, united by language. Whether 'Germany' was born at the partition of Charlemagne's empire at Verdun in 843 and the election of Louis the German as ruler of the Germanic part or at the election of Henry the Fowler as king in 918 is disputed. There is ample evidence that pride in Germany's association with the Holy Roman Empire and a passive awareness of distinctiveness existed among Germans in the Middle Ages, though there were still wide differences between the Germans of different regions, for example the Netherlands and Switzerland, and tribal consciousness remained alive in spite of nominal unity under the Holy Roman Empire. The idea of Germany as a geographical area appeared early: the *Annolied*, an epic poem produced in the late eleventh century, designated the German lands as the area where the 'German language' was spoken. Walther von dern Vogelweide in his *Deutschlandlied* of 1203 defined Germany as stretching from the Elbe to the Rhine and down to Hungary.[28] There is recorded anti-Slav feeling among Germans in the Teutonic Order colonizing the eastern provinces in the fourteenth century and during the Hussite wars, though religion probably played a large role in this, and there was recorded ill-feeling between the French and Germans taking part in the Third Crusade.

The period of instability and fear preceding the Reformation called forth other nationalistic statements.[29] An important element

[27]K. Pastenaci, *Das viertausendjährige Reich der Deutschen* (Berlin, 1940).
[28]J.A. Armstrong, *Nations before Nationalism* (Chapel Hill, 1982), p. 27ff; S. Reynolds, *Kingdoms and Communities in Western Europe 900–1300* (Oxford, 1986); J.G. Robertson, *A History of German Literature* (6th edn, Edinburgh, 1970).
[29]See A.G. Dickens, *The German Nation and Martin Luther* (1974) chaps. 1 and 2 and G. Strauss, (ed.), *Pre-Reformation Germany* (1972) and *Manifestations of Discontent in Germany on the Eve of the Reformation* (Bloomington, 1971).

in this outburst of national feeling was plain xenophobia, which had been a constant feature since the fifteenth century, if not earlier, manifesting itself in turn as anti-Czech, anti-Italian and anti-French sentiment. The strange view appeared that the Germans were simple, honest and courageous people, whose increasing problems were all caused by the machinations of crafty foreigners. This strengthened existing xenophobia and deepened resentment against the outside world. It was often accompanied by a romanticized view of the German past, with figures like the Emperor Frederick I Barbarossa portrayed as great heroes. Briefly Martin Luther became the hero of the German nation in its fight against the oppression of Rome. His attack on papal power ran through Germany like wind-driven fire. The late fifteenth century also saw something recognizable as pan-Germanism, the desire to see all German-speaking lands in a spiritual and intellectual union, even though their political unity had been shattered. This was to be achieved by *renovatio imperii*, the revival of a powerful Holy Roman Empire. The Emperor would take back his lost power and come down like *deus ex machina* with magic solutions to Germany's problems.

In the early modern period there were some expressions of German national sentiment which sound startlingly modern. For example, the *Book of a Hundred Chapters*, (*Buch der hundert Kapitel*), the work of the anonymous Revolutionary of the Upper Rhine, was published around 1500 in the Colmar area.[30] Supposedly the record of an apocalyptic vision given to the author by the archangel Michael, it was one of many such works, calling for a social and moral revolution in Germany. The Germans, it explained, were a chosen people. Before the building of the Tower of Babel all people on earth had spoken German, the *Ursprache*, the language spoken by Adam and Eve in the Garden of Eden. The great classical heroes had all been German, including Alexander the Great. The Latin peoples were shallow and corrupt while the Germans were the repository of all virtues. Thus the only salvation for the world was for the Germans to reassert their superiority: the German Emperor was to replace the pope as the figurehead of a new Church to be based in Mainz instead of Rome. This was part of a generalized wave of discontent which swept Germany before the Reformation, at its most extreme taking the form of revolutionary millenarianism. A common ingredient in these writings was the notion of a mystic Emperor, Barbarossa or Frederick II, asleep under a mountain and waiting to return to destroy the French, Slavs, Magyars and Jews, to elevate the Germans above all peoples

[30]N. Cohn, *The Pursuit of the Millenium* (1952).

of the world, to create a new German *Reich* covering the whole of Europe and to prepare the way for the Second Coming. This became known as 'Kyffhäuser Yearning' (*Kyffhäusersehnsucht*), after the mountain in the Harz where the mystic Emperor was supposed to sleep. Such notions were, of course, not restricted to Germans.

Statements like these were not evidence of anything recognizable as mass national feeling, cultural or otherwise, before the nineteenth century. The factors dividing the German people, regionalism, religion and political divisions, were strong while the factors unifying them were very weak. There was not even linguistic unity; the German language was still in the process of formation in the late medieval period.[31] It was only then that a standard written German emerged as a result of the rise of an educated bureaucracy, to be established finally in the Reformation—though as late as the eighteenth century the Bavarian Wittelsbachs were still trying to make the Bavarian dialect the German literary standard.[32] In spite of a great expansion of vernacular publishing after about 1520, Latin and later French were to enjoy greater prestige than German for a long time. It is well-known that Charles V claimed to use it only to speak to his horse and that Frederick the Great considered a German-speaking librarian worth only half the salary of a French-speaker. In the eighteenth century it was reported that the nobility's fondness for French was spreading down to the lower orders. Peasants' daughters in Schleswig-Holstein used French phrases in their conversations, without understanding what they meant. It was partly in reaction to this that a self-consciously German cultural movement appeared in the later eighteenth century. Only then did language become one of the main criteria of nationality; until then the language a man spoke did not have the significance it was later to acquire.[33] Nevertheless a passive awareness of distinctiveness, the sentiment of Germanness, existed.

This sentiment was strengthened and reinforced and the other ingredient needed to create German nationalism, the desire for change in national terms, was produced in the period of French

---

[31]F.R.H. Du Boulay, *Germany in the Later Middle Ages* (1983), p. 3. This illustrates well the difficulty of attempting to use language as a basis for the definition of nationality. Over the centuries several population groups, originally part of the German-speaking stock, have broken away and elevated their versions of the German language into separate languages, such as the Dutch, the Luxemburgers and the Swiss Germans, though the last two also still use the high literary language.

[32]P.C. Hartmann, *Karl Albrecht-Karl VII* (Regensburg, 1985), pp. 98-9.

[33]There *are* exceptions: in May 1302 the Flemish population of Bruges massacred Frenchmen in the city, the so-called Matins of Bruges, during which they are said to have selected their victims by forcing men to say something in Dutch. Failure to achieve the correct pronunciation meant death. There was national friction in fourteenth-century Bohemia and under the terms of the Golden Bull of 1356 German princes were required to ensure their heirs learned a Slav language: Kedourie, *Nationalism*, p. 60.

domination after the French Revolution. It is generally held that nationalism, in Germany and elsewhere, was a product of the period of the French Revolution and the reign of Napoleon I. Starting from the Aristotelian postulate that men must have a rational political order in which to organize their existence, something which only gods and animals do not need, this view argues that since the Middle Ages Europe had tried to organize itself on the basis of a great variety of feudal, imperial and dynastic arrangements, none of which had proved satisfactory. By the nineteenth century the nation state seemed increasingly the only means of achieving sound government in a modern society. This, supposedly, was a general lesson learned in Europe in the period after the French Revolution, which produced the Liberal concept of national self-determination but also a powerful combination of national sentiment and reaction. The first sentence of Elie Kedourie's study of nationalism states: 'Nationalism is a doctrine invented in Europe at the beginning of the 19th century.' Benedict Anderson places the 'creation' of national sentiment towards the end of the eighteenth century.[34]

The events of the French period forced many to think about the basic question of what Germany was, because the traditional political framework of the German nation, the Holy Roman Empire, disappeared and Germany came under foreign control. This period also saw the emergence in German society of groups whose solution to problems centred on the achievement of some form of national unity. The impact of such ideas was limited to a minority of Germans and they did not attract a mass following in the early nineteenth century. None the less they were important. They appealed in particular to a group of growing significance in German society, unemployed intellectuals, or those who felt themselves employed below their deserved status and frustrated by their inability to achieve anything. These people formed a kind of all-German community above the individual states made up of men like students, officials, army officers, academics, musicians, projectors and teachers. Through university education and the opportunities for mobility which it provided in Germany, they had broken out of the regional, group or employment restrictions which marked traditional society and cut themselves off from 'ordinary people'. They had often risen out of the 'narrow fatherland' but were not accepted into the noble-dominated ruling classes.[35] Such

---

[34]See note 4 above for Anderson's work.
[35]L. O'Boyle, 'The Problem of an Excess of Educated Men in Europe' *JMH* 42 (1970) pp. 471–95. There was a developed 'common market' for educated men between the German states and it was not unusual for men of talent to serve several different rulers during their careers. In pre-revolutionary France similar groups existed, which challenged the claims of the crown and nobility to be 'the nation'.

men felt themselves morally and intellectually superior both to nobles who aped the French and in many states enjoyed unearned privileges such as a monopoly of high office in Church, state and army, and to established intellectuals who fostered cosmopolitanism. High expectations of change aroused initially by the French Revolution among many of these people were deeply disappointed and many frustrated intellectuals began to look increasingly to a new single German state, which was seen as capable of achieving more, in practical and spiritual terms, than the individual German states.

From its origins in the early years of the nineteenth century German nationalism was never a single united movement.[36] For the sake of convenience and at the risk of considerable simplification, it is possible to distinguish from the beginning two main strands of nationalism, with variations within each. They can be called Liberal nationalism and Romantic nationalism. They shared certain common roots. Disillusionment among German intellectuals at the abandonment by the French of the principles of their revolution played a large part in the growth of national consciousness in Germany. Some clung to the model of a state and society supposedly present in the early days of the Revolution but later betrayed and, as Liberals, sought to realize it on German soil. Others reacted by becoming reactionary Romantic nationalists, seeking a return to a mystic medieval Germany, strong and united, built on Catholic Christianity and a powerful Emperor. Both were very much minority movements, affecting the political attitudes and behaviour of only small groups in German society. Both centred on a vision of a changed Germany in the future and both contained a large element of Utopianism. This haloization of the nation, the idea that the achievement of national goals would be the gateway to a perfect world, was a common feature of all nationalisms. Liberal nationalism was to remain predominant until the late nineteenth century, when it was replaced as the leading form of the movement by a variant of Romantic nationalism. In addition to these two, there were always other forms of nationalism present in German society: after 1871 the whole picture became even more complex with even greater divergence of views as to what form the German nation should take. Socialists, Liberals, democrats, agrarians, anti-Semites and Pan-Germans all had very different visions of the ideal German nation-state.

Liberal nationalism was an extension of the main tenets of the Liberal ideology from the individual to the nation. It was held that the nation, like the individual, should be allowed to develop to the

[36]H. Kohn, 'The Eve of German Nationalism', *J. Hist. Id.* 12 (1951), pp. 256–84.

limit of its potential in a framework of freedom. The oppression of a nation by foreign rule or the artificial division of the nation, as in the case of Germany, were seen by Liberals as barriers to the achievement of individual liberty. Whereas before 1789 those desiring progressive changes had looked to enlightened rulers to achieve these on a piecemeal basis state by state, they now saw a short-cut to their achievement by means of national unity. The abolition of the separate states or their substantial weakening in some kind of federal Germany was seen as the easiest means of destroying the things Liberals regarded as barriers to what they saw as progress, that is monarchial absolutism, noble privilege and clerical obscurantism, and of achieving individual freedom, free institutions and free trade and enterprise. They believed in freedom of enterprise and equality of opportunity. They opposed democracy in the modern sense of one-man-one-vote and German Liberal nationalism is not always easy to fit into a model of nationalism as an democratizing movement. They rejected a Germany of equal citizens and the hierarchical Germany of traditional society and had a vision of a classless bourgeois society. These were ideas which were already germinating before 1789 and their progress was speeded up in the years 1792 to 1813, when Germany was effectively controlled by the French.[37] There was no united Liberal party and no all-German Liberal programme. The movement was very vague and disunited, with its strongest support among the educated middle class in the Rhineland, Baden and some large cities, especially in the areas which came under the strongest French influence. The Liberal nationalists, therefore, saw national unification as a means to an end, not an end in itself.

For Romantic nationalists this was not the case. There was always a Romantic thread in German nationalism alongside the Liberal form and the line between them was often very blurred, especially in the years after the French Revolution. The Romantic Movement was primarily a cultural movement, a reaction against the cold rationality of the Enlightenment and the revived Classicism of the late eighteenth century. It sought to bring back colour and emotion to artistic creation and enthusiasm and faith to human life. It also gave rise to a new view of history which had important effects on the rise of nationalism. Some Romantics were reactionaries in that they worked for the restoration of a lost Golden Age of pre-revolutionary Germany while others dreamed of creating a completely new kind of society and state. Both groups were susceptible to irrationality and metaphysics and both glorified an idealized

[37]J.J. Sheehan, *German Liberalism in the Nineteenth Century* (Chicago, 1978); E.K. Bramsted and K.J. Melhuish (eds.), *Western Liberalism* (1978), pp. 80–90.

German past of wise and powerful Emperors, fatherly princes and happy peasants and townsmen. The notion of the mystical nation (*Volk*) also played a major role in the Romantic concept of the nation. The poet Novalis portrayed an idyllic lost world of the Middle Ages, an age of unity and faith, when the national spirit (*Volksgeist*) had bloomed at its purest.[38] A future Empire (*Reich*) would recreate this. In Romantic thinking the role of the individual was degraded. It was held that the individual was capable of achieving fulfilment or freedom only by identifying with the greater whole, the nation or state. The state was seen as the agent for the realization of the individual's potential not just as a collection of individuals who have come together for a purpose. It was held that the nation or state was higher than the individual and had a total claim on his allegiance. A favourite analogy for a collection of individuals without the glue of nation or state was a heap of loose sand. This was the exact opposite of Liberal thinking.

In examining the rise of these different forms of nationalism it is necessary to look briefly at some of the intellectual contributions to the development of the ideas and attitudes associated with it, bearing in mind the earlier warning about overestimating the importance of intellectual views in the development of mass nationalism. Too many studies of German nationalism have taken the form of lists of writers and resumés of what they wrote. The assumption is made that their views must have had an impact on the behaviour of their fellow-countrymen, which is not easy to demonstrate.[39] Certainly there was among German intellectuals a deep and traditional interest in philosophy, which was often seen as offering a blueprint for practical action and which produced a love of abstraction: in 1828 Goethe was reported as wishing that the Germans might become less philosophical and more active, less theoretical and more practical, like the British. There is also a danger in placing the writers in rigid categories such as 'Enlightened' or 'Romantic'. The boundaries between them were often vague and shifting. Frequently the ideas of major thinkers were taken up and distorted by lesser minds and used for purposes their originators would never have dreamed of. Typical was the case of Johann Gottfried Herder, seen as the father of modern

[38]Novalis was the pen-name of Friedrich von Hardenberg (1772–1801), a leading poet of the Romantic movement, whose reputation was much enhanced by his early death.
[39]There have been some studies of German popular journalism attempting to show how attitudes changed: J. Tiäinen, *Napoleon und das napoleonische Frankreich in der öffentlichen Diskussion des 'Dritten Deutschland' 1797–1806* (Jyväskylä, 1971) emphasizes the limited circulation of newspapers and pamphlets and the weakness of German national sentiment in them. H. Gruppe, *'Volk' zwischen Politik und Idylle in der Gartenlaube 1853–1914* (Frankfurt, 1976) is a study of *Die Gartenlaube* (The Summer House), a magazine for all the family. Reference will be made to this in a later chapter.

nationalism.[40] Herder's ideas were set out in his *Another Philosophy of History* (1774) and *Outlines of a Philosophy of the History of Man* (1784–91), in which he described history as a story of progress and improvement achieved by struggle and not, as the Enlightenment postulated, by Reason. Diversity he saw as a fundamental feature of the universe; the cosmopolitanism of the Enlightenment was therefore unnatural. Nations had existed before the state and were an organic part of this diversity, each being endowed with a unique character, the national spirit (*Volksgeist*). The most important symbols of this distinctiveness were language and the culture of those who spoke it. This gave rise to the idea that the mother tongue expresses the nation's soul. The work of philologists in the early nineteenth century in demonstrating the divergence of languages played an important part in making language a major criterion of nationality and national distinctiveness.[41] Herder did not find the purest expression of the *Volksgeist* in the products of high culture but in folklore and folk tales. It was no coincidence that a marked revival of traditional German epics and folk tales took place around 1800, for example the *Nibelungenlied*, *Des Knaben Wunderhorn* (old German songs), the *Minnelieder* (works of medieval minstrels) and the fairy tales collected by the Grimm brothers. Herder also described the nation as a community of blood (*Blutsgemeinschaft*). Unlike the dynastic states of the *ancien régime*, which had been based on force and compulsion and had moved bodies of people around like pawns in a manner repugnant to nature and liberty, the nation-state would be natural. As a practical step Herder suggested the creation of a German Academy to promote German culture. His ideas were basically philosophical, humanitarian and apolitical, arising as they did from an attempt to make sense of history, but they proved very congenial to many Germans, who, living as they did in a fragmented country, were able to identify with his vague definition of Germanness.

Such ideas were taken up, expanded and sometimes changed by later thinkers, from whose work a further refinement of ideas important in the development of nationalism resulted. A well-known statement of such views came in Fichte's *Addresses to the German Nation*,[42] a collection of 14 lectures in fact delivered to an audience of academics and students in Berlin in the winter of 1807–8. It is interesting that a document later regarded as a clarion call of German nationalism was passed by the French censorship,

[40]R.R. Ergang, *Herder and the Foundations of German Nationalism* (New York, 1931).
[41]J.A. Fishman, *Language and Nationalism. Two Integrative Essays* (Rowley, Mass., 1972).
[42]J.G. Fichte, *Reden an die deutsche Nation* (edited and introduced by I.H. Fichte) (Leipzig, 1871). An English edition, *Addresses to the German Nation* (transl. by R.F. Jones and G. Turnbull) (1922).

which saw it as simply a work on education. Fichte, like most German intellectuals, was initially a great admirer of the French Revolution but, also like many, changed his mind when Bonaparte established his rule. The *Addresses* were an attack on Napoleon's supposed plan to create a universal empire and to impose a French monoculture on all the peoples of the Continent. They combined an appeal for the creation of a German state with further exposition of the idea of the state as an agent of perfection, an instrument 'to allow the eternal and divine to blossom in the world'. The Germans, as a uniquely original and uncorrupted nation, had a special duty to preserve their culture and defend it against foreign influences and to regenerate themselves spiritually by regaining their national liberty. This was an obligation not only to themselves but also to all humanity because the Germans had a special world-historical leadership mission. Unlike 'pure' Romantics such as Novalis, Fichte did not totally reject the Enlightenment and retained a large element of Enlightenment cosmopolitanism in his thinking: the victory of the German nation would allow all nations to enjoy freedom. He also extended Herder's ideas on language, arguing that the moral standing of a nation is damaged if it allows its language to be contaminated by foreign words or if it abandons its own language and adopts someone else's. German was the original pure language of mankind, the *Ursprache*, while other languages were borrowed or mongrelized and therefore inferior. It was easy to apply this to the French, who had abandoned their original Germanic Frankish tongue and adopted a Latin language. This seemed to provide pseudo-philosophical evidence that the French were a trivial light-weight people and offered a convenient explanation of other events. Prussia under Frederick II had allowed itself to become frenchified and this process reached its inevitable dénouement in defeat by the French at Jena in 1806. According to Fichte, no culture can survive unless it has a sovereign state exclusively its own; the vital next steps for Germany were the union of the whole nation in a single state, free of foreign domination, and the creation of a national education system to teach the next generation of leaders not just traditional subjects but national history and consciousness.

Fichte was an intellectual and his idea of national sentiment was not rooted in political realities. His ideas on economics were thoroughly unsophisticated.[43] He and others emphasized the spiritual and cultural character of Germany's mission, seeing it as a

[43]Fichte's only work on economics, *Der geschlossene Handelsstaat* (Tübingen, 1800), proposed a system in which international trade would cease as would be individual's right to choose his own occupation. The whole thing was wildly Utopian.

cultural nation (*Kulturnation*) and not a state nation (*Staatsnation*). He offered no concrete policies for the achievement of his ideas but his rhetoric struck a responsive chord in many Germans.

Also significant in the development of nationalist ideas were the so-called 'Awakeners to Germanness' (*Erwecker zur Deutschheit*), especially Friedrich 'Father of Gymnastics' (*Turnvater*) Jahn (1778– 1852) and Ernst Moritz Arndt (1769–1860). Jahn, a Prussian patriot before his conversion to German nationalism about 1806, founded a gymnastic movement to encourage young Germans to make themselves fit to liberate their country. He was also the author of *Deutsches Volkstum* (*German national Character*, 1810), in which he emphasized the need to preserve the racial purity and the customs and usages of the German people, a perversion of the humane ideas of Herder. He warned Germans that anyone who allowed his daughter to learn French was delivering her up to prostitution. The reputation of Arndt, a versifier, impresario of folk festivals and academic political commentator, has suffered from the fact that selective quotation from his substantial writings has made him appear a precursor of Nazism. He seems often to have been carried away by the splendour of his own rhetoric. His poetry or doggerel, often chauvinistic and fiercely anti-French, embodied the vision of a Germany one and indivisible. He taught the cult of action, racial and linguistic purity, anti-Semitism and anti-capitalism, together with a fierce patriotism: 'The highest religion is to love the fatherland above law and princes, fathers and mothers, wives and children.' His *Catechism* of 1813 contained a famous definition of the fatherland:[44]

> Where God's sun first appeared to you, where the stars of heaven first twinkled at you, where lightening first revealed to you God's almighty power and where his storm-winds roared through your soul producing holy terror, there is your love, there is your fatherland. Where the first human eye bent longingly over your cradle, where your mother first held you joyfully on her lap and your father burned into your heart the lessons of wisdom and Christianity, there is your fatherland.

Young Germans were urged to love iron above gold and to hold German national rights more dear than individual liberty, equality or the rights of man. Like Fichte, Arndt emphasized the innate

[44]A.G. Pundt, *Arndt and the Nationalist Awakening in Germany* (New York, 1935). Arndt's *Catechism for the Teutonic Warrior and Soldier* (1813) was one of a large number of pamphlets he produced between 1812 and 1814. Elsewhere he defined Germany as 'Wherever the German language rings, and God songs in Heaven sings' (*So weit die deutsche Zunge klingt, Und Gott im Himmel Lieder singt*).

superiority of the Germans, if only they could throw off corroding *Welsch* or foreign influences, which had crept in after the end of the Hohenstaufens in the thirteenth century. He saw in the original Germanic tribes a model of freedom, courage, manliness, purity and discipline, which should be recreated by German youth. His views were oddly ambivalent: sometimes he called for a restoration of the medieval Germany of Estates and sometimes he expressed support for the idea of individual freedom, especially in his more mature writings in the 1840s and 1850s. His importance lay more in influencing attitudes than in the formation of practical policies for the achievement of national goals. It is hardly surprising that he found an enthusiastic audience among young people and it was among academic youth that his influence was greatest.

Claims that the Germans, in spite of everything, were a special people perhaps also helped to compensate for the manifest weakness of Germany. The works of Fichte, Jahn and Arndt also contributed to a growing belief among Romantic nationalists that Germany should not look outside her own borders for help in the solution of her predicament but must help herself. At the same time as writers condemned the subjection of German lands to foreign occupation and German culture to foreign fashions, they also condemned the subordination of her ideas to foreign models, such as French rationalism or English constitutionalism. Among a lunatic fringe of Romantic Nationalists, the Teutomaniacs, extreme forms of such ideas remained alive into the late nineteenth century. The supposed deviation of Germany from western Europe from the beginning of the nineteenth century, the notion of a German special road (*deutscher Sonderweg*), will be a theme in this study. Liberal Nationalists, on the other hand, continued to look to France, Britain and, after 1830, to Belgium for answers to Germany's problems; but after 1848 they too began to regard German power and German greatness as ends in themselves, requiring no mission or message to justify them.

Mixed in with such ideas a much older sentiment, which could be called negative or anti-foreign nationalism, survived and grew stronger. This was nothing new but a development of traditional xenophobia. It enjoyed the largest numerical support among the German people but was ephemeral in its manifestations and remained essentially negative, hardly fitting into the definition of nationalism as sentiment and action combined. It expressed itself in hatred of the French and a desire to see them removed from Germany but it put forward no concrete proposals for a new Germany to replace the Holy Roman Empire after it came to an end. If this sentiment did have political expression, it seems to have been reactionary or restorative, that is a vague desire to return to things as they had been before. In 1814–15 there is evidence of some yearning for a restoration of the Empire but this was made impossible by the changes which had taken place during the French period.

3

Germany before 1815: Rebirth of a Nation?

Germany on the eve of the French Revolution was politically fragmented, economically weak, socially divided and, in spite of growing support for religious toleration in many parts of the country, troubled by religious divisions.[1] Although many commentators at the time bewailed the decline in Germany's European position, there is no evidence of anything recognizable as nationalism in a modern sense. It could be argued that there was no real need for a nationalist movement as Germany already had an acceptable political framework in the shape of the Holy Roman Empire, which symbolized the unity of the nation and enjoyed the prestige of association with the Roman Empire and Charlemagne. For many contemporaries the Holy Roman Empire, combining as it did unity and diversity in correctly balanced proportions, was the ideal constitution for Germany. A weak 'Germanic space' in the centre of Europe was also convenient for Germany's neighbours. The survival of the Empire was vital to the maintenance of the balance of power, which would be dangerously disturbed if it dissolved in anarchy or if it was absorbed by a neighbouring great power. The Holy Roman Empire was a German habit and a European necessity. When, after the French Revolution, the French effectively destroyed the balance of power, the need for the Empire disappeared.

A number of factors accumulating over centuries promoted disunity among the Germans and worked against the development of nationalism. Politically, the Holy Roman Empire was fragmented into a large number of states with all the attributes of sovereignty except sovereignty itself, which belonged to the Emperor. The Empire was based on the feudal relationships and legal norms of the late Middle Ages, a remarkably stable though flexible structure which survived until the great changes of 1803–6. The religious peace, the political boundaries and the peace-keeping apparatus of

[1]General works on Germany in this period: K. Epstein, *The Genesis of German Conservatism* (Princeton, 1975); J. Gagliardo, *Reich and Nation. The Holy Roman Empire as Idea and Reality 1763–1806* (Bloomington, 1980) and *From Pariah to Patriot* (Lexington, 1969); J.M. Diefendorf, *Businessmen and Politics in the Rhinland 1789–1834* (Princeton, 1980); G.P. Gooch, 'Germany's Debt to the French Revolution', *Studies in German History* (1948), pp. 190–209; A. Menhennet, *Order and Freedom. German Literature and Society 1720–1805* (1973), esp. pp. 3–43.

the Empire were consolidated by the treaties of Westphalia in 1648, which gave it another century and a half of life. Political fragmentation, in itself, need not have been an unclimbable barrier to the growth of national feeling. Indeed, it could have acted as a spur to it, as was the case after 1815, but there was no clear idea of what should replace the Empire. In addition, many of the larger individual states were actively promoting state patriotism and deliberately seeking to wean their subjects away from any lingering attachment to the Holy Roman Empire, using the clergy, schools and army to this end. In Prussia Frederick II employed the clergy of the Lutheran Church to preach Prussian rather than German patriotism and he abolished the long-standing practice of saying prayers in Prussian churches for the family of the Holy Roman Emperor, the nominal overlord of Germany. The rise and growing particularism of the states and the further decline of the Holy Roman Empire were accelerated by the Reformation and the Thirty Years War and were codified in the treaties of Westphalia in 1648. All this further stunted German national feeling. Germany lacked a powerful centre around which it could cohere. The Empire remained a focus of patriotism and popular emotion but was unable to do anything to strengthen Germany. The Empire was concerned only with tradition while most positive aspects of life — government, commerce, defence and education — passed totally under the control of the princes. There was no German national dynasty to act as a focus for national sentiment. In the seventeenth and eighteenth centuries there were periods of national solidarity associated with heroes or anti-heroes like Louis XIV or Frederick II, on whom the Germans could concentrate their hatred or affection, but such periods were brief and had no lasting effects, though anti-French feeling was to remain a major element in German nationalism into the nineteenth and twentieth centuries. There was from the later seventeenth century a great revival of interest in German history and law and the eighteenth century saw the publication of massive volumes on the imperial constitution and law[2] but no active desire to change the German political system. There is some danger in exaggerating the extent to which the Empire lost significance for ordinary Germans.[3] Prayers for the imperial family were said in all churches in the Empire, except Prussia, and the imperial courts continued to dispense justice until 1806.

[2]M. Walker, *Johann Jakob Moser and the Holy Roman Empire of the German Nation* (Chapel Hill, 1981).
[3]For example, H.A. Winkler, in his introduction to the collection of articles edited by him under the title *Nationalismus* (2nd edn, Königstein, 1985) states that the Germans 'had no political and institutional medium which could have provided them with an awareness of community, only a cultural one, language.' This ignores the Empire.

A more serious barrier to unity was the existence of dualism, the domination of the 'Germanic space' by two powers, Austria and Prussia, neither of which was wholly German in character or interests. Both states had important concerns outside Germany and since the seventeenth century both had behaved increasingly like foreign powers, pursuing interests outside Germany, building up spheres of influence among the smaller German states and using German national feeling when it was in their interest. In the seventeenth century Louis XIV had posed as the defender of 'German liberty', that is the liberties of the princes, against imperial encroachments; in the eighteenth this role passed to Prussia. In his League of Princes (1785) Frederick II cynically exploited the tradition of German liberty to sabotage Habsburg attempts to absorb Bavaria. The Habsburgs were equally ready to use the small reservoir of imperial loyalty when it suited them.[4] Not surprisingly, such behaviour was imitated by second-rank German states. Only among the miniature states, free cities and smaller ecclesiastical territories, especially in the south-west, did genuine imperial loyalty remain alive but the Empire was no longer able to protect them and in the late eighteenth century its importance was declining even as a symbol of German unity. Only the rivalry between Prussia and Austria enabled the Empire to survive for as long as it did.

The predominant political system in most of the German states was some form of bureaucratic monarchical absolutism, which grew up partly as a result of the weakness of the Empire and partly contributed to that weakness. In 1758 the Württemberg philosopher Friedrich Karl Moser wrote: 'Every nation has its principal motive. In Germany it is obedience; in England freedom; in Holland trade; in France, the honour of the king.' This was an exaggeration and oversimplification but contained an element of truth. The old view that the period after 1648 was 'the age of absolutism' in Germany, or in Europe as a whole, now needs considerable modification. The absolutist apparatus of government represented a system imposed over an existing framework of loyalties and institutions. Even powerful rulers in Germany had to live within the realities of the social and political situation in their states. The old Estates and corporate bodies like the guilds, nobility and even, in some cases, the peasants retained considerable influence. Regionalism and localism remained powerful forces into the nineteenth century and they, rather than national feeling, were strengthened by the constitutional battles against the imposition

[4]For example, the instructions for Austrian archdukes drawn up in the 1790s emphasized the importance of the imperial crown for the Habsburgs: W. Wagner (ed.), *Das Staatsrecht des Heiligen Römischen Reiches Deutscher Nation* (Karlsruhe, 1968).

of absolutism in many states in the seventeenth and eighteenth centuries.[5] Certainly, the rising absolutist states exercised more and more control in the daily lives of their subjects and demanded their loyalty exclusively for the local ruler. In the eighteenth century absolutism was in many German states transformed into its sanitized form, enlightened despotism. Although, under the influence of this movement, some rulers achieved significant improvement in their subjects' lives, as a whole Germany remained economically backward.[6]

In spite of this backwardness, enlightened despotism remained a source of great pride to Germans, who saw it as their own special form of government. It is significant that the initial reaction of many Germans to the French Revolution was that it was an attempt by the French to achieve the benefits of enlightened government, which they could attain only by violence. Germany enjoyed a period of peace between 1763 and 1792 and this influenced political attitudes. Although the situation varied from state to state, in the years leading up to the French Revolution several German states had experienced substantial reforms, which had improved their subjects' lives. The foundations of the state based on law (*Rechtstaat*) were firmly laid and written law codes had been introduced in many states to regulate relations between rulers and ruled. Social reforms had also taken place attacking discrimination and injustice. The *ancien régime* was popular with the majority of Germans on the eve of the French Revolution.[7]

Enlightened despotism, like the absolutism from which it developed, was based on the elevation of the state and the dynasty to a position of primacy. Bureaucratic government and cameralism, state direction of economic life, left no room for the concept of the nation. In countries other than Germany the absolutist monarch often acted as the unwitting father of the nation-state as a result of institutional centralization and the subjection of the population to greater control and more frequent direct contact with the organs of the state. The nation was also to inherit the mystical authority, and many of the ambitions, enjoyed earlier by monarchs and dynasties. For example, in France the attempts of Louis XIV to promote centralization of government and the increased use of French rather than local languages anticipated the policies of revolutionary governments after 1789. In Germany the progress of government growth solidified the states at the cost of the idea of

[5]F.L. Carsten, *Princes and Parliaments in Germany* (Oxford, 1959).
[6]H. Böhme, *An Introduction to the Social and Economic History of Germany* (Oxford, 1978), chap. 1.
[7]T.C.W. Blanning, *Reform and Revolution in Mainz 1743–1803* (Cambridge, 1974) and *The French Revolution in Germany* (Oxford, 1983).

the nation. It also layed the foundations for a peculiarly German view of the state and its role, which was to be very significant throughout the period we shall be looking at. Absolutism also hindered the growth of national feeling in other ways. It preserved the social primacy of the aristocracy, in Germany a cosmopolitan class susceptible to the lure of French fashion, fond of using the French language and tied to the dynastic state as the source of its status and employment. Other social groups and institutions were not inclined or were not able to act as promoters of nationalism. The Churches, Catholic and Protestant, were little more than departments of state. The peasantry were voiceless. Most towns were sleepy decaying places, usually controlled by conservative oligarchies of the guilds or state officials. The middle class was overwhelmingly a service class of lawyers, teachers and administrators, dependent for their employment on the state or the nobility, or members of the guilds, by the late eighteenth century bastions of reaction. An economic middle class in the sense of the modern capitalist bourgeoisie existed in only a few centres in Germany, like Berlin, Munich, Hamburg and Frankfurt, and they were weak and isolated.

In cultural terms Germany at that time was not fertile soil for the growth of nationalism. The predominant cultural movement was the Enlightenment, which, based as it was on the notion of an International Republic of Letters, was essentially cosmopolitan and a vehicle for foreign influences. It only touched the top layers of society directly and resistance to attempts to put its tenets into practice often stiffened localism rather than promoted German national feeling.[8] Among many educated Germans the notion of *ubi bono, ibi patria* was taken for granted. Goethe summed up the situation well when he wrote in 1772: 'Have we a fatherland? If we can find a place where we can rest with our possessions, a field to sustain us, a home to cover us, have we not there a fatherland?' The basic concern of the Enlightenment was man as an individual, not as a member of a class or nationality. Among the majority of Germans untouched by the Enlightenment, religion remained of prime concern and the Churches emphasized the desirability of individual morality and perfection. The nation had no place in their world view.[9]

In spite of this, the new attitudes associated with the Enlightenment did contribute to the rise of nationalism in that they promoted

[8]M. Walker, *German Home Towns. Community, State and General Estate 1648–1871* (Ithaca, 1971) and Helen Liebel, *Enlightened Bureaucracy versus Enlightened Despotism in Baden. 1750–92* (Transactions of the American Philosophical Society 55, Philadelphia, 1965).
[9]H. Holborn, *A History of Modern Germany* ii 1648–1840 (1965), p. 308; E. Kedourie, *Nationalism* (1961), p. 12.

a growing concern with this world rather than the next, with human happiness and fulfilment on earth and a belief in man's capacity to make his own future. Human reason, the argument ran, is capable, by its own power, of understanding and mastering the world. These ideas produced a new critical attitude towards aspects of traditional government and society. Reform was not to be simply in the gift of rulers but could be achieved by the people. In spite of that, the German Enlightenment remained essentially apolitical, concerned primarily with religion and philosophy. This is not to say that political discussion did not take place within the German states. Within bureaucracies there was often a lively if subterranean debate on policy and the aims of government, which was political in that it derived from different principles. The progress of enlightened reform in many states had slowed down somewhat in the years before 1789 as rulers began to lose their nerve or as opposition appeared. It is not too fanciful to see in some of this opposition in the years before the French Revolution the first faint stirrings of Liberalism in Germany. In the 1770s mild dissatisfaction with traditional forms of government had begun to be expressed in some states and long-accepted and unquestioned institutions and practices had come under challenge. Ironically, this had been encouraged by some of the German princes, among whom support for the Enlightenment was seen as modish. Just as in the seventeenth century they had aped Louis XIV and Versailles, so now they looked as their models to Frederick II and Berlin, which had claims to be the intellectual capital of Germany. They allowed their middle-class citizens to found reading circles, built their courts into cultural centres and encouraged the foundation of libraries and learned journals − some commentators talk of a 'publishing revolution' in Germany in the 1770s − clearly seeing no threat to their own power in such proceedings. Monarchy which did not make itself the instrument of progress, a nobility which did not earn its privilege by service, religious exclusiveness and intolerance, superstitious practices tolerated by the clergy, persecution of the Jews and barriers to a free economy were all being questioned and at the same time vested interests were beginning to fight back against enlightened reform, causing social tensions.[10]

Calls for greater social mobility, the abolition of guild restrictions, equality of opportunity and liberation of the economy − the voice of individualism − began to be heard. The ideas of Adam Smith

[10]Epstein, *Genesis of German Conservatism* and J. Whaley, *Religious Toleration and Social Change in Hamburg 1529−1819* (Cambridge, 1985).

spread quickly in Germany after the appearance of the first translation of *The Wealth of Nations* in 1776. The economic backwardness
of Germany was manifest. Only a few areas, the northern Rhineland, Saxony, Silesia and the Hanseatic ports, had some share in
the Atlantic economy, the rise of which had been one of the causes
of Germany's economic stagnation. The American Revolution in
the 1770s had a limited impact in Germany but enough to worry
some rulers. This is not to say that there was anything resembling
an organized opposition party with an articulated political programme, just the expression of vague and unco-ordinated discontents. Only when free discussion at an academic level began to
turn into criticism of the prevailing situation did German rulers
begin to question the wisdom of their earlier laxity. As the French
Revolution became more violent, such doubts began to turn into
fear and Germany was to be swept by reaction.

Very little of this reaction concerned itself with the political
structure of Germany as a whole. Some commentators, such as
F.K. von Moser in his work *On the German National Spirit* (1765),
called for a strengthening of the *Reich* and a modernization of its
creaking Gothic structures as a means of promoting general progress
in Germany. They were calling for a rational rather than a national
Germany and might be linked to the Patriot movements in other
parts of late-eighteenth-century Europe, such as Ireland and the
Netherlands, groups of people who believed that they had the
right policies for their countries and were not, like their political
opponents, motivated by sectional or selfish considerations.[11]

The French revolutionary period was important in changing all
this. In examining the rise of German nationalism the events of
the French period, 1789 to 1814, are of primary importance in
establishing the conditions in which nationalism could grow, in
providing the model of a new political, economic and social organization as an alternative to the *ancien régime*, in fostering new
ideas and in creating legends on which nationalism was later to
feed. During this period the whole of Germany came under direct
or indirect French military, political and economic control. While
Napoleon Bonaparte was in power, major changes took place in
Germany. The Holy Roman Empire, which had been the political
framework for the German nation for over a thousand years, was
abolished. The period also saw rapid and kaleidoscopic territorial
and political changes. It is also said to have witnessed the first
clear manifestations of modern German nationalism. In considering
the effects of the French Revolution in Germany one basic point
must be borne in mind: Germany as an entity did not exist,

[11]R.R. Palmer, *The Age of the Democratic Revolution* I (Princeton, 1959), p. 324ff.

politically, economically or even psychologically. In each German state the political, social and economic facts of life were different. To the great majority of Germans the concept of 'Germany' was something vague and very remote from their daily lives. Different areas, groups and classes in Germany were affected by the French domination of Europe in different ways.

The details of the period are complex and are not in themselves important if certain broad trends are understood.[12] When news of the first stages of the French Revolution arrived in Germany, the overwhelming reaction was indifference. Among the minority of educated Germans the events in France received an approving but passive welcome. France seemed to be in the process of acquiring by revolution the benefits of the Enlightenment which many Germans already enjoyed or hoped to enjoy thanks to their generous princes: written constitutions, law codes, the abolition of privilege, equality before the law and a career open to talents. The early optimism and confidence in the power of Reason and the principles associated with the Revolution continued to influence educated Germans but there was no attempt to imitate the French, except for a few isolated outbreaks of peasant rioting in areas close to the French borders. Conditions were different in Germany, with the absence of a Paris and a middle class in the French mould. More significant was what has been described as the 'spectator psychology' of the Germans: they enjoyed watching exciting events without desiring to take any part in them. Perhaps there was also some hope that events in France might breathe new life into reform in Germany.

The first effects of the Revolution were felt quickly as a marked reaction set in among the German rulers and they made determined efforts to prevent the contamination of French ideas spreading into Germany. The growing radicalism of the revolution in France intensified this reaction. It was particularly strong in Austria under Emperor Francis II after the troubled years of Joseph II's reign and was to endure for 50 years. It was unfortunate that Leopold II reigned for only two years (1790–2) as his previous activities as Duke Peter Leopold of Tuscany had earned him a reputation as one of the most enlightened rulers of the eighteenth century.[13] The reaction was part of a tide of feeling against the *philosophes* which had begun before the Revolution and was now reinforced by

[12]C.P. Gooch, *Germany and the French Revolution* (repr. 1965); O. Connelly, *Napoleon's Satellite Kingdoms* (New York, 1965); S.S. Biro, *The German Policy of Revolutionary France 1792–7* (Cambridge, Mass., 1957); H. Kohn, 'Napoleon and the Age of Nationalism', *JMH* 22 (1950), pp. 21–37 and *Prelude to Nation States. The French and German Experience* (Princeton, 1967).
[13]E. Wangermann, *From Joseph II to the Jacobin Trials* (Oxford, 1959); A. Wandruszka, *Leopold II* (2 vols., Vienna, 1963–5).

mounting xenophobia, anti-French sentiment, which identified the ideas of the Enlightenment with foreign atheism and subversion.

The principles of the French Revolution were eventually imported into Germany by force of arms. As a result of military victory, the French were able to dictate a settlement by right of conquest. The outbreak of war between France and the Emperor in April 1792 initiated a military revolution on the battlefields of Europe.[14] The *Amalgame*, a mixture of half-trained conscripts under amateur officers, stiffened with the remnants of the old royal army, smashed the cream of the professional armies of the *ancien régime*. As a result Paris, rather than Vienna or Berlin, became the place where the future of Germany was decided. The outbreak of war was a decisive turning point. Although there was growing friction between the French government and the Emperor in the months before over a variety of causes, the desire for war came from France not from Germany.[15] The prime cause of the war lay in French internal politics: the Gironde party preferred fireworks abroad to fireworks at home and promoted an aggressive foreign policy leading to war as a means of keeping the royalists and the Jacobins out of power. In their propaganda they portrayed war as a means of cleansing the revolution and forcing traitors to reveal themselves. They dressed their foreign policy in the clothes of principle, claiming the natural frontiers of France, including the Rhine, and preached the mission of the French to bring liberty to all those suffering tyranny and yearning to be free.[16] When France declared war on the Emperor in April 1792 it was not unwelcome. Both Austria and Prussia saw war as a chance to make easy gains from a France disrupted and, it was assumed, weakened by revolution. They were encouraged in this by Russia, anxious to distract them from Poland and the Balkans, leaving her a free hand there.

The war did not turn into the military promenade the allies had expected. After initial setbacks, the French won a great victory at Valmy in September 1792, after which they drove back their enemies. By the end of 1794 all of Germany west of the Rhine was in their hands and it was to remain so until 1814. They immediately began to introduce reforms, probably in preparation for the eventual annexation of the area. Guilds were abolished, there was a

[14]G. Best, *War and Society in Revolutionary Europe 1770–1870* (1982), chaps. 7–9.
[15]T.C.W. Blanning, *The Origins of the French Revolutionary Wars* (1986), p. 75.
[16]By a decree of 19 November 1792 the French assembly proclaimed the national mission of helping all peoples to regain their liberty and by one of 15 December 1792 French military commanders were instructed to declare to 'liberated' peoples that the French had come to bring peace, help, liberty, equality and fraternity and popular sovereignty. In reality, as soon became clear, liberation mean annexation, sometimes legitimized by very suspect plebiscites.

reorganization of administrative, judicial and legal systems and feudalism, or what the French regarded as feudalism, was abolished in all its forms. There was opposition from the main casualties of these changes, the clergy, the nobility and guild masters, but the overwhelming reaction to all this on the part of the population was indifference, a tribute to the success of absolutism. The French were regarded as new 'authority' or *Obrigkeit*, to be obeyed like the old. A few pro-French intellectuals emerged to form a puppet government, the most noted of whom was Georg Forster, the former scientist and librarian of the archbishop of Mainz.[17] These people were completely untypical of the population of the area.

In December 1794 the Prussian government entered secret negotiations with the French out of fear that Austria and Russia were conspiring against her, which they were. These negotiations culminated in April 1795 in the peace of Basel, under the terms of which Prussia withdrew from the war and the whole of northern Germany, which Prussia regarded as her sphere of influence, was neutralized. This arrangement with Prussia was very important to the French as it effectively guaranteed the security of the Rhine frontier. For over 10 years after this Prussia remained isolated and passive as she abdicated her role in Germany in order more easily to digest her gains from the partitions of Poland. More significant for Germany as a whole was the provision in the agreement that Prussia would be compensated for her land on the left bank of the Rhine, held by France, within the body of Germany. The cession of the left bank to France was confirmed in the treaty of Lunéville in 1801. This was to become the basis for subsequent massive territorial reorganizations, the first of which took place in 1803, by which time the French had defeated all the German states. Taken together, the changes of the years 1803 to 1806 can be described, as Heinrich von Treitschke was later to do, as 'the revolution of the princes', the final throwing off of the authority of the Emperor and the Electors and the conversion of the *Reich* into a confederation of sovereign rulers.

Although in theory the details of the changes were resolved by a committee of the imperial diet (*Reichstag*), the *Reichsdeputation*,[18] in reality it was the work of France and the larger German states, with Russia, linked by marriage to many of the German dynasties,

---

[17]Forster had the distinction, rare among leaders of puppet governments, of having had his dog eaten by the English explorer Captain Cook, whom he and his father accompanied on a voyage of exploration. The emperor penguin, *Aptenodytes forsteri*, is named after him. J. Cook, *A Voyage towards the South Pole* I (1779), p. 275; G.A. Craig, 'Engagement and Neutrality in Germany: The Case of Georg Forster 1754−94', *JMH* 41 (1969), pp. 1−16.
[18]The document embodying the changes was known as the Main Resolution (*Hauptschluss*) of the *Reichsdeputation*.

taking an interest. The French foreign minister Talleyrand made a fortune from the bribes offered by German states anxious to gain the choicest bits. Several states occupied and began digesting their gains long before the *Reichstag* ratified the settlement, which was based on the principle resolved at Basel, that compensation for those who had lost land to the French was to be found in the rest of the Empire. The obvious victims were the smaller states and, in particular, the ecclesiastical states, whose seizure had long been prepared for by attacks on them, in some cases undeserved, as badly-governed bastions of obscurantism. In the same way the French had long been preparing the way by attacks on the Holy Roman Empire as an institution. The *Moniteur* of 21 October 1797 described the German imperial constitution as 'the centre for all noble and feudal privilege' and stated that it must be the aim of the French republic to destroy it. France was anxious to build up a system of client states in Germany and territorial grants were an easy way of buying them. Even enlarged German states with no cohesion between them would represent no threat to France.

As a result of these reorganizations the famous patch-work of the old Empire disappeared. In all 112 political units disappeared, including 20 archbishoprics and bishoprics, 40 abbeys and convents and all the free cities except six. Also 350 free counties and knightly states were mediatized, handed over to other rulers. It was like a gigantic birthday party for the larger German states at which they could take any presents they wanted. They could now gobble up territory they had long coveted and rob their neighbours at will, something which the Empire, for all its manifest weakness, had long been able to prevent. France presided to prevent squabbles and mediated exchanges of territory to remove enclaves and anomalies. At the same time a political reorganization of the imperial constitution was carried through, under which extra Electors, the princes who chose the Emperor, were appointed and a Protestant majority in the imperial diet guaranteed. As it turned out, the settlement of 1803 was to last only three years.

Under Napoleon I France abandoned any pretence that her German policy was based on an altruistic desire to export the principles of the French Revolution and returned to traditional aims, the Rhine frontier and a protectorate over the rest, to use Germany as a milch cow for the benefit of the French military and political system, as a source of useful satellites and to deny German resources to the enemies of France. Napoleon made available to German governments the new methods of administration and organization which had made France such a formidable power and cloaked imperialism behind the pretence that membership of a French super-state under *la grande nation* would bring great benefits.

In exile on St Helena he liked to claim that he had planned to establish a federation of European nation states and that it was the nationalism, which he as heir of the Revolution had helped to foster, which eventually destroyed his empire. In this respect he quoted the examples of Spain, Germany, Italy, Poland and Hungary. There was little truth in this. Napoleon offered Europe a powdered instant form of the French Revolution solely with the aim of bringing benefit to France. If his regime did provoke German national feeling, it was essentially anti-French and not in any sense creative or progressive. There is still dispute among historians about Napoleon's ultimate aims, whether there was a blue-print for a new Europe or whether he was led on by pure ambition and expediency. Napoleon turned Germany into a great French prefecture. He went far beyond the traditional policies of Richelieu and Louis XIV. He had no concerted plan of reform for Germany and any reforms which did take place were incidental and designed to make it easier to cement Germany's colonial status. Strategic concerns played an important part in his policies. He toyed with the idea of joining northern Germany to the kingdom of Holland but in 1810 annexed it, as far as the Baltic, to the French Empire.

The constant warfare and frequent territorial reshuffles which took place subsequently gave the whole settlement an air of impermanence; a longer period of peace might have made lasting change possible. The reforms of the French period had the overall effect of strengthening the rulers and governments of individual states and did nothing directly to increase popular participation in decision-making. Most typical were the changes associated with the period of so-called neo-absolutism in the south German states. Among all Napoleon's policies, two in particular were of lasting importance, the enlargement of the south German states and the abolition of the Holy Roman Empire. After 1803 the south German states were allies of France. Austria was extremely unhappy about the 1803 settlement as the enlarged south German states were a barrier to her influence in the *Reich*. She had plans to consolidate her scattered possessions in the south, *Vorderösterreich*, into a powerful territorial block. The south German states were afraid of Austrian ambitions, a continuation of the expansionist policies of Joseph II. In January 1804 the Emperor tried to stop further changes in the Empire by judicial decision, a *Conservatorium*, and, when the opportunity arose, went to war against the French again. After the defeat of the Austrians and Russians at Austerlitz in December 1805, the southern states were rewarded with more territory. Prussia was enlarged by the acquisition of Hanover. Napoleon also set up the League of the Rhine (*Rheinbund*), an enforced union of German states and the grand duchy of Warsaw, excluding Austria and

Prussia. The League was originally planned as a genuine confederation with an assembly like the old *Reichstag* and a common law code, but these proposals met massive opposition from the larger members, especially Bavaria, jealous of their new power, and Napoleon dropped his plans. The League was eventually set up as a perpetual alliance between the Emperor of the French and 16 German rulers. It had a common army under the control of France, which also took care of foreign policy. Members were not permitted to enter any alliances outside the League. All seceded from the Holy Roman Empire and France issued an ultimatum compelling Francis II to abdicate. The title was offered to the king of Prussia, who refused it. The Holy Roman Empire ended on 6 August 1806. Germany, like Poland after the Partitions, had ceased to exist.

This is as convenient a date as any from which to begin a study of German nationalism because the end of the old Empire created the modern 'German problem'. That is perhaps a misnomer because in reality it was far more of a problem for the rest of Europe rather than for the Germans themselves. After 1806 there was no longer any political expression of the unity of the German nation and this was resented by a small minority of Germans, whom one could label 'nationalists'. Far more important than the aspirations of this group was the need to find a political arrangement of Central Europe acceptable to Germany's neighbours.

Although anything recognizable as modern nationalism was very weak during the French period, it was to give birth to a number of myths and legends important in the development of nationalism and for later generations of German nationalists. This was particularly true of the so-called War of Liberation, 1813–14. G.L. Mosse sees the War of Liberation as one of the most important events in modern German history and a major formative influence on German nationalism.[19] If so, it was more important for the legend than the reality. Goethe's scepticism about the 'national awakening' of 1813 is significant. He saw it as the affair of only a few thousand educated men while millions remained soundly asleep. The war began in December 1812 when the Prussian General York withdrew his contingents from the French army returning from defeat in Russia and moved into East Prussia. There he entered the convention of Tauroggen with the Russians without the consent of his government. The Prussian king hesitated a long time before deciding to fight the French. In the course of the subsequent war the French were driven out of Germany. Nationalist enthusiasm centred particularly on the battle of Leipzig, 16–19 October 1813, the so-called 'Battle of Nations', which made general

[19]G.L. Mosse, *Nazism* (Oxford, 1978), p. 33.

Blücher a national hero. There was certainly genuine patriotic enthusiasm for war against the French but later descriptions of the event as a 'people's war' or 'popular rising' (*Volkskrieg* or *Volkser-hebung*) are misleading. Part of the myth was created very quickly after the events. On the first anniversary of the battle E.M. Arndt organized a festival in Leipzig, described by a contemporary as a celebration by 'the German people rescued from 20 years of French slavery by princely unity and the power of the people' (*Fürsten-Eintracht und Volkskraft*). Unlike in Spain, there were no spontaneous popular uprisings. Far from being the great popular crusade against foreign domination portrayed in nationalist legend, the war was in reality a cabinet war, that is a war fought in pursuit of narrow state interests and initiated by German rulers when they felt safe enough to leave their alliance with France after the defeat of Napoleon's army in Russia, an army which, interestingly, con-tained a substantial number of Germans. Rulers now saw the writing on the wall and turned on the French. Typical was Metter-nich, foreign minister of Austria. When he decided to join the anti-French coalition in June 1813, German national considerations played no part in his careful calculations and he was afraid that French domination of Europe might be replaced with Russian. Bargains over future exchanges of territory, regardless of nationality, were struck before the war finished.

Although the motivation behind the German states' participation in the war was very much in the eighteenth-century tradition, the unprecedented scale of the conflict, the size of the forces involved and the financial burdens it produced, forced German rulers to try to imitate the mass mobilization of society seen in France after the Revolution. In 1813 rulers were prepared to use the age-old hostility of the Germans to the French but the actual campaigns were fought mainly by professional armies. The idea of mobilizing the people had been circulating for some time. In 1794 the *Reichstag* agreed, against fierce Prussian opposition, that the raising of militias would be a cheap way of supplementing professional armies on the model of the French *Amalgame*, but the intitiative was left to individual states. Under the influence of events in Spain, the idea was taken up in Austria with the foundation of a militia in 1808, which fought alongside the regulars in the war of 1809. Although popular, this was, like the later Prussian *Landwehr*, very carefully controlled by the military authorities. In the battle of Leipzig there were substantial numbers of Germans on both sides. The role of the Free Corps was marginal and they were made up of an unrep-resentative minority of students and middle-class youth under radical officers. They are better known for poetic celebration of their exploits than their real achievements, which were very small.

The popular militias recruited by German governments were adjuncts of the regular armies, though the fact that the German states needed mass conscript armies was a sign of how things had changed.

The size and coherence of the German nationalist movement at this time has been much exaggerated. The war was not the work of peoples but of states, strengthened and consolidated during the French period, and it was fought for particularist not nationalist motives. During it individuals like Baron von Stein, by then working for the Russian government, proposed the formation of a new federal German state with a single parliament but this idea enjoyed little support. Some historians, especially from the German Democratic Republic,[20] argue that the German rulers, by diverting their subjects' legitimate discontents against the French, were enabled to preserve the existing social system based, as it was, on exploitation of the lower orders; there may be something in this. Most Germans had little direct experience of French rule but lived under their own governments and remained docile until called upon by their rulers to rise up. German governments had done nothing to encourage resistance before 1813 in the conviction that it was wrong to encourage opposition to any authority. French domination of Germany had not produced any great popular discontent until the effects of an economic recession made themselves felt after 1810. There was no terrible oppression under the French, though after 1799 their rule did mean higher taxes more efficiently collected, higher prices, especially in the west (though in the areas annexed to France real incomes probably rose until the onset of the recession in 1812), the operation of the Continental System and conscription. The last was very unpopular; an estimated 120,000 Germans were conscripted in the *Rheinbund* states for service with the French army. There were outbreaks of violence before 1813, mainly among the peasantry, but they often arose in opposition to the modernizing policies of governments, that is in defence of local interests, and were in no sense part of a 'national' movement. The docility of the middle classes, the supposed standard-bearers of nationalism, was noteworthy. In Westphalia they supported French troops in putting down outbreaks of lower-class unrest and middle-class civic guards were organized after the departure of the French to preserve order until representatives of the new authorities arrived.

Other nationalist legends should be mentioned here. Jahn's *Deutscher Bund*, a student movement, operated mainly in the form

---

[20]A. Dorpalen, 'The German Struggle against Napoleon. The East German View', *JMH* 41 (1969), pp. 485–516.

of discussion groups and a few conspiracies. The German Societies (*Deutsche Gesellschaften*) in the Rhineland and the Hoffmann Society were short-lived and achieved little. In the Tyrol a force of peasant guerillas waged partisan warfare and their executed leader Andreas Hofer was later praised as a hero of German nationalism. In fact he fought against Bavarians, fellow Germans, in the cause of Tyrolean separatism, dynastic loyalty and the Catholic faith; against the reforms brought in by the Bavarian government, not for the cause of German freedom or a German national state. The rising was planned and directed from Vienna, which supplied propaganda material and built up contacts with the Tyrolean clergy and peasant leaders.[21] The Nuremberg bookseller Palm, executed by the French in 1806 after publishing a pamphlet, *Germany in her Deepest Humiliation*, bewailing the end of the Empire is remembered because so few copied his example. There were a few isolated attempts to stir up risings in parts of Germany, associated with the names of Dörnberg, Schill and the Duke Frederick William of Brunswick-Oels, all later nationalist heroes, but they came to nothing.

There is in nationalist legend much quotation of the Prussian king's proclamation 'To My People', issued in Breslau on 17 March 1813 and couched in vaguely nationalistic terms. Reference is also made to the reforms and a movement of national revival associated with Count Stadion and the Archduke Charles in Austria.[22] In 1809 Charles issued a much-quoted proclamation, including the statement: 'our affair is Germany's affair ... only with Austria's support can Germany again be independent and happy'. This was more a declaration of Austria's German role than a nationalist pronouncement. Such appeals served to arouse expectations of change but did not produce a mass movement for national unity or civil freedom. There was massive indifference to the 'national question'.

Later the liberals were to create their own myth of the war: to them an integral part of the whole affair was an implied promise of internal reforms after the defeat of the French. If some saw the war of Liberation as containing the implicit promise of progressive change, others saw it as fought on behalf of prince and religion. This view was summed up in the cry 'With God for king and fatherland!' used at the time; 'fatherland' could apply as well to the 'narrow fatherland' or state as to the German nation. The destruction of foreign oppression was seen as an opportunity to

[21]There was a strange echo here of a rising by Bavarian peasants against an occupying Austrian army in 1705–6, which combined local patriotism with social grievances.
[22]W.C. Langsam, *The Napoleonic Wars and German Nationalism in Austria* (New York, 1930).

restore the divinely ordained established order in state and society, far more German than the alien ideas and practices brought in by the French. There is evidence of a belief that the princes, when restored, might show gratitude to their people but the great majority of Germans seem to have been influenced by a vague yearning for a return of the good old days rather than a new form of Germany. If an alliance of progressive and reactionary forces was forged in opposition to the French it was very short-lived. The solution of the German question was eventually worked out by German and foreign rulers without reference to the wishes of the German people, whatever those wishes were.

Traditional views have placed great emphasis on the role of the Prussian Reform Movement in the development of German nationalism.[23] The Reform was the work of a group within the Prussian bureacracy, a highly educated class, drawing its ideas from a variety of sources, including the Enlightenment, the French Revolution and Adam Smith. The university of Königsberg in East Prussia was an important centre for the spread of Smith's ideas in Germany. The reformers, many of whom were not native Prussians, were able to gain the support of a small section of the nobility and the queen of Prussia and had tried to institute changes in the 1790s but they had to be very circumspect during the period of reaction. They were given their chance by the catastrophic defeat of Prussia at Jena in 1806. France had been prepared to allow Prussia to grow and dominate northern Germany while her hold on the left bank of the Rhine was insecure. After Austerlitz this was no longer the case and the French were not happy about Prussian ambitions to create a north German sphere of influence for herself. After Jena the whole structure of the Prussian state crumbled, though it was not rotten. Most striking was the total collapse of morale, comparable to that experienced in France in 1940. There was no resistance after the defeat of the army, fortresses surrendered at the first appearance of the French and the whole system of Frederick II, on whose laurels, according to the queen, the Prussian state had gone to sleep, fell apart. The apathy of the people was encouraged by the government, its attitude symbolized in the famous proclamation after Jena that the first duty of the citizen was to keep quiet (*Ruhe ist die erste Bürgerpflicht*).

The disaster of Jena, followed by substantial territorial losses

---

[23]H.W. Koch, *A History of Prussia* (1978); G.S. Ford, *Stein and the Era of Reform in Prussia* (Princeton, 1922); E.N. Anderson, *Nationalism and the Cultural Crisis in Prussia 1806–1815* (New York, 1939); P. Paret, *Yorck and the Era of Prussian Reform 1807–15* (Princeton, 1966); M.W. Gray, *Prussia in Transition: Society and (Politics under the Stein Reform Ministry* (Transactions of the American Philosophical Society 76, Philadelphia, 1986).

and a French military occupation of the country, enabled the reformers to capture the king's ear and to attempt to put into effect
a comprehensive programme of reforms designed to change the
basic nature of the Prussian state and Prussian society. It was not
the result of popular demand, a factor singularly lacking in Prussia,
but the work of a small section of the Prussian ruling class. It was
the aim of this group to destroy for ever the notion that the state
and army were alien corporations, whose fate was of no concern to
the people. They planned, in the words of the Nassau Memorandum
of June 1807, issued by one of the leaders of the Reform, Baron von
Stein, 'to reawaken a spirit of community and civic pride, the
employment of dormant or misapplied energies and of unused
knowledge, harmony between the views and desires of the nation
[Prussia or Germany?] and those of the administrative authorities
of the state, the revival of patriotism and the desire for national
honour and independence.' The practical steps proposed included
the abolition of serfdom, the introduction of free enterprise, equality before the law and of opportunity and major reforms in the
army and government.

The Reform Movement failed. They were not able to put their
ideas into practice in full. Their achievement was, in the light of
their ambitions, incomplete but they were able to bring about a
renaissance and modernization of Prussia with important long-
term consequences. They introduced the ministry system and cabinet government under the influence of Napoleon's legislative
council, strengthening the Prussian state and modernizing its absolutist system of government. They made Prussia a more efficient
and coherent state but they did not fundamentally change the
nature of the state, as they originally intended. The Reform failed
because of its inherent weakness: it had no mass following, the
king was a weak and hopeless ally and the opposition was strong,
influential and articulate. When later in the nineteenth century
Prussia began seriously to challenge Austria for power in Germany,
the work of the Reform Movement took on a new historical importance but one must beware of accepting the legend that the
Reform leaders were German nationalists.[24] There was no unity of
purpose and deep divisions on principle and policy within the
Reform Movement. Stein, who could be seen as on the 'right' of
the movement, was a free count of the Empire from the Rhineland,

[24]W.M. Simon, 'Variations in Nationalism during the Great Reform Period in Prussia',
Am H.R. 59 (1953−4), pp. 305−21, and *The Failure of the Prussian Reform Movement 1807−19*
(Ithaca, 1955); H.A. Schmitt, 'Stein, Alexander I and the Crusade against Napoleon', *JMH* 31
(1959), pp. 325−8.

an area where imperial loyalty was strong — 'I have only one fatherland and that is Germany. To it, and not to a part of it, I am fully devoted' — but his political ideas were complex and ambivalent, combining reactionary and progressive ideas. He recognized the need to take account of the realities of the German situation, the existence of the states. After his dismissal, on French insistence, as prime minister of Prussia in November 1808, he entered Russian service and in 1812 organized a Committee for German Affairs to organize opposition to French rule in Germany. This was responsible for the clandestine distribution of E.M. Arndt's writings. In a memorandum of 18 September 1812 he called for a restoration of a modernized and strengthened Holy Roman Empire, with fewer and larger states and a common German parliament or *Reichstag*. In 1813 he wrote in favour of the division of Germany into Austrian and Prussian spheres of influence with some kind of central authority, to begin its activities in a common occupation of the liberated *Rheinbund* states after the deposition of the collaborationist rulers.

Stein's 'Liberalism' has been much exaggerated in German historiography, for which he has been a redeeming feature, a kind of father of democracy. In reality he was no such thing. Another prominent leader from the 'centre' of the movement, Hardenberg, was strongly influenced by the French model and seems to have wanted to see a Germany divided into Austrian and Prussian spheres of influence, an institutionalization of the dualism of pre-1789 Germany, in itself a barrier to the creation of a truly unified nation-state. His prime concern was with the strengthening of Prussia in Germany, though after 1815, when he had lost most of his power, he became associated with the Hoffman Society, devoted to the creation of a united constitutional Germany. Wilhelm von Humboldt, one of the more radical Reformers, desired the reform and modernization of Prussia, especially in education, to enable her to make 'moral conquests' in Germany. It is significant that the fall of Prussia caused a far greater reaction in Germany than the end of the old Empire and it became for many patriots the focus of attention as the agent for Germany's rebirth. In spite of that, the Prussian Reform hardly amounted to a serious nationalist movement.

Its achievements were, even if incomplete, important in the long term in preparing the way for the economic modernization of Prussia. Legal serfdom was abolished in 1807 but the Reformers' aim to create a large, free and independent landowning peasantry was not realized because most peasants lacked the capital to take advantage of their freedom. The abolition legislation was modified by regulations issued in May 1816, which were very unfavourable to the peasantry. The main beneficiaries of the free trade in land were the nobility, who were to benefit further after the war from government-sponsored rural credit agencies, rural industry and a revival of the grain trade. Substantial landed estates were built up in the eastern provinces and large increases in output were achieved by the application of new methods. This provided a life-buoy for the large-scale landowners. From 1808 Prussia had elected town governments and councils, which were later to become important training schools for Liberal politicians, though the system was not extended to the Rhineland and Westphalia when they became Prussian in 1815. There the French system of government-appointed town officials was retained until 1845. There was no all-Prussian parliament, no written constitution and no rural self-government. The dominance of the nobility in the Prussian countryside remained intact. Class privileges were abolished but important noble privileges, including tax exemption, abolished in 1810, were restored in 1819. The nobility exercised civil jurisdiction over its former serfs until 1848 and retained police powers in rural areas until 1872 and special administrative powers until 1891. In theory after the Reform the civil service and the officer corps were open to all men of talent but in reality they were not and remained preserves of the nobility and upper middle class. The eastern provinces continued for a long time to set the tone for the whole state. Important educational reforms were achieved with the foundation of a university at Berlin and a system of *Gymnasia* on the model of Napoleon's *lycées*. The restrictive powers of the guilds and internal barriers to trade were abolished, including the urban excise, which had erected toll barriers between town and countryside, and Prussia enjoyed in theory a system of free enterprise, though it would be a long time before she was wealthy enough to take advantage of it.

Equally if not more important were the military reforms. Scharnhorst and Gneisenau wished to convert the army into a 'school of the nation', teaching civic virtues as well as soldiering. In 1813 a system of universal conscription was introduced along with the militia or *Landwehr*. The last was to become a great Liberal legend later in the nineteenth century, when it was seen as a people's army under middle-class officers available to defend constitutional rights against tyranny. The role of the *Landwehr* in the war of Liberation was minimal and it became a shadow after 1819. Although the Army Law of 1814 remained in effect in Prussia, the high-minded intentions of its framers were not achieved. After 1815 conscription, universal in theory, became increasingly selective in practice.

The Reform removed some of the more glaring faults in the old

Prussian system and cleared the way for an eventual industrialization of the country. Most important, it left a legacy of brilliant
young officers and civil servants, imbued with the ideal of service
to the state and committed to the concept of the state based on
law (*Rechtstaat*).[25] They were also responsible for Prussia's later
achievements, including the establishment of the German Customs
Union (*Zollverein*) of 1834 and, because of the industrial modernization of the 1850s and the brilliant works of Moltke's General
Staff, for the military victories between 1864 and 1871. But these
men were not German nationalists and their work in strengthening
Prussia could have laid the foundations of a distinct Prussian
nationhood, making German unification more difficult. Other larger
states, for example Bavaria, could also have created nationhood of
their own, as Austria was eventually to do.

Just how different was the Germany of 1815 compared with that
of 1789? In addition to the obvious territorial changes and the end
of the Holy Roman Empire, the French period saw a general
modernization of government. The extent of other aspects of change
varied from region to region. The effects were deepest in the area
west of the Rhine, annexed to and completely incorporated into
France. After initial problems, the population became reconciled
to French rule, which brought benefits such as inclusion in the
highly protected French market. In 1815 there was some opposition
in the area to proposals to cede it to Prussia, which was seen as a
backward state, and to Bavaria. Its economy remained vigorous
and it remained under French law until 1900. It was from the
Rhineland that some of the leading Liberals of the early nineteenth
century were drawn.

Major changes in other parts of Germany arose from the fact that
Napoleon's system of control was based on co-operation with the
existing rulers, who were subject to increasing pressure to make
their administration more efficient in order to meet the costs of
French garrisons and mounting French demands on them for men
and money. French agents were sent into the satellite states in
large numbers to keep Paris informed of what was going on. The
reforms were not motivated by concern for the rights of man,
popular democracy or German unity but by the needs of the state.
Napoleonic Germany was made up of artificial states with an
artificial boundary, the Rhine. The need to contribute to the French
war effort considerably limited the impact of modernization and
many German states were still paying off the accumulated debts
years after 1815. The reforms which were carried out have been

[25]J.R. Gillis, 'Aristocracy and Bureaucracy in Nineteenth-Century Prussia', *P. and P.* 41
(1968), pp. 105–29.

grouped together under the name late absolutism or neo-absolutism, though in many of the states absolutism had remained an aspiration rather than a system before 1803. The work is associated with the names of Maximilian de Montgelas in Bavaria, Sigismund von Reitzenstein in Baden and King Frederick in Württemberg. Reforms on the French model were also carried through in the French-ruled states Westphalia and Berg.[26] The changes were not as marked in northern Germany, where territorial changes were less substantial. Only the tiny state Anhalt-Köthen voluntarily introduced a copy of the French administrative system. The southern states were faced with the problem of incorporating the new lands given to them by France, lands with widely differing social and political systems. The easiest way to achieve this was to issue new unitary constitutions and uniform legal systems, to construct new bureaucracies and to introduce a system of equality before the law and general religious toleration. Centralization, cabinet government, state control of Churches, the removal of internal barriers, the abolition of personal unfreedom where it survived, common currencies and weights and measures systems and local government reforms were also introduced. These states were thus able to acquire many of the benefits of the French Revolution without any of the inconveniences. They also enjoyed the time to concentrate on internal affairs, as diplomacy and foreign policy were generously taken over for them by the French, and the state began to penetrate more deeply into the lives of subjects than before. The unprecedented upheaval of the French period enabled many of the barriers which had earlier prevented the complete victory of centralization to be thrown aside. Great strides were made in Bavaria, Baden and Württemberg, which acquired assemblies and were by 1815 taking their first steps on the road towards parliamentary government. Another result of the reforms was a further strengthening of states, princes and bureaucracies, which made the achievement of national unity more difficult. It was most unlikely that these new, stronger and more self-conscious states with modern administrations would be ready to submit themselves to any new federal systems of government in Germany.

The Germany which emerged in 1814 from a period of French control was further away from unity than before. It was made up of states with widely differing legal systems, economic laws, currencies and weights and measures systems. The old ruling groups

---

[26]H.C. Vedeler, 'The Genesis of the Toleration Reforms in Bavaria under Montgelas', *JMH* 10 (1938), pp. 473–95, W.O. Shanahan, 'A neglected source of German nationalism: The Confederation of the Rhine 1806–13', in M. Palumbo and W.O. Shanahan (eds.), *Nationalism* (Westport, 1981), pp. 103–30.

were still in power as Napoleon had found it most convenient to run Germany in collaboration with the established authorities. There had been no great economic changes and no powerful middle class had emerged. Free-trade ideas were spreading but the success of the concept demanded a free economy, a strong economic middle class and ample capital, all lacking in Germany. Capital released by the abolition of serfdom in the form of compensation paid to former lords by governments, for example, found its way overwhelmingly into land purchase or government stocks in the good old *ancien régime* fashion and the role of the state in the economy remained paramount. The Napoleonic code did not, as in France, produce a strengthened class of substantial peasant farmers and middle-class land-holders. 'Feudalism' was nominally abolished in Germany but the effects varied from place to place and many 'feudal' relics lasted well into the nineteenth century. The lords' lost rights were often simply converted into payments, which strengthened noble landowners. The freeing of the serfs also had a limited effect: most former serfs remained in their villages, habits of deference towards former owners remained and high taxation and limited capital resources prevented the great majority of freed serfs from taking advantage of their freedom. Free enterprise was introduced and the guilds abolished or weakened but the effects of this were very limited in an economy still dominated by agriculture. After 1815 many German states had free enterprise but there was a considerable time-lag before this was exploited on any substantial scale. Even in the states controlled directly by the French, for example the kingdom of Westphalia and the duchy of Berg, there was no introduction of institutions to permit wider participation in decision-making, though the French may have planned this.

The 'reforms' introduced during the French period were not always seen as beneficial by everyone, especially when they assaulted the rights of vested interests. Ironically, the main effect of the French-sponsored modernization was to increase yearning for a restoration of the 'good old days' and to strengthen regional and group loyalties, and this was to remain the case after 1815. In addition, the departure of the French was followed by a reaction against them. Many of the reforms they had introduced were regarded as unpatriotic and there was a widespread desire for the restoration of traditional conditions. It is argued, for example by some East-German historians, that anti-French feeling engendered during the French period blunted the social awareness of the Germans, as a result of which they longed for a return of a romanticized old regime not the creation of a new unified Germany; and there is something in this argument. The changes brought in by the French in the areas under their direct control were regarded with great suspicion by many of the rulers who returned after 1814 and most aimed to restore as much as possible of the pre-revolutionary order. The situation differed from state to state. In some, for example the kingdom of Hanover, the French legislation was abolished and there was a return to the old system, with all its local and regional differences. Financial pressures forced some governments to retain the French reforms in land-holding, taxation and administration, at least in part, and there was no general restoration of the pre-revolutionary powers of the guilds. Long before 1789 German rulers had sought to reduce the political and social power of the guilds, a powerful vested interest with cross-border connections. Where changes originating in the French period were retained after 1815 it was because they were in the interests of the larger German states or of European powers not because of German nationalism.

It now seems to be accepted that the French period retarded the development of the German economies and caused considerable distortion. Maritime trade and all that depended on it were hard hit. The new sophisticated administrations were a costly burden. Napoleon's Continental System, the closing of the Continent to British imports, did not last long enough to promote German manufactures and after 1815 Germany was again exposed to the cold wind of British competition and the effects of the British Corn Laws. Most German states lacked the capital to sustain exports.[27] There were no incentives for economic co-operation between the German states before or after 1815 when depressions led to increasing concentration on narrow state interests. In the Rhineland and Baden the operation of the Napoleonic code, which remained in force there until 1900, led to subdivision of holdings, which, because of a shortage of capital to buy out younger siblings, led to a development of dwarf holdings and rising emigration from the 1830s. Only in the Rhineland, which for 20 years had benefited from inclusion in the protected French market, was there any substantial industrialization and a strong economic middle class. The rest of Germany remained firmly pre-capitalist until the middle of the nineteenth century. The deep differences between east and west became more marked during the French period. Most German towns remained sleepy and conservative, devoted to the negative virtues of stability, loyalty and security rather than enterprise and

[27]F. Crouzet, 'Wars, Blockade and Economic Change in Europe 1792–1815', *Journal of Economic History* 24 (1964), pp. 567–88; F.L. Ford, 'The Revolutionary–Napoleonic Era: How Much of a Watershed?', *Am. H.R.* 69 (1963–4), pp. 18–29; H. Kisch, 'The Impact of the French Revolution on the Lower Rhine textile districts', *Ec.H.R.* 15 (1962–3), pp. 304–27.

individual effort. Germany was to experience economic change and progress in the period 1815 to 1848 but it was to be patchy and the states were to play a substantial part in taking the initiatives.

Nevertheless, the French period did have long-lasting political, social and cultural results. It gave rise to new thinking about society and after it the clock could not be put back to 1789. Legitimacy had been challenged as hundreds of German rulers lost their territories in the great changes after 1803. Only the most powerful, or those with foreign friends, were restored after 1814. A new model of a social and political system was created in an idealized version of the French revolutionary state, though many German Liberals saw the French as having 'betrayed' their revolution, a return to the rather patronizing attitudes apparent in 1789. It soon became clear after 1815 that the main beneficiaries of the French period were not German nationalists but the German governments. The German nationalist movement remained vague and had no realistic scheme of reorganization to offer as an alternative to the individual states. The local prince, not the German nation, remained the focus of popular sentiment.

4

Germany 1815–1850: The Rise and Fall of Liberal Nationalism

The years 1815–50 were a key period in the development of German nationalism.[1] Germany experienced the first stages of social and economic modernization to complement the administrative modernization achieved during the French period. This produced new movements and tensions in society. In the absence of developed political institutions in most of the states, there was no readily available means of articulating dissatisfaction with the prevailing situation. These years also saw the appearance of a number of important legends to join those already accreting on the Germans' view of their own past, the conservative view of revolution and its causes and the Liberals' view that the triumph of their ideology was somehow inevitable. Both the major strands of nationalism, Liberal and Romantic, also experienced important changes. Nationalism began to change from the creed of a small minority and to acquire a wider popular following.

As part of the general European settlement negotiated at Vienna in 1815 Germany was given a new political framework, the *Bund* or Confederation. This has been the victim of nationalist value judgements, that anything which promoted national unity was good while anything else was bad. It has suffered from a very bad press and has been castigated as a total failure, a kind of stop-gap system only waiting to be replaced with something more attuned to German 'realities' or a better expression of German nationalism. It has no real history but is usually written off as the codification of particularism or a tool of the 'System' of the Austrian foreign minister Metternich, designed to crush Liberalism and nationalism. It is also viewed with hindsight as a prelude to the revolutions of 1848, a view symbolized in the description of the period 1815–48 as the Pre-March (*Vormärz*). In fact the Confederation lasted from 1815 until 1848 and from 1850 until 1866, longer than Bismarck's Second *Reich*, the Weimar Republic or the Third *Reich*. It collapsed for essentially the same reasons as the Holy Roman Empire, its inability to control its powerful members, especially Prussia, rather than the inherent weaknesses of its constitution. To

[1]General works on the period: T.S. Hamerow, *Restoration, Revolution and Reaction. Economics and Politics in Germany 1815–71* (Princeton, 1958); A. Ramm, *Germany 1789–1919. A Political History* (1967, pb. edn, 1982).

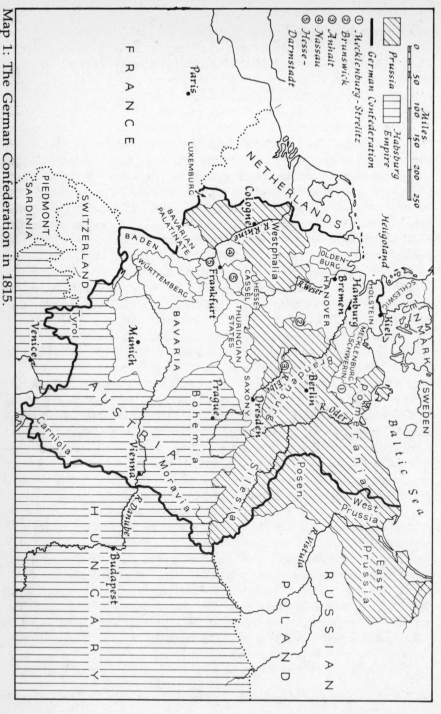

Map 1: The German Confederation in 1815.

Prussia

German Confederation

Habsburg Empire

① Mecklenburg-Strelitz
② Brunswick
③ Anhalt
④ Nassau
⑤ Hesse-Darmstadt

Miles
0 50 100 150 200 250

FRANCE

Paris

NETHERLANDS

LUXEMBURG

BAVARIAN PALATINATE

Cologne

R. Rhine

Westphalia

OLDEN-BURG

Heligoland

Bremen

Hamburg

MECKLENBURG-SCHWERIN

HOLSTEIN

SCHLESWIG

DENMARK

SWEDEN

Baltic Sea

Kiel

Pomerania

①

Berlin

R. Oder

West Prussia

East Prussia

R. Vistula

RUSSIAN POLAND

Posen

Silesia

Dresden

SAXONY

THURINGIAN STATES

HESSE CASSEL

④

⑤

Frankfurt

⑤

HANOVER

R. Weser

SWITZERLAND

PIEDMONT SARDINIA

BADEN

WÜRTTEMBERG

BAVARIA

Munich

AUSTRIA

Tyrol

Venice

Carniola

Prague

Bohemia

Moravia

Vienna

R. Danube

Budapest

HUNGARY

Brandenburg

R. Elbe

view the Confederation as an unrelieved failure is to subscribe to the Borussian and nationalist legends. Arguably the Confederation was the most appropriate constitution Germany has had in its recent history, the political framework best suited to the circumstances of the time. To condemn it because it was not an expression of nationalism is to misunderstand totally the circumstances of 1815.

The Confederation was not without possibilities of development. It is interesting to compare Germany with Switzerland: in 1815 both set out from the same starting point but, whereas in 1848 Switzerland was converted into a federal state, Germany was not. Like the Holy Roman Empire, the Confederation survived as a factor in the European balance of power. Its major weakness was its inability to accommodate change and its failure to cope with the political and social results of economic modernization. This led to the revolutions of 1848. The Confederation survived these, only to be destroyed, as the Holy Roman Empire had been, by the collapse of Austro-Prussian dualism and the political ambitions of the Prussian prime minister Bismarck, not as a result of nationalism.

It is necessary to examine the genesis of the Confederation, which was the product of a long development. The German question took up a considerable amount of time at the congress of Vienna and many divergent interests had a say in the settlement.[2] The overwhelming motive behind it was a desire for peace and quiet and the Confederation of 1815 was part of a collective security system. The future of Germany was a common European problem, as a weak Germany was an open road into Europe for France or Russia, as had been shown after 1789. Suspicion of Russia was strong after 1815, made worse by its military power and Alexander I's unpredictability. In the eyes of the European powers the prime need was for a strong buffer not a strong Germany. It was therefore a European necessity to devise some form of German unity. The question was not whether Germany should be united but in what form. Article 6 of the First Treaty of Paris of May 1814 said: 'The states of Germany shall be independent and united by a federative bond'. To have expected a reorganization on the basis of popular sovereignty and nationalism would have been quite unrealistic; these were the very ideas which the French Revolution claimed to have been spreading in Europe. The powers at Vienna were, anyway, not totally deaf to national claims.[3] The German states enlarged

[2]E.E. Kraehe, *Metternich's German Policy* (2 vols., Princeton, 1963–83). Vol. 2 deals with the Congress of Vienna.

[3]Under the influence of the British foreign minister Castlereagh, the powers which had partitioned Poland agreed to introduce some form of autonomy for the Poles in their territories. Metternich himself favoured self-government for the Italian provinces acquired by Austria as part of the Vienna settlement: A.C. Haas, *Metternich. Reorganization and Nationality 1813–18* (Wiesbaden, 1963); E.L. Woodward, *Three Studies in European Conservatism* (1929); A. Palmer, *Metternich* (1972).

by Napoleon were to survive because there were international agreements to that effect and because it was in no one's material interest to dismantle them. In addition, nationalism was very weak in Germany in 1815 and very few wanted a single unitary state, as the Liberal newspaper from the Rhineland, the *Rheinischer Merkur*, admitted with regret. There was, no doubt, great disappointment among progressive nationalists at the settlement of 1815 and wider regret that Germany made no territorial gains,[4] but far more common was a desire for a restoration of the Holy Roman Empire, especially amongst those who had lost their imperial immediacy, that is their status as direct subjects of the Holy Roman Emperor, during the French period and the small states who feared their larger neighbours. Such remote possibilities were anyway vetoed by the governments of the larger German states. For example, Bavaria banned all propaganda calling for a restoration of the Old Empire or the creation of a German union. The particularism of the larger south German states also extended to resentment of domination by Austria and Prussia. In 1822 politicians in Bavaria and Württemberg floated the idea of a *Trias*, a closer union of the 'Third Germany' to resist the two German great powers.

The actual decisions on the future of Germany at Vienna were left to a committee of the larger states, Austria, Prussia, Hanover, Württemberg and Bavaria, which met several times between October and November 1814. The main factor at work was the political jealousy between the states, especially between Austria and Prussia. Austria, assuming the role of the policeman of Europe, expected the main threat to international order to come from Italy and regarded a tranquil Germany as essential. The *Bund* came into existence as an extension of Austrian foreign policy and it was envisaged from the start that the whole thing would be within an Austrian sphere of influence in Europe, with Britain and Russia in a secondary role. There is some irony in the fact that Metternich had to fight hard until 1819 against those in the Austrian government, including sometimes the Emperor, who believed that Austria, far from trying to control Germany, should detach herself completely from what was seen as a blister on the heel of Austrian progress.

With the decline in the influence of the Reform party, the second German great power, Prussia, was interested in Germany only as far as she could gain advantages there to strengthen her European

[4]In the years 1813–14 there was some hope that Alsace and Lorraine, separated from Germany since the seventeenth and eighteenth centuries, would be restored, but, in accordance with the wishes of the inhabitants, they remained French. It is anyway hard to see which German state or states would have absorbed them without offending others.

position. Since the 1770s Prussia's policies had had an eastwards orientation: her main ambition lay in the retention of as much Polish land as possible and she was prepared to play German politics in the hope of gaining bargaining counters to put pressure on Austria. The main motives behind her policies in Germany were the same as before 1789. The geographical determinant, arising from the scattered nature of her lands, remained strong. She had ambitions to acquire the whole of Saxony (an old ambition of Frederick II), which had remained an ally of France for too long and ended up on the losing side.[5] She wished to turn northern Germany into a Prussian sphere of influence and to gain some institutional recognition of her equality with Austria in any German political structure, especially in military matters. During the nego- tiations at Vienna the Prussians floated a number of schemes for a federal Germany with strong central organs run by a committee of the larger states but it is very doubtful that these were intended to be taken seriously. Prussia was not able to make the gains she had anticipated. Austria and France collaborated to stop Prussia seizing the whole of Saxony and she was forced to accept a part of it and the Rhineland and Westphalia, seen by Prussia as an expensive nuisance and by Austria as a means of weakening her. This was ironical because possession of the Rhineland forced Prussia back into Germany and gave her the basis of her later industrialization.[6] The population of Prussia was doubled by the settlement of 1815 to some 11½ million, of which about 8 million were in the Confed- eration. (The population of the Austrian Empire in 1815 was about 30 million, of which about 10 million were in the Confederation, which had a total population of about 31 million.) The kingdom of Hanover, in personal union with the British crown until the un- foreseen breach of the link in 1837, was much enlarged to balance Prussian power in north Germany. The union of Belgium and the Netherlands was also envisaged by Austria as a check on Prussia as well as a barrier against French aggression.

The long-winded negotiations in Vienna were interrupted by Napoleon's return from Elba and the Hundred Days, after which the German Committee resumed under Metternich's presidency and was clearly under pressure to settle things quickly. After eleven days' meetings a settlement was rushed through, leaving major items over for later arrangement, including Jewish rights,

[5]G.A. Craig, *The Politics of the Prussian Army* (Oxford, 1955), pp. 65—75, has a good analysis of Prussian politics at this time. See also L.J. Baack, *Christian Bernstorff and Prussia. Diplomacy and Reform Conservatism 1818—32* (New Brunswick, 1980).
[6]J.M. Diefendorf, *Businessmen and Politics in the Rhineland 1789—1834* (Princeton, 1980), p. 334f.: Prussia very quickly overcame initial hostility in the area and won over influential people by a careful policy, including leaving much of the French system intact.

military arrangements, press rights and economic co-operation. Matters such as religion, citizens' rights and constitutional provisions were specifically left to the decision of individual states as any attempt to lay down a common system would have caused far too much trouble. Austria was prepared to accept limited collaboration with Prussia as a means of controlling her and both states were very conservative in domestic politics. In practice dualism was restored in the form of common action against nationalist and democratic movements. Control of Germany was shared informally between the two on the basis of advice, influence, dynastic links and economic interdependence. After 1819 Prussia seems to have abandoned all plans for activating the Confederation and thereafter her German policy was restricted to the construction of a loose party among the smaller north German states. Austria did not make a great fuss about her primacy in Germany and preferred to work quietly among the other governments, using influence and fear of the revolution to maintain her control The Habsburgs still enjoyed the prestige associated with the old Empire and this aided the maintenance of their leadership of the Confederation. Metternich also remained afraid of Prussian ambitions and a revival of demands for formal dualism, which, he believed, must mean a partition of Germany.[7]

Foreign interference, a permanent feature of German political life under the Holy Roman Empire, was less obvious but still an important factor after 1815. During the periods of repression after 1819 and in the early 1830s Britain and France tried to exercise some mild pressure on behalf of Liberalism. After 1815 the French government quickly reverted to traditional policies in Germany. Its opposition to various repressive anti-Liberal policies of the Confederation was largely motivated by fear that Austria was becoming too dominant in German affairs. Russian influence, though inconsistent while Alexander I was on the throne, was usually in support of repression.

The structure and institutions of the Confederation do not need detailed analysis here. It has been described as a modernized and streamlined version of the Holy Roman Empire and there is something in this, though now the member states were fully sovereign. Like the Empire, it contained foreign monarchs, the kings of Britain, Denmark and the Netherlands, as rulers of territories inside the Confederation. It was more German in character than the Empire. It did not, for example, include northern Italy, but its borders were as anomalous as those of the Old Empire, in that it contained large

[7]R.D. Billinger, 'The War Scare of 1831 and Prussian—South German Plans for the End of Austrian Dominance in Germany', *Cent. Eur.H.* 9 (1976), pp. 203—19.

non-German minorities and excluded substantial bodies of Germans in Schleswig and East and West Prussia. The Confederation was a perpetual alliance of 34 monarchs (35 after 1817) and the governments of four free cities. It involved no surrender of sovereignty by any of its members, except that there was no right of secession from the union. It existed among the member states but not over them. It had no head of state, no common administrative organs, no common citizenship, no national flag and no common law courts. In these respects it was much less of a state than the Holy Roman Empire. The Act of Association by which it was established contained vague promises of future common action to promote all-German economic interests but nothing was done, largely because of the opposition of Bavaria. Immobilism seemed to be built into its structure. The diet in Frankfurt was, like the old *Reichstag*, an assembly of ambassadors, under the presidency of the representative of the Emperor of Austria, dependent on instructions from their governments. Both the standing committees, which prepared material for debate, and the full diet were dominated by the larger states, which had more votes. Votes were anyway usually a formality as decisions were worked out in advance by secret conferences and diplomacy. Its permanent staff was very small. It had no seal of office and sat in a rented building, the former palace of the counts of Thurn and Taxis. Any decisions reached had to be put into effect by the individual states as the Confederation had no executive organs. This did not matter much as the assembly reached very few decisions. The publication of its debates ended in 1828.

The Confederation only seemed to act as an all-German body when it came to repressing movements for change as an extension to Germany of the so-called Metternich system, the censorship, secret police and mail-interception system established in Austria since the reign of Joseph II. Eighteen-nineteen, the year of the Carlsbad decrees placing strict controls on the press and universities, can be regarded as a turning point. Up to then the Confederation was evolving with different forces at work within it and it could have developed in the direction of a more unitary state. The years 1814 to 1819 also saw relative press freedom in most of the German states. Afterwards the Confederation seemed devoted only to repression. Metternich's reaction to the murder of the writer Kotzebue by a student in March 1819 and to an attempt on the life of the chief minister of Nassau shortly afterwards was out of all proportion to the acts themselves. They were not the first blows in a revolutionary rising but the work of unbalanced individuals. Metternich typified the eighteenth-century view of the Revolution as the result of the machinations of an evil 'intellectual proletariat' and under his influence the main targets of repression were the writers, universities and clubs. In the eyes of Liberals, at least, this made Germany a much more visible political entity than the old *Reich* had been.

The final form of the Confederation was established by the Vienna Final Act of May 1820, worked out at a long conference of the leading states and accepted by the diet in July. This brought to an end all attempts to give the organization a wider competence in all-German affairs. In 1821, after Prussian agitation, the organization for a German confederate army was created. This was designed only for defensive war and was only to come into existence in case of an external attack on a member state or to undertake federal execution against a member state to prevent its secession from the Confederation. Prussia was understandably anxious that her own security should not depend on allies whose military arrangements were inadequate but Prussia's ambition to take charge of military arrangements in the North as a tangible symbol of its equality with Austria was vetoed by Metternich, with the help of Prussia's jealous neighbours. A confederate military commission was set up to standardize military arrangements in the states but nothing was achieved. The first, last and most spectacular action of the confederate army was in carrying out a federal execution against Prussia in 1866. Its total defeat heralded the end of the Confederation.

Under the Confederation Germany became in some respects more variegated rather than more unified. Regionalism remained very powerful and local loyalties rather than German sentiment were reinforced by the further development of more modern and more clearly defined states, whose activities had a more immediate impact on their citizens' lives. In general there was an emphasis on tradition and a conservative ideology seemed to be hardening. Friedrich Gentz, an enthusiastic supporter of Metternich's policies speaking at the conference of 10 leading states called in 1819 at Carlsbad to discuss the repressive measures, urged respect for Germany's past rather than imitation of foreigners. He unsuccessfully pressed for a tightening up of Article 13 of the Act of Association, which laid down that each member state was to have a 'constitution based on Estates' (*landständische Verfassung*), to exclude the more modern constitutions of some of the states. This vague provision may have been a sop to English constitutionalism and, more importantly, probably derived from a desire to rob revolutionary movements of an excuse for action. It was intended that the German princes should seek the advice of representative corporations and the use of the word *landständisch* is pre-revolutionary, redolent of the world of medieval orders. In fact, a wide range of different constitutions emerged under the vaguely worded Article 13. In most, the old Estates remained in existence and continued to act as fora for localism and group loyalties. In a few nothing was done to fulfil Article 13. For example, Oldenburg had no Estates and in the kingdom of Hanover, much enlarged in 1815, the various component provinces which made it up retained their separate Estates. Where the old Estates were restored there was no great resistance to this. A few states were able to advance constitutionally after 1815. In some, particularly in the south, modified versions of the modern constitutions issued during the French period, and usually based on the French *Charte* of 1814, survived and were extended, for example in Saxe-Weimar in 1816, in Baden and Bavaria in 1818, in Württemberg in 1819 and in Hesse-Darmstadt in 1820. Their parliaments were elected on very narrow franchises, had very limited powers and seem to have aroused massive apathy among the population, judging by the low turn-out for elections and evidence of some resentment of them as a waste of money, but they represented a beginning, a foundation. Certainly they were not linked to past traditions and had no connections with the old pre-revolutionary Estates. They may have been training schools for Liberals but this was rarely obvious. Governments were able to make life very difficult for those who wanted to extend parliamentary powers. Polls were often rigged, parliamentary debates were not published and state employees were often refused leave for political activities. There were usually upper houses dominated by the nobility and appointees of the crown. The 1820s saw constitutional squabbles in the four south German states. Princes and parliaments long tended to view one another as opponents, not a good basis for parliamentary government.

In the years after 1815 Germany presented an odd spectacle, often administratively progressive but politically conservative. This served to make problems for the Liberals and to strengthen the existing tradition of state power. The strong state was increasingly seen as essential to preserve order in human society, containing as it does so many contradictory, divergent and potentially disruptive elements. Politics in the Third Germany took the form of struggles within the bureaucracies between progressive and conservative elements or three-sided battles between groups usually linked together under the name Liberals, reactionary vested interests, like the guilds or rural nobility, and the bureaucracies. It has been shown that the south German parliaments were often dominated by reactionary interests, devoted to looking after local or sectional interests;[8] it was among the bureaucracies that progressive opinions

[8]M. Walker, *German Home Towns* (Ithaca, 1971) and 'Home Towns and State Administrators: South German Politics 1815–30', *Political Science Quarterly* 82 (1967), pp. 35–60.

and the strongest reservoirs of Liberalism were found.[9] It is argued that Baden, reputedly the most Liberal state in Germany, apart from a brief period of reaction from 1825 to 1831, became Liberal because the bureaucracy was keen to protect its special position against both the grand duke and the conservative masses.[10] In many states the years after 1815 saw serious disputes over the retention or abolition of the taxation systems brought in during the French period. A substantial vested interest, especially in Baden, was represented by the mediatized nobility, the rulers who had lost their sovereignty under the Emperor in the great territorial reorganizations after 1803. Under Article 14 of the Act of Association their special rights were guaranteed. It is interesting that this group produced some prominent leaders of the Liberal nationalist movement, for example Heinrich von Gagern, prime minister of Germany during the revolution of 1848–9, a former count of the Empire. This was perhaps a sign of their abiding hostility to the states that had mediatized them.

The two leading German states had no common parliaments. The Prussian reform Movement expired with the dismissal of Humboldt and Boyen in 1819 and the death of Hardenberg in 1822. In 1823 the advisory council set up during the Reform period as the embryo of a parliament was abolished under Austrian pressure and the old provincial assemblies were reinstated. This symbolized the waning of the Prussian national idea and the reassertion of provincialism. The constitution promised during the Reform period did not come into existence. After 1820 the nobility's hold on the army and the administration became firmer, a process also seen in other states. Although Prussia was among the more backward states in Germany in constitutional terms, the Reform spirit lived on in the civil service and in the Rhineland, which retained the French law code. Politically, Prussia remained an

[9]J.J. Sheehan, *German Liberalism in the Nineteenth Century* (Chicago, 1978), 'Liberalism and the City in Nineteenth-Century Germany', *P. and P.* 51 (1971), pp. 116–37 and 'Liberalism and Society in Germany 1815–48', *JMH* 45 (1973), pp. 583–604; M. Salvadori, *The Liberal Heresy* (1977); M. Duverger, *Modern Democracies: Economic Power versus Political Power* (Hinsdale, Ill., 1974); J.H. Hollowell, *The Decline of Liberalism as an Ideology, with particular reference to German politico-legal thought* (1946); J.L. Snell and H.A. Schmitt, *The Democratic Movement in Germany 1789–1914* (Chapel Hill, 1976); L. Krieger, *The German Idea of Freedom. History of a Political Tradition from the Reformation to 1871* (Chicago, 1972). There is also useful material in T. Schieder, *The State and Society in Our Times* (Edinburgh, 1962), which makes available in English some of the work of a leading German historian of nationalism. The papers 'The Problem of Revolution in the nineteenth century', 'The Theory of Party in Early German Liberalism' and 'The Political Party in Germany. Historical Bases and Stages' are valuable. There is a continuing historical debate about the nature of German Liberalism provoked by L. Gall's article 'Liberalismus und bürgerliche Gesellschaft', *Historische Zeitschrift* 220 (1975), pp. 324–56. Sadly, little of this is available in English.
[10]L.E. Lee, *The Politics of Harmony. Civil Service, Liberalism and Social Reform in Baden 1800–1850* (Newark, N.J., 1980).

adjunct of the Metternich 'system' but at the same time economic growth in Prussia continued and by the time of the foundation of the German Customs Union (*Zollverein*) in 1834 it had emerged as the leading German economy. This was partly the result of luck, in particular the acquisition of almost the whole Rhineland and the Ruhr, where the firm of Krupp was established in 1827, and partly the work of progressive officials like Eichhorn, head of the German Affairs department in the Prussian Foreign Ministry, the finance minister von Motz, and Maassen and Beuth of the Ministry of the Interior, who promoted economic progress by government action. In one of the last major acts of the Reform, all internal economic barriers were removed in 1818 and the whole kingdom became a single economic unit. Other reforms, including reductions in in-direct taxation, gave Prussia sound finances. Agents were sent to study the progress of industrialization in Britain and machines were bought there. It is interesting that the campaign to establish the *Zollverein* was accompanied by a great deal of anti-English propaganda and calls to end Germany's economic dependence on Britain. The state encouraged industrialization by, for example, sponsoring exhibitions, founding a technical commission and funding railway construction.[11] The level of technical education in Prussia was high. The system of chambers of commerce created by the French in the Rhineland was retained and extended to the whole kingdom.

These measures were designed to strengthen the Prussian state and were in no sense a preparation for German unification, though individual civil servants like Motz may have seen them as steps towards an assertion of Prussian political leadership in the Con-federation. Prussia's initial measures to strengthen her economic power in north Germany by pressurizing the little states on or within her borders to enter a customs union, were attacked as 'economic terrorism' and increased traditional mistrust of Prussia in the rest of Germany. Saxony, for example, fought hard to strength-en her economy in rivalry with Prussia and in 1830 Hanover, Hesse-Cassel and other north German states formed an overtly anti-Prussian economic union. In spite of this, Prussia quickly grew into the most vigorous economy in the region,' the German land of opportunity'. The economic benefits of union with her became obvious and in 1828—9 Hesse-Darmstadt, Bavaria and Württemberg entered the Prussian customs union. With the foundation of the *Zollverein* in 1834, bringing in Saxony and Hesse-Cassel, and the

[11]W.O. Henderson, *The State and the Industrial Revolution in Prussia 1740—1870* (Liverpool, 1958) and *The Rise of German Industrial Power 1834—1914* (1975); J.R. Gillis, *The Prussian Bureaucracy in Crisis 1840—1860* (Stanford, 1971).

accession of Baden and Nassau in 1836 and of Brunswick in 1842, two thirds of Germany came together in a common market. The Prussian economy benefited from the development of the Cologne– Antwerp railway line, the 'Iron Rhine', opened in 1843 after the Belgian revolt weakened the hold of the Dutch on the Rhine. This led to the development of Antwerp, a major *Zollverein* entrepôt. Free enterprise flourished, especially in the Rhineland, and a wealthy and confident middle class began to emerge. It was ironic that such a politically backward state should emerge as the focus of the hopes of Germans with the most advanced political views. The alternative, Austria, seemed hopeless.

Austria, unlike most of the other German states, had not experienced reform and modernization of its administrative and financial structure during the French period.[12] There too the provincial diets remained in existence. Her backwardness and financial weakness in comparison with most of the German states, which increased in the years after 1815, were an important factor in determining her policy towards the rest of Germany. Austria retained internal customs barriers when they were being removed elsewhere and manufacturing was seen as potentially dangerous to political and social stability. A system of chambers of commerce was not established until after 1850. The birth rate was lower in the Austrian than in the non-Austrian parts of the Confederation. Metternich was aware of Austria's relative backwardness and was not initially a rigid opponent of change but he faced powerful opposition from the deeply conservative Emperor Francis I, the native nobility, who resented him as a non-Austrian, and the influential finance minister Count Kolowrat. The stagnation of the Austrian government became worse after the death of Francis in 1835 and the accession of his epileptic son Ferdinand I. Metternich's awareness of the vulnerability of an unmodernized Austria contributed strongly to his increasingly rigid attitudes after 1819.

The Confederation froze Germany in an attitude which was convenient for the circumstances of 1815, when the desire for stability was strong and the Liberals and nationalists weak. The traditional description of Germany between 1815 and 1848 is the age of the *Biedermeier*, an untranslatable word redolent of uniform stagnation, petty-bourgeois respectability and middle-brow culture. It may be useful as the designation of a style of furniture but it conceals the truth about what was happening in Germany in that period. In the 1830s and 1840s many parts of Germany were in

[12]General works on Austria: C.A. Macartney, *The Habsburg Empire 1790–1918* (1968); R.A. Kann, *A History of the Habsburg Empire 1526–1918* (Berkeley, 1974); P.J. Katzenstein, *Disjoined Partners: Austria and Germany since 1815* (1976).

social and economic transition, the pre-industrial stage of development.[13] Important relics of the old pre-revolutionary order remained. Industrialization, when it came, was concentrated in a few centres and substantial parts of the country remained technically backward, with agriculture and traditional small enterprises predominating. There was still no developed national market. In spite of a shortage of reliable statistics, certain trends can be seen. The old bonds were beginning to break down with the abolition of serfdom and the decline of the guilds and a new potentially more mobile society was emerging with improvements in transport, especially the railway network after 1835. Just *how* mobile it was is not clear. Under Article 18 of the Act of Association free movement was allowed between member states, subject to differences in local residence qualifications, but, apart from guild journeymen and the 'top people', there is no evidence of any large-scale movement within Germany at this time. Before 1850 the German railway system was very regional in character, being made up of a Prussian and Central German network linking Prussia with the Rhineland, a south-western line from Frankfurt to Basle and a local Bavarian network. Harmonization of the systems came in 1847. Physically and economically non-Austrian Germany was beginning to 'grow together' but the development was limited. State and regional 'capitals' retained their political, economic and social status and nothing like a single German centre was emerging before 1848.

Increasing differentiation was developing with the emergence of new elements within broad social groups, such as the middle class, the peasantry and the guilds. Large traders and manufacturers were often close in social origins to the university-educated upper middle class. The term 'guild master' covered a wide range, from large-scale manufacturers to men whose standard of living was lower than that of skilled factory workers. Within groups like masters and apprentices there were marked divisions. Some were progressive in views and others reactionary, depending on local circumstances, and it is a mistake to talk of such groups as in any sense united. Technical changes in agriculture, new crops, methods and breeding techniques, were producing much increased yields. Demand was also growing as Germany's population rise continued. Between 1815 and 1845 the population of the Confederation, including the whole kingdom of Prussia, grew from about 31 million

[13]H. Böhme, *Introduction to the Social and Economic History of Germany* (Oxford, 1978); M. Kitchen, *The Political Economy of Germany 1815—1914* (London, 1978), chap. 3; R. Tilly, *'Soll und Haben*. Recent German Economic History and the Problem of Economic Development', *J.Ec.H.* 29 (1969), pp. 298—319.

to about 46 million and óverpopulation was a serious problem in the west, which experienced mounting land-hunger and emigration in the 1830s. A reservoir of urban discontent was building up among guild artisans, the *Handwerker*, suffering economic distress even in cities where the guilds were still powerful. Even limited factory development hit them hard and foreign competition was a constant problem. The prevalence of the truck system of paying workers was a major cause of discontent. The bad harvests of 1831 and 1832 produced serious political troubles in many parts of Germany, sparked off by riots of starving artisans unable to meet higher food prices. Guild journeymen, a mobile group obliged to travel between the states, played a prominent part in this violence, as their chances of becoming masters were declining. One sign of increasing social tension was a sharp rise in crime rates and violence in the 1830s and 1840s, attributed by some conservatives to the greater freedom allowed in some states. Violence and riots in the Pre-March period have been studied in detail,[14] as a result of which it is clear that they were caused by a great variety of different factors, among which local issues were overwhelmingly important. National issues or the German question played virtually no part in them. Most common were crimes against property, especially infringements of the forest and hunting rights and theft of firewood. There was growing publicity about the 'social problem' and an intense debate on pauperism.

The position of the peasants, the majority of the population (only in Saxony and the four city states were they a minority), was also not rosy. They enjoyed personal freedom but for many the ending of serfdom during and after the French period simply meant exposure to the cold winds of a free economy, for which they were unprepared. The situation varied from state to state. Often the lands of former rulers mediatized during the French period were specifically exempted from government legislation designed to protect the peasantry and relics of unfreedom persisted there. In some areas emancipation brought few benefits as the peasants lost their land and could not make a living. In the west land-hunger was common, with the growth of uneconomic dwarf holdings (for a few the cultivation of grapes provided a way out), while in the east large estates farmed by landless labour were more the rule. Even the great rural capitalist landowners of the east were under-capitalized and susceptible to crisis. Many were hard-hit by the

---

[14]H. Zehr, *Crime and Development of Modern Society: Patterns of Criminality in Nineteenth-Century Germany and France* (1976); J. Mooser, 'Property and Wood Theft: Agrarian Capitalism and Social Conflict in Rural Society 1800–50', in R.G. Moeller (ed.), *Peasants and Lords in Modern Germany* (1986), pp. 52–80.

depressions of 1816—17, 1825 and 1834—5. As formerly noble land was transferred into middle-class ownership (a continuing process: by 1860 out of 12,000 knight's fees in Prussia 57 per cent were in non-noble ownership) and was more efficiently exploited, so old lord—tenant relationships broke down and there was even less protection for the rural poor. There remained a growing reservoir of rural poverty as there was no large-scale migration into the towns. Only the wealthier, more enterprising or more fortunate peasants were able to take advantage of opportunities and cash in on access to growing urban markets or the brief boom in grain exports in the early 1840s. The majority remained groaning under the burden of commutation fees, compensating their former lords for the abolition of serfdom, taxes and mortgage payments. In some states the game laws were a running sore; the retention by former lords of their hunting rights was the last relic of feudalism in the west and was bitterly resented by farmers unable to control game which attacked their crops. Cottage industry was increasingly resorted to as a vital supplement to incomes from land.

When conditions changed, the Confederation was unable to adapt and became increasingly out of step with the economic and social realities in Germany. There was enormous diversity within Germany between progressive states like Baden and the thoroughly backward Mecklenburgs, for example, but by the 1840s Liberalism and nationalism, progressing hand in hand, were becoming potent ideas among certain groups and in certain regions of Germany. This was in spite of repressive policies. In reality, repressive measures, for example the Carlsbad decrees of 1819, were not applied in all the German states with the same rigour, though in some they were used to unleash a minor White Terror. Metternich had achieved the establishment in Mainz of an investigation committee to monitor individual states' enforcement of the decrees and there was always diplomatic pressure and the ultimate threat of armed action to compel states to toe the line laid down by the Confederation.[15] The political troubles of the early 1830s in Hanover, Hesse-Cassel and Brunswick, following the French and Belgian revolutions and the passage of the English Reform Bill, revealed the strains beginning to build up in German society.[16]

Against this background the Liberals began to emerge as the main standard-bearers of German nationalism and an alternative ruling group with at least the skeleton of a political

[15]Sheehan, *German Liberalism*, p. 10: 'Liberalism took shape in a climate which had enough restrictions to be frustrating but not enough to cut off political life entirely'.
[16]R. Hinton-Thomas, *Liberalism, Nationalism and the German Intellectuals 1822—47* (Cambridge, 1951).

programme. To the Liberals the attainment of national unity and self-determination was desirable for practical and ideological reasons. Only a united Germany could achieve the prosperity and weight in world affairs which it merited and Germans could only be free in a free Germany.[17] There was also a measure of cosmopolitan idealism is this: Liberals saw themselves as part of a kind of international liberation movement − 1848 was to be described as the 'Springtime of Nations' − and usually evinced great sympathy for oppressed peoples like the Greeks and the Poles (though less for the Italians) and dreamed of a Europe of free nation states in an era of perpetual peace. They held that instability in the European states system would only be eliminated by the national consolidation of Germany, the division of which created a vacuum attractive to aggressors.

The reasons for the rise of the Liberals were economic developments, the growth of government and various discontents. Liberalism was usually the creed of those excluded from power or people with legitimate grievances about the arrogance of the nobility[18] or officialdom or about restraints on enterprise, and who wished to express these grievances through meetings, a free press and representative assemblies. Ironically, many looked back with nostalgia to the Napoleonic period as a lost Liberal age. Their main support came not so much from the top rank of the middle class but from the next level down: there was often a strong element of religious, status or class resentment, for example among the Protestant minority in Bavaria and among primary-school teachers, in most states an underpaid and unregarded group. Groups who saw themselves as suffering restrictions on their freedom regarded the attainment of national goals as a means of achieving personal emancipation. There was also an important idealistic or moralistic element. The German bourgeois saw himself as better and less corrupt than the nobleman, the wage-slave or the foreigner.

Economic circumstances seemed to be working for the Liberals. According to some economists, especially the Württemberg political exile Friedrich List, Germany was a natural economic unit crying out for the removal of the artificial barriers which were hampering growth. Certainly there were burdensome physical barriers not only between states but, in some cases, between town and country in the form of border poles, passport checks, searches and payments of duty. The emerging economic middle class needed a

[17]On the influence of Mazzini's ideas: H. Kohn, *Prophets and Peoples: Studies in Nineteenth-Century Nationalism* (1966), which contains studies of Mazzini and Treitschke.
[18]Thomas Mann, *Buddenbrooks* (1901), part 8, chap. 2 has an account of the resentment felt by a Lübeck patrician faced with the condescension of a petty Mecklenburg nobleman.

government to protect economic endeavour while leaving the conduct of it in the hands of individuals. The German Commerce and Manufacturing Society (*Deutsche Handels- und Gewerbeverein*), set up in 1819 among traders and manufacturers in the south and west, acted as an early pressure group representing such views. It did not last long in the face of opposition from governments. Specific Liberal demands included a common external tariff to nurture German industry, the abolition of internal barriers, the creation of common transport, coinage and weights and measures systems and unified insurance and business laws. Many acts of economic unification were carried through as a result of 'bourgeois self-organization', private rather than state initiatives, beginning with professional groupings, such as the Society of German Scientists and Doctors (1822) and the Society of Book Dealers (1825). One of the earliest developed national markets in Germany was the book trade, centred in Leipzig.

At the same time there were growing disputes between those favouring Protectionism, mainly manufacturers, and Free Traders, mainly large-scale agrarians cashing in on markets in Western Europe, and those engaged in commerce. Economic growth was also hampered by a severe shortage of capital: manufacturing was still seen as too risky an investment and land and government stocks were preferred as safer. In many cities the restrictive guilds retained their power. In spite of this, free enterprise and industry did develop in Germany, often outside city walls, though in 1848 in most of Germany factories were still a rarity and factory workers a small minority, usually highly paid and looking forward to joining the middle class. More common was a mixed system in which certain processes, spinning and weaving for example, were put out to cottage workers while expensive finishing processes were concentrated in factories. Only in the Rhineland and around Berlin were there substantial concentrations of modern industry, encouraged by Prussia's increasingly liberal tariff policies and large French investments in the 1830s. The basic problem was that industrialization in Germany was too slow and distressing aspects, such as unemployment among those involved in traditional forms of manufacture, were chronic and long-drawn-out while the benefits were slow in appearing. It is estimated that in 1847 only about 3 per cent of the employed population of the *Zollverein* worked in factories. In 1850 about 60 per cent of the working population were still engaged in agriculture and forestry. Even a minor crisis could do great damage to an undercapitalized industry in its early stages. The putting-out system had the great advantage that the workers could be laid off in bad times.

Economic change was not the only factor promoting Liberalism.

It was also fostered by an expansion of the functions of government, which provided more opportunities for civil servants, judges, lawyers, teachers and administrators as states expanded their functions. There never seemed enough jobs and problems of an excess of educated men remained.[19] Many of those excluded from power came firmly to believe that they could run things better. Liberalism was also helped by an expansion in education and new attitudes in universities stemming from the ideas of the Prussian reformer Wilhelm von Humboldt. There is evidence of growing interest in German history and German linguistics from the 1820s and of an expanding readership, catered for by an increase in the number of books, newspapers and journals, especially in the 1840s, in spite of censorship. In the 1840s the German governments agreed to accept common copyright rules for the whole Confederation. There are no reliable statistics on literacy in the first half of the nineteenth century. In most states a basic education system for all existed on paper but not in reality. In Prussia, thanks to a sharp increase in school attendance between 1800 and 1850, illiteracy was as good as eliminated.

Such developments and circumstances certainly speeded the rise of Liberalism but it is wrong to overestimate its strength. It was neither an all-German nor a mass movement. Liberalism was very much a regional movement and was to remain so after 1848. A rounded picture of the movement must wait for more detailed studies of the Liberals in local politics. Some earlier studies tried to divide the German Liberals into two 'schools', those who looked to England as a model and those who looked to France, but this is oversimple. In reality German Liberalism varied widely in ideas and membership from state to state, with the basic difference from, for example, British Liberalism that civil servants played a much more important role. Also German Liberalism did not develop a right of resistance theory on the English model. The French, British, American and, after 1830, Belgian systems were admired in Germany, though often misunderstood, but they were not seen as instantly transplantable to Germany. Individual Liberal leaders played a major role in defining the form the movement took in a given locality. Liberalism had a hard fight in most parts of Germany. Apart from repression and the fact of government leverage over important instruments of political influence and control like clergymen, school teachers and local officials (though some of these

[19]L. O'Boyle, 'The Problem of an Excess of Educated Men in Europe', *JMH* 42 (1970) and 'The Democratic Left in Germany 1848', *JMH* 33 (1961), pp. 374–83.

groups were important elements in the Liberal movement[20]), Liberals had an up-hill battle against tradition. The legacy of absolutism died hard and dynastic loyalty remained a powerful force.

The continuing importance of religion in the daily lives of most Germans (the *Life of Jesus*, a major theological work by David F. Strauss published in 1835, was a best-seller) also acted as a barrier to the spread of new ideas and it is not surprising that anti-clericalism was a significant factor in German Liberalism. The Churches' control of basic education in most states remained intact until 1848. The Protestant Churches were state institutions and overwhelmingly conservative. Only in the case of Württemberg has evidence been produced showing significant support for Liberal nationalism among the clergy and Württemberg was unusual in that, as a matter of policy, clergy were not appointed to posts in the areas of their upbringing.[21] The union of throne and altar was seen as a vital element in the preservation of the established order. In 1817 the Prussian government pushed through the creation of a unified Protestant Church against the opposition of Lutheran and Calvinist clergy and this example was followed in other states. The Catholic Church too was very conservative, though in the 1840s some echoes of the Catholic Liberal movement growing in France and Belgium began to be heard in Germany. In 1815 agreements between the papacy and state governments produced a reorganization of the German Catholic Church making the boundaries of sees coterminous with state borders and giving the governments wider powers over the appointment of bishops. In spite of that the Church remained strongly orthodox and ultramontane. Religious divisions also weakened the national idea. Protestant celebrations in 1830 of the anniversary of the Lutheran Augsburg Confession and the landing of Gustavus Adolphus in Germany began a period of sharp confrontation with the Catholics, in the course of which they were accused of not being fully German because of their links with Rome. There a was brief attempt in the 1840s to create a separate German Catholic Church but it attracted minimal support, as did the Liberal movements within the Protestant Churches, the Friends of Light and Free Congregations. Hostility was increased by a long struggle between the Prussian state and the Catholic Church in the 1830s over the issue of mixed marriages, in the course of which two archbishops were imprisoned. This led to the emergence of a Catholic mass movement, beginning in the Rhenish

[20]A.J. La Vopa, *Prussian School Teachers 1763–1848* (Chapel Hill, 1980), esp. chap. 7.
[21]R.J. Evans, 'Religion and Society in Modern Germany', *Europ. Stud. Rev.* 12 (1982), pp. 249–88.

provinces, sustained by a rapidly expanding press and highly organized mass pilgrimages. This presented Liberals with the di- lemma of choosing between their belief in religious freedom and their hatred of an obscurantist clergy, especially when the move- ment was mobilized against non-confessional education and econ- omic modernization — so dear to Liberals — as it was in Baden and Bavaria in the 1840s.

The rise of the Liberals also suffered serious setbacks. The period 1830—2 has been described as 'Germany's forgotten revolution'. These years saw a rash of violent outbreaks across Germany fo- mented by the revolutions in France and Belgium and the crisis surrounding the Reform Bill in Britain. Great nervousness in Germany about the likely behaviour of revolutionary France added to the atmosphere of instability and there was a genuine fear of general revolution among the German governments. These troubles were caused primarily by economic and social dissatisfaction but they quickly acquired a political colouring. There were risings in the badly-governed states of Brunswick, Hesse-Cassel and Han- over in 1830 and outbreaks in Saxon cities in 1831, which resulted in some social reforms and the granting of more liberal consti- tutions. In the south German parliaments a sharper note entered debates. In 1832 half the Polish revolutionary army crossed Germany on its way into exile in France and this again produced sporadic violence, including riots in Berlin and Vienna. The city of Aachen experienced serious machine-breaking riots. In 1833 a group of Heidelberg students and guild artisans attempted a *putsch* in the free city of Frankfurt.

The best-remembered manifestation was the Hambach festival of May 1832, at which some 30,000 people gathered to listen to patriotic speeches on a hill in the Bavarian Palatinate, an area where there was strong resentment of 'alien' rule from Munich. The splendour of the speeches, calling on the German princes to 'adopt the manly toga of German national dignity' and to establish 'the united free states of Germany', was matched only by the lavishness of the refreshments. No practical measures were pro- posed.[22] More significant and a clearer sign of the abiding weak- ness of German Liberalism at the time was the short-lived political organization, the Patriotic Society for the Support of a Free Press (*Vaterlandsverein zur Unterstützung der freien Presse*), which organ- ized the Hambach meeting. This body lasted a bare 12 months. Its

[22]A great gathering of political parties and movements reassembled on the Hambach in 1982 on the 150th anniversary of the festival. The ruined castle on the site has been expensively restored and is now, quite spuriously, labelled 'the cradle of German democracy'. Ashtrays and other souvenirs bearing this legend are on sale there: the knick-knack as myth.

aim was to mobilize opinion in favour of a free press, seen as the only means of achieving a 'spiritual reunification' (*Wiedervereinigung im Geiste*) of Germany, in the cause of which it collected money and published pamphlets. It was reformist and thoroughly unrevolutionary. It attracted some 5,000 mainly young (25—35 years of age) members, including large numbers of small shopkeepers and master artisans, and was strongest in the south-west and the Rhineland towns. It was destroyed by the arrest of its leaders and military repression in the Rhineland in 1833 and 1834.

The troubles of 1830—2 provoked an overreaction on the part of German governments. A confederate garrison was stationed in Frankfurt and it was made illegal to send in petitions to the Assembly. The Carlsbad decrees were reissued with the additional Six Articles of 1832, which increased confederate supervision of the internal affairs of member states, and in 1834 the Confederation acquired a Secret Committee to spy on potential revolutionaries. Again the application of these measures varied but in some states it resulted in savage repression. Simple membership of banned societies or putting one's signature to a petition could earn severe punishment.

In spite of these factors, Liberalism was able to advance in some places in the 1830s and 1840s, notably in some cities like Berlin, Munich and the Hanseatic ports and regions like the Rhineland and Baden, where French, Belgian and Swiss influences were strong and the ruling houses were of recent vintage and therefore dynastic loyalty was weak. The wave of repression in the early 1830s forced many with progressive views to keep their heads down but illegal publication of their views continued and the more relaxed atmosphere of the 1840s saw the foundation of a number of Liberal associations and newspapers. The universities of Heidelberg and Freiburg in Baden were important centres. Individual rulers like those of Saxe-Weimar also promoted Liberalism. The accession of Ludwig I to the Bavarian throne in 1825 roused Liberal hopes as he was thought to have advanced views. They were to be disappointed. Liberalism also had supporters among groups like the nobility of E. Prussia and Silesia — many of whom believed in free trade and practised rural capitalist manufactures of brewing, distilling, brick-making and timber working on their estates (the influence of the university of Königsberg also played an important part) — civil servants and members of chambers of commerce, railway associations and cultural societies.[23]

Liberalism continued to make gains especially as some of the

[23]F.G. Eyck, 'English and French Influences on German Liberalism before 1848', *J. Hist. Id.* 18 (1957), pp. 313—41.

north German states began to catch up with the south constitution-ally. Parliaments meeting regularly and with the right to consent to taxation and legislation were more common as were equality before the law, freedom of conscience and some civil rights. The accession of the old and unbalanced duke of Cumberland as King Ernest Augustus of Hanover in 1837 was a serious setback. He at once annulled the constitution granted in 1833, mainly to recover his domain lands which had become state property in 1833, and dismissed seven Göttingen professors of mildly Liberal views who protested against his action. This did not arouse much protest in Hanover itself as Ernest shrewdly combined his action with tax reductions. The 'Göttingen Seven' were not active political Liberals and had little popular support. But it was significant that behav-iour such as Ernest's was regarded as egregious even in conserva-tive Germany and provoked an outcry, a sign that political standards were rising and that mindless repression was no longer accept-able. Moves were made to involve the Confederation against Ernest's unilateral abrogation of an established constitution, an attempt to revive the judicial activity of the old imperial aulic council (*Reich-shofrat*) in constitutional disputes. As a result of Austrian pressure the diet refused to intervene, though Bavaria, Saxony, Württemberg, Baden, the Saxon duchies and the free cities voted in favour.

Liberalism still remained a loose and divided movement with no all-German organization and with only the skeleton of a com-mon programme, though the publication between 1834 and 1844 of the *Staatslexikon* of Rotteck and Welcker, both academics at the university of Freiburg in Baden, provided the framework for such a programme: freedom of the press, assembly and conscience, free enterprise, parliamentary participation in government, equality of opportunity, army reforms and a reform of the Confederation to give Germany more practical unity. A wide variety of opinions, including a non-national cosmopolitanism, was accommodated within Liberalism before 1848 and the revolutions of that year revealed deep divisions on basic questions, which helped to weaken the Frankfurt Parliament. A deliberate vagueness and avoidance of concrete policies were cultivated in order to avoid possible splits. In spite of this, the movement continued to appeal overwhelmingly to notables, people of education and property (*Bildung und Besitz*). In a way the fundamental tenet of the Liberal ideology, individual-ism, hindered the formation of a disciplined and organized party; party was still regarded as synonymous with faction. Liberals tended to rely on the press, petitions or *ad hoc* organizations set up for electoral purposes or operated through existing non-political bodies, such as the association of Germanists, teachers and students of German, whose congresses in the 1840s heard calls for national unity. As administrators they were able to achieve something in individual states but they remained frustrated by opposition from above and below. They claimed to speak for 'the people' but their definition of this was very narrow, excluding as it did the uneducated masses and the feudal aristocracy. This was shown in the *Song of the Leipzig Citizens' Guard* (1830), which contained the words: 'The citizens' guard only wants what's right. Not the madness of the mob but also not a tyranny.'[24] By 1848, however, when Germany faced a major crisis, the Liberals were strong enough to be regarded as the only available alternative to the prevailing system of bureaucratic absolutism and their promise to reconcile order and progress seemed to offer an answer to Germany's problems.

If Liberalism was weak and divided in pre-March Germany, other manifestations of nationalism were even weaker and more marginal.[25] As an organized movement, Romantic nationalism barely existed. In the past much attention has been given to the *Burschenschaften* (university fraternities), against which the Carlsbad decrees were aimed.[26] Their significance was exaggerated at the time, for example by Metternich who regarded all the leaders as dangerous criminals, and has been exaggerated since. In spite of a rising population, German student numbers stagnated in the pre-March period. Before 1806 Germany had 45 universities but 22 closed after that year. The *Burschenschaften* were more important for what they symbolized than for what they achieved: while earlier fraternities had been provincial, the new *Burschenschaften* were organized on national lines. In 1818 a united German fraternity was set up with branches in 14 universities but it seemed to concern itself more with pursuit of the Romantic *Volksgeist* than with any concrete political programme. Like the older fraternities, they were part of the German 'old-boy' network (*Altherrenschaft*), a system designed to build useful contacts to last a lifetime. One section of the movement issued in 1817 a statement of principles, *Grundsätze und Beschlüsse*, calling for a democratic federation, the preservation of German customs and usages and the maintenance of the purity of the German language. It revealed a large measure of anti-foreign sentiment and a rather naïve faith in the good will of the German rulers. It was also exclusively Protestant. The famous Wartburg meeting in October 1817 in Saxe-Weimar was called to commemorate the beginning of the Reformation as well as the Battle of

[24]E.N. and P. Anderson, *Political Institutions and Social Change in Continental Europe in the nineteenth century* (Berkeley, 1967).
[25]W.M. Simon, 'Variations in Nationalism during the Great Reform Period in Prussia', *Am.H.R.* 59 (1953–4), pp. 305–21.
[26]C.E. McClelland, *State, Society and University in Germany 1700–1914* (Cambridge, 1980).

Leipzig in 1813 and it did not have the political significance sometimes attributed to it. Nationalist writings had a paltry circulation,
for example Arndt's *Catechism* (1813) of less than 30,000 and Follen's
German Youth to the German Masses (1818) about 6,000. Perhaps the
exaggerated importance attributed to the whole movement was
due to the extremist lunatic fringe of Karl Follen's General German
Fraternity at Giessen and the Unconditionals at Jena, who preached
the cult of violence and unrestricted free will. A member of the
latter group, Carl Sand, was responsible for one of the outrages
which led to the Carlsbad decrees. In the last decades of the
nineteenth century the site of Sand's execution became a nationalist shrine though it is impossible to discern the motives behind
the assassination.

Mass nationalism, in its traditional negative xenophobic form,
occasionally appeared, for example during the post-war economic
depression of 1815–19, the French revolution in 1830 and the
Rhine crisis of 1840, when calls in France for a revision of the 1815
settlement and return of the Rhineland to French rule were answered
with a great outpouring of patriotic songs and poems, including
the *Watch on the Rhine* (*Die Wacht am Rhein*) (1840) and the *Deutschlandlied* (1841), the later national anthem, and with cries that the
Rhine was Germany's river but not Germany's border. (This was a
revival of a poem written by Arndt during the War of Liberation.)
Old horror stories about three centuries of French atrocities against
the German nation were revived, along with calls for the return of
the lost lands, Alsace and Lorraine. Some of these expressions took
pride in Germanness to extreme lengths, portraying the nation as
an outpost of superior civilization threatened on one side by
Welsch or Latin and on the other by Slavic barbarism. The possibility of war against the French was welcomed by many. Similar
emotions arose over Schleswig-Holstein in the late 1840s.[27] Such
outbreaks were passionate but ephemeral and were as likely to
strengthen loyalty to individual princes as to win support for more
progressive nationalist movements.

Some nationalists gravitated into shooting circles and gymnastic
and musical societies, sometimes given to the wearing of ancient
'Germanic' costume. Some of these were harmless and apolitical.
More detailed recent studies of these groups have attributed a
more important role to them, seeing in them a substitute for weak
or non-existent political institutions, able to involve wider sections

[27]W. Carr, *Schleswig-Holstein 1815–1848* (Manchester, 1963), an excellent study of the rise of
nationalism, showing how one nationalism fed and grew off another.

of the middle classes in the national issue.[28] In the 1840s they were beginning to organize on a wider basis, recruiting in the lower middle class, and becoming more overtly political. Their participation in local celebrations played a role in creating an all-German consciousness and weakening localism. There is some danger in exaggerating the significance of this development. The Austrian middle class did not become involved and some sharp-shooters' groups were conservative. The societies did not become a bourgeois mass movement and they did not have a clear programme for national unity. Attitudes among active nationalists tended to be negative and restricted to making attacks on the Confederation rather than putting forward positive schemes for change. In the late 1840s there were some signs that they were becoming more organized. The first all-German singing festival in Würzburg in 1845 called for the unity of Germany in song. A congress of gymnasts from all parts of Germany, held at Frankfurt in the summer of 1847, set up a national Gymnastic League organized on military lines. Some governments encouraged them as a means of diverting political activities into safe channels but others, always suspicious of large numbers of people getting together in organized activities not initiated and supervised by them, harrassed the societies.

Again a lunatic fringe was thrown off by these movements, the so-called Teutomaniacs. These went in for what came to be known as *Deutschtümelei*, an untranslatable word perhaps best rendered by 'ultra-Germanness' or hypertrophe of the national ego. This involved a sincere conviction that German things were superior to everything else, incessant praise of all things German and claims that German wine was more vinous, German virgins more virginal and German loyalty more selfless, and so on, than their non-German equivalents. The composer Richard Wagner sometimes went in for it. For example, in his 16 volumes of collected writings, *German Art and German Politics*,[29] he frequently claimed that, unlike all other peoples, the Germans do things for their own sake and not for gain[30] and that German achievement was the pinnacle of human achievement. Much of this crazy emphasis on Germanness

[28]P. Düding, *Organisierter gesellschaftlicher Nationalismus in Deutschland 1808–47* (Munich, 1984). The various organizations liked to describe themselves as a 'people's movement' (*Volksbewegung*), which meant exclusively middle-class. By emphasizing the factors which united them and ignoring those which divided them, the middle classes were able to create the myth that they were the united *Volk*.
[29]E. Goldman and E. Sprinchorn (eds.), *Wagner on Music and Drama* (1970) (extracts from Wagner's writings).
[30]This was to become a self-definition of Germanness: '*Deutsch sein heisst, eine Sache um ihrer selbst willen tun*', alongside the 'Nation of Poets and Thinkers'.

was in itself a sign of inner feelings of national inadequacy and it disgusted and exasperated many Germans. For example, the Teutomaniacs came under frequent attack from the Young German writers, attached to the Mazzinian concept of national freedom as the basis for universal peace. There was in fact no united Young German movement except in the eyes of governments, which exaggerated their significance. Leading spokesmen of the group were the poets Ludwig Börne and Heinrich Heine, who chose to spend most of their time in France after their writings were banned in Germany in 1835. In his *The Romantic School* (1836) Heine drew attention to the difference between French patriotism, which broadens the heart and embraces everyone, and the German version, which, based as it was on hatred of foreigners, narrows the heart and behaves like frost on leather.[31] The Young Germans' admiration for France and their mockery of bombastic nationalism earned them the hatred of many German nationalists and the accusation that they were 'fellows without a fatherland'.

There were also occasional manifestations of what could be described as conservative nationalism. This started from the premise that Germany as it existed, a loose union of separate states with a long historical existence, was the ideal political expression of the nation. For supporters of this view nationalism consisted in the loyalty of Germans to their rulers and their states. This form of nationalism was active in that it sought to defend the *status quo* against perceived threats to it. A leading representative of this view was Wolfgang Menzel,[32] whose writings expressed hostility to foreigners, especially the French and the Jews, accused of importing ideas dangerous to 'sound German views'. Occasionally individual rulers made use of it for their own purposes. King Ludwig I of Bavaria was responsible between 1830 and 1842 for the building of the huge Valhalla monument near Regensburg. This 'temple' in memory of great Germans, which did not include Luther, was supposed to make those who visited it leave 'better and more German' than when they arrived. As part of the same policy the Germanic National Museum (*Germanisches Nationalmuseum*) was opened in Nuremberg in 1843. It served the purpose of asserting the claims of the Bavarian dynasty, apart from the Habsburgs the only Catholic ruling house in the Confederation, to primacy among German rulers and was an echo of the Bavarian imperial ambitions of the eighteenth century. When it suited them, for example when trying to persuade German rulers to toe the repressive line

[31]A selection of Heine's prose writings is available in English: *It will be a Lovely Day* (E. Berlin, 1965). His attack on the extreme nationalists, 'Why Did the Germans Take to the Romantic School?', is pp. 302–17.
[32]On Menzel see H. Kohn, *The Mind of Germany. The Education of a Nation* (1962), pp. 94–8.

against Liberalism, the Austrian government was also prepared to use the reservoir of imperial nostalgia which existed in Germany.

Against this background the revolutions of 1848 broke out.[33] Expectations of change had been aroused in the years before 1848, especially in Prussia. King Frederick William IV came to the throne in 1840. He was brilliant, unstable and romantic and wanted to restore the personal links between the crown and the people which, he believed, had been eroded by bureaucratic rule. One of his first acts was an amnesty releasing those convicted of political crimes in the early 1830s and he quickly brought to an end the dispute with the Catholic Church by making concessions. That he was born to be a king was a great loss to the German theatre. He was a deep believer in divine-right monarchy and enjoyed histrionic performances, like the personal act of oath-taking arranged in Berlin after his accession. He also instituted an annual reception at court for all recipients of honours, including many non-nobles. He later became clinically insane but was probably seriously unbalanced throughout his reign. He listened to a wide range of different opinions and allowed himself to be influenced by them but from the beginning there was a lack of consistency in his behaviour. If he had any coherent ideas on German politics, he seems to have dreamed of a recreation of some form of the Holy Roman Empire under a Habsburg Emperor with the king of Prussia as hereditary arch-general in charge of the armed forces. Frederick William certainly raised nationalist hopes. He gave E.M. Arndt and the Grimm brothers university posts. He took practical steps to revive interest in Prussia's German role; in 1846 he commissioned the publication of the works of Frederick the Great in 30 volumes (a project completed in 1857) after a nine-volume biography by J.D.E. Preuss (1832—4) had re-established Frederick as an all-German hero figure. Under the influence of the war-scare of 1840 Austria agreed to a tightening up of the confederate military arrangements, long desired by Prussia. In 1842 he used the ceremonial surrounding the laying of the foundation stone for the last stage of Cologne cathedral (known as the *Dombaufest*) as the occasion for an orchestrated theatrical demonstration of the Christian-monarchical principle combined with Prussian—German national enthusiasm. The cathedral, he said, was to be the 'door to a new great and good era

---

[33]On the 1848 revolutions see: P.N. Stearns, *The Revolutions of 1848* (1974); P. Jones, *The 1848 Revolutions* (1981); P. Robertson, *Revolutions of 1848: A Social Interpretation* (Princeton, 1952); R. Stadelmann, *Social and Political History of the German 1848 Revolution* (Columbus, Oh., 1975); T.S. Hamerow, '1848', in L. Krieger and F. Stern (eds.), *The Responsibility of Power* (1968), pp. 145—61, and 'History and the German Revolution of 1848', *Am.H.R.* 60 (1954), pp. 27—44; R. Pascal, 'The Frankfort Parliament, 1848, and the *Drang nach Osten*', *JMH* 18 (1946), pp. 108—22; H. Rothfels, '1848—One Hundred Years After', *JMH* 20 (1948), pp 291—319.

for Germany.' At the dinner afterwards the Austrian representative, the Archduke John, gave a speech, subsequently much misquoted in the nationalist press, which seemed to be in favour of German unity. An all-German industrial exhibition was held in Berlin in 1844. The medal struck to commemorate the occasion bore the figure of Germania with the inscription 'Be United'. In 1844 Prussia suggested the adoption of the red black and gold tricolour, colours associated with the Free Corps in the War of Liberation, as a common German flag to be flown on the confederate fortresses but this was vetoed by Austria.

From the beginning of Frederick William's reign there was a serious and complete misunderstanding between ruler and people. The belief that there was at last a king on the throne sympathetic to their views gave the Prussian Liberals new confidence and the movement grew rapidly in the 1840s, especially in the Rhineland, where it was led by wealthy and respected figures from industry and commerce like Ludolf Camphausen, David Hansemann and Gustav Mevissen. Younger and more radical Liberals, including briefly the young Karl Marx, were also making their mark. Published demands that Prussia should take the lead in achieving more unity for Germany became frequent. This led in 1843 to the re-imposition of strict censorship.

In 1842 the king called together members of the eight provincial Estates to Berlin for consultation and in 1844 announced plans for a Prussian United Diet, seen as the basis for a Prussian parliament. The basic motive for this lay in the state's growing financial problems but appetites were much whetted. In spite of its limited functions it strengthened links between the state and society. When the United Diet met in April 1847, the majority of its 612 members were Liberals. It immediately began to try to block government plans to float a large loan for a new railway construction until constitutional concessions were given. The issue did not matter; the assembly, in which, significantly, members sat in provincial rather than party blocks, wanted to flex its muscles. Under pressure from Vienna and St Petersburg, Frederick William dismissed the diet and dropped plans for the railway. The failure of the United Diet caused great disappointment in Prussia and northern Germany generally.

The Liberals were also on the offensive in the south. By the 1840s the Liberals were in government in Baden but the old generation of moderate and cosmopolitan Liberals was passing away and new more radical figures were emerging, like the Badenese politicians Friedrich Hecker and Gustav von Struve, leaders of the German Radical Movement during the 1848 revolution. In September 1847 these Liberals of more advanced views met at Offenburg in Baden. The meeting put forward a programme of 16 articles, including demands for free trade, a free press, all the usual Liberal freedoms, speech, press, assembly and so on, the abolition of all privileges, the creation of a citizens' militia instead of standing armies, which were unpopular with the Liberals, trial by jury, a graduated income tax, 'an equalization of the imbalance between capital and labour', the abolition of the repressive laws of the Confederation and an elected central parliament for Germany. Nationalism was most clearly expressed in Article 6: 'The German wants one fatherland and a voice in its affairs. It befits us as a nation to have internal justice and liberty and a firm attitude towards the rest of the world.' The hint of xenophobia is interesting as it shows that even advanced Liberals were not free of the oldest and most visceral form of German national feeling. In October more moderate Liberals from Baden, Württemberg, Hesse-Darmstadt and Prussia met and produced the Heppenheim programme. They proposed interparliamentary action to secure an eventual reform of the institutions of the Confederation, an elected parliament and a central government. They also demanded, as more immediately achievable, an extension of the *Zollverein* to cover all Germany except Austria, an elected toll parliament to discuss common economic matters, elected local councils, the abolition of medieval survivals, a citizens' militia and the Liberal freedoms. Among the Heppenheim Liberals there was already a substantial group looking to Prussia as a potential leader in the movement towards German unity. Although neither programme was revolutionary, the two meetings showed that there was a growing division between radicals and moderates among German Liberals, especially in Baden and the Rhineland.

In 1847 Germany was hit by the severest economic crisis so far experienced in the century. It approached the universality of crisis which had preceded the French Revolution in 1789. The resulting distress was so serious that even those German governments that were highly organized and efficient could not cope. Much of the economic growth achieved earlier had been at the cost of the workers. There was a high level of female and child labour and a large section of the population lived a marginal existence facing the constant threat of being thrown into total destitution by a natural or family disaster. There had been a foretaste of the problems in 1844 when a bad harvest and industrial depression led to a revolt by starving Silesian handloom weavers, which had to be put down by troops. A further series of natural disasters occurred in 1846. Harvests failed, especially the potato on which large numbers of people had become dependent. A long hot summer and a very cold winter deprived industry of water power. Germany was swept by severe epidemics. There was heavy unemployment and bread riots broke out in several German cities in early 1847.

But the revolutions of March 1848 were not caused directly by the economic trouble of the preceding years. There was no revolutionary situation between summer 1847 and spring 1848. During the riots of 1847 middle-class Liberals supported the violent suppression of the rioters — they did not jump on to a rolling bandwagon to make political demands. Rather, the instability caused by economic problems and the revolution in France in February encouraged the German Liberals to make their demands. The economic crisis had passed its worst when the revolution broke out but its destabilizing effects lingered on. Certain groups remained economically damaged and an air of expectation remained. A political ferment began in the south-west before February under the influence of the civil war going on in neighbouring Switzerland between Liberal and Conservative cantons, won by the former. The scandalous affair between King Ludwig I of Bavaria and the dancer Lola Montez, which brought down governments and outraged Liberal and Catholic opinion, produced an explosive situation in Munich before February 1848. Ludwig was eventually prevailed upon to abdicate on 20 March. In the winter of 1847–8 a severe financial crisis struck Austria, already under pressure as a result of growing effervescence in Hungary, Galicia, Bohemia and the northern Italian provinces. Liberalism was also growing among the Germans in Vienna and the Austrian archduchies, long dominated by the nobility.

The actual revolution began in March 1848 when meetings, petitions and demonstrations escalated into isolated outbreaks of rioting in towns and cities and in the countryside. Liberal groups took advantage of the violence in France in February 1848 to organize a movement calling for constitutional reforms and national unity, which was especially strong in southern Germany and Prussia. A mixture of local and national issues, economic and political, was revealed in the meetings, demonstrations and petitions. It would be wrong to see the outbreaks of violence as motivated by a desire for national unity or Liberal government, though the Liberal nationalists were the main beneficiaries from it. It is interesting that 'German' demands were strongest in areas like Baden and Brunswick, where local constitutional disputes had not been so acute in the 1840s. The causes of unrest varied from place to place and local factors played a major part. In the urban areas the main participants in the violence were the artisans or *Handwerker*, suffering unemployment and venting their grievances against factories, machines or the Jews. In the case of rural disorders, long-growing divisions between richer and poorer peasants were often as important a cause of violence as the sufferings of the peasant class as a whole. Traditional urban/rural hostility also played a part, with the rural population turning their hatred against the town-based agents of oppression like tax collectors and lawyers. Perhaps also the breakdown of traditional poor-relief systems, which were usually based on networks of local influence, helped to break down localism. Large areas of Germany did not have any direct experience of revolutionary violence, outbreaks of which were very short-lived and restricted to a few cities and regions. The old regime collapsed in Germany more as a result of a loss of nerve by rulers than of violence. There was in Germany no centre equivalent to Paris and political developments varied from state to state. Indeed, even before the outbreak of violence in Paris in 1847, a number of German princes saw trouble coming and installed Liberal governments. News of riots in Berlin, Vienna, and the Rhenish and Saxon cities or of peasant risings in Baden, the Palatinate and the Rhineland, in the course of which troops had fraternized with the rioters, was enough to persuade many German rulers to sack their conservative ministers and install leading local Liberals as the saviours of society. The fall of Metternich on 13 March was widely seen as the symbolic end of the old order. When more governments began to make concessions in March and April, it was this which provoked the wave of violent outbreaks: a perceived loss of authority by the governments made the situation worse by raising expectations further. The old rulers and the old ruling class were not destroyed in the revolution but were left intact, ready to take over again when order returned and the Liberals were no longer seen as the only barrier between Germany and anarchy. In particular the armed forces of most of the States remained largely untouched by the revolutions.

The expectations of change were also felt in the confederate diet, as representatives of states in which the Liberals had gained influence pressed for reform of the German constitution. A large number of schemes for reform were floated in February and March, usually involving the addition of an elected parliament to the existing structure and all-German standardization of legal, military and economic arrangements. There was a debate on freedom of the press and it was resolved to allow each state to decide on this with some restrictions. Bavaria, as in 1815, was still at the forefront of opposition to standardization as an affront to states' rights, even a common postal and telegraph system, which Austria was ready to accept. On 10 March Metternich agreed to a meeting of all the German rulers to be held at Dresden two weeks later. This was overtaken by events.

In the earliest stages of the revolution the focus of attention shifted from the individual states to Frankfurt, which became the temporary capital of Germany. The new governments instructed their representatives in the diet to begin the work of reform of the German institution. The majority of Liberals were thinking in terms of a federal state based on the American model. On 1 March the diet declared itself 'the legal organ for national and political unity'. The tricolour flag was adopted and a committee of 17 men 'enjoying public confidence' was set up to work on details of reform. Heinrich von Gagern, the moderate Liberal first minister of Hesse-Darmstadt, emerged as leader of this. On 30 March the diet instructed the state governments to arrange elections to a German Parliament, which was 'to establish a German constitution between the governments and the nation'. It is significant that Austria, Prussia and Bavaria played no part in these decisions.

Simultaneously a parallel 'revolutionary' movement was working out its own plans for reform of the Confederation. The end of repression allowed various associations to operate without restraint, leading to a greater mobilization of the lower middle class, a phenomenon still not sufficiently investigated. A campaign to organize petitions and demonstrations developed from a series of mass meetings held in the south-west in late February and early March. This culminated in a meeting of representatives of various groups in Heidelberg on 5 March to discuss German unity. Deep divisions at once appeared. Hecker and Struve wanted a German republic while the Liberals held out for an elected parliament to devise the constitution for a new *Reich*. Early plans by some to create a united Germany by acclamation without the inconvenience of electing a parliament were dropped because of fear of the growth of the Radical Movement. The small committee entrusted by the meeting with making the arrangements was dominated by the moderate Liberals, as was the Pre-Parliament, a self-appointed body which sat from 31 March to 3 April and organized elections to a national constituent assembly. The emerging Radical movement wanted the Pre-Parliament to rule as a provisional government but it restricted itself to arranging the elections, drafting a list of fundamental rights and declaring in favour of the admission of Schleswig and East and West Prussia to the Confederation. It refused to purge the Confederate Diet, which continued to sit. A large group of Radicals left the Pre-Parliament and launched their first attempt to seize control of the revolution by a *coup*. A rising in Baden, in the course of which a German republic was proclaimed at Constance, was put down by troops between 20 and 27 April.

1848 saw the first mass nationalist experience in German history. Mass enthusiasm for national unity was a growing force in the early stages of the revolution, when it was briefly seen as the gateway to all manner of individual and group Utopias. Such enthusiasm was certainly visible in towns and cities; there is less certainty that it was present in rural areas. It waned quickly, leaving the Liberals isolated in their identification of general progress with the achievement of national goals, though the memory of the heady days of March and April 1848 lingered for a long time and the tricolour flag remained a very important symbol. In early 1849 workers in south Germany were still collecting money for the construction of a German navy. Enthusiasm revived in some places in April 1849 in support of the constitution eventually drawn up at Frankfurt. After the passing of the euphoria of early March, mass nationalism only appeared again in the form of anti-foreign sentiment over Schleswig-Holstein, which was also present at the beginning of the revolution. The Schleswig-Holstein affair was not of the formidable complexity sometimes attributed to it. The two duchies were separate entities in personal union with the Danish crown and, since 1460, in legislative union with one another. They shared common Estates. Holstein, wholly German, was in the Confederation while Schleswig, with a substantial Danish minority in the north, was not. The years before 1848 had seen mounting national friction between the two peoples. After a revolution in 1848, which ended absolutism in Denmark, Danish nationalists claimed Schleswig as part of the new constitutional Danish state. In March representatives of the duchies met, introduced Liberal reforms and resolved to seek the admission of Schleswig to the Confederation. On 24 March they proclaimed a provisional government and asked the diet for military help against Danish attempts to coerce them. Prussia, as keen as ever to have an excuse to extend its influence into a desirable area, at once sent troops into Holstein without waiting for authorization from the Confederation. This was ratified by the diet not, significantly, in order to remove the duchies from the sovereignty of their Danish ruler but to preserve their union by admitting Schleswig to the Confederation. Skirmishing between Danish and German troops in April was watched with avid interest in Germany. This whole problem was to be inherited by the Frankfurt Parliament.

The revolution is seen by some as a break in German history, the acid test of German Liberalism and 'the last chance for Germany to catch up'. As usual, myths quickly obscured the reality, which was that there was no possibility of a united Germany with a Liberal constitution in 1848. The revolution showed up clearly some of the characteristics of Liberal nationalism. It has become a commonplace that the Parliament was overwhelmingly made up of educated upper-middle-class deputies, obsessed with resolutions and paper constitutions which had little if any impact on the real Germany outside Frankfurt. Throughout the crisis the Liberals were most successful when they worked at a local level within the states; their attempt to create an artificial Paris in Frankfurt proved a fatal trap. From the outset there was always something artificial about the Frankfurt Parliament; it took leading Liberals away from the places where they had some power and influence and isolated them in an ivory tower of their own making. Their consciousness of their own isolation was shown in their attitude to the franchise. The Parliament was elected under a wide variety of suffrages in the different states as the Pre-Parliament's decision to give the vote to all independent adult males was open to wide interpretation. In many states some form of property or educational franchise was employed to keep out 'undesirables', the vote was often withheld from all employees without property and, in some cases, poll-rigging was employed.[34] When the Liberals spoke of the 'the people', the majority continued to think in terms of people with property and education. Some 80 per cent of the members had university degrees and were middle-class professionals like civil servants, lawyers, doctors, teachers and journalists but the problem of the Liberals was not lack of experience but a lack of policies. It soon became clear that many of the Liberal deputies, even if schooled in the politics of civil service committees, lacked parliamentary experience, this being shown in the rapid fragmentation of the Parliament into a fluid and unstable system of groupings or *Fraktionen*, divided by principle, geographical origins or religion or attached to influential individuals. These 'parties' took their names from the Frankfurt hotels where they met to concert policy. Moderate Liberals made up the largest group.[35] There were very deep divisions concerning the shape and form of the Germany they were trying to create. There was also no agreement on who were the enemies of the *Volk* — the princes, foreigners or Austria — and dispute about whether Austria was any longer a German state. Disputes over the details of the constitution for a new united Germany, for example between federalists and centralists, and even the exact geographical limits of this new Germany, took up the time which might have been used to convert the Liberals' moral authority into real power, though it is hard to see how.

The reforms eventually enacted in Frankfurt, including a bill of rights, a new federal constitution strongly influenced by the American and Belgian models, ministerial responsibility, the take-over of the domain lands of the German rulers, the abolition of all privileges, local self-government, free enterprise and judicial reforms illustrate what the mainstream Liberal nationalists wanted. The committee which drafted the list of fundamental rights was

[34]T.S. Hamerow, 'The elections to the Frankfurt Parliament', *JMH* 33 (1961), pp. 15–32.
[35]F. Eyck, *The Frankfurt Parliament 1848–9* (1968).

dominated by the moderate Liberals and this led to a statement of the classical Liberal freedoms but an almost complete absence of social provisions in the final version, accepted by the rump of the Parliament in December 1848. The changes enacted by the Parliament were accepted by a majority of the German governments but very little was put into effect. On 12 July the Confederate Diet formally handed over its functions to the new provisional central government, which was set up with, at its head, an Administrator (*Reichsverweser*), the 66-year-old Austrian Archduke John, and ministers but without the means to put its decisions into force. The Parliament's lack of real power was shown clearly in August, when Austria and Prussia flatly refused the Administrator's order that their troops were to perform a kind of oath-swearing to him. Other large states complied only partially. There was also powerful resistance from the states to the provisional central government giving direct orders to their civil services. Financial contributions from the states for the maintenance of the Parliament and provisional government were often not paid. The states also maintained their own independent diplomacy. This took on great importance in August, when the king of Prussia, under pressure from Britain and Russia, signed the Malmö armistice with the Danes, under which he agreed to withdraw his forces from Schleswig and Holstein and to dissolve the provisional government of the duchies in Kiel. This produced outrage in Frankfurt and the resignation of the German provisional government.

A new government was formed in September after the Parliament accepted the armistice by one vote. This was to have a lasting effect: consciousness of having been defeated by a small state was seen as very demeaning to the German nation. Only in October did the Parliament begin to debate the nuts and bolts of a German constitution, by which time the forces of reaction were already beginning to recover power in many German states. After debates, which were as long and intricate as those on the bill of rights, a constitution was agreed by a tiny majority on 28 March 1849. Initially the great majority of the deputies favoured the inclusion of German Austria in the new German state but from late autumn vigorous debates between the *kleindeutsch* and *grossdeutsch* parties, those who favoured a German state without Austrian lands and those who supported Austria's inclusion, revealed that there was no unity among them as to exactly what 'Germany' consisted of. This question was closely involved with religious considerations: a Germany without Austria would have a large Protestant majority and this, added to the known anti-clericalism of most Liberals, was very worrying to Catholics. There were bitter debates on the powers to be left to the individual states and whether Germany was to have an hereditary Emperor, a president or a committee as head of state. By March 1849 the Austrian government had made it clear that the unity of the Austrian Empire would be preserved. This forced the Parliament to drop its initial scheme for the German provinces of Austria to be detached and to remain in only personal union with the rest and allowed the pro-Prussian party to carry the day.

Considerable resistance to Prussian control of Germany had to be overcome. Under the constitution the head of the new state was to be the king of Prussia as hereditary Emperor with a suspensory veto over legislation. Germany would be a federal state, coterminous with the old Confederation with additions, in which the individual states would devolve important powers upwards to a central authority, answerable to an elected parliament. The new state would be called the German *Reich*, a symbol of its links with the old Empire rather than the Confederation. Although the constitution contained a large measure of compromise, it retained essential Liberal features: an elected assembly with a generously wide franchise, an advanced code of basic rights and a strong central authority.

The king of Prussia torpedoed the whole constitution on 2 April 1849 by refusing 'the crown from the gutter' and the larger German states rejected the constitution. By then the Parliament was beginning to disintegrate as states ordered their deputies to leave. By May only the deputies of the Left remained. The legal existence of the Parliament ended on 18 June, when the Württemberg government prevented the few remaining members assembling in Stuttgart, but it was clear long before then that it had failed.

The complexities of the Austrian 'problem' were a major factor in explaining the failure of the revolution. There were severe practical difficulties in placing part of a unitary state under a new German government while leaving the rest to be ruled from Vienna. Even among Liberal Austrian Germans there was marked reluctance to see their state lose its identity through being submerged in Germany. The government which took over after the fall of Metternich ordered elections to the Frankfurt Parliament but issued a declaration on 21 April reserving all Austria's state rights. The non-German inhabitants of the parts of Austria inside the Confederation had their own national demands and many did not welcome the prospect of being outsiders at the German family birthday party. Events in Bohemia in the first days of the revolution showed that not all Germans shared the enthusiasm for national unity. On 11 March Czech and German representatives meeting in Prague called for autonomy for the Bohemian lands within a federal Austrian Empire, the preservation of which was seen as vital to the defence of Central Europe against Russia. Eventually the Czechs refused to send representatives to Frankfurt, as did many of the Slovenes of Carinthia, and the summer of 1848 saw growing friction between Czechs and Germans quickly replacing the earlier Bohemian regional solidarity. The Austrian government was to exploit growing ethnic disputes very skilfully in restoring its authority in its territories.

There were similar problems with the Polish minority in Prussia. In the province of Posen, where Poles were in a majority, a Polish national committee was established to resist German influence. The initial sympathy of the Liberal Prussian government quickly evaporated and, after violent clashes between Poles and Germans, troops were sent in to restore order. The Poles boycotted the elections to the German Parliament in large numbers. The Prussian Liberals were quite unprepared to make any concessions to the Polish minority in East and West Prussia.

Also revealed was the fact that the majority of Liberals, faced with the choice between national unity and power or Liberal freedoms, opted for the first. Instead of seeing national unity as a means to an end, they were now moving closer to the nationalists who viewed German power as an end in itself and who were obsessed with the need to catch up and overtake others. The notion of Germany as a 'belated nation' was appearing very clearly. A leading Liberal, F.C. Dahlmann, speaking in the Frankfurt Parliament on 22 January 1849, summed this up: 'The road to power is the only one which will satisfy and assuage our desire for freedom ... Germany must finally join the ranks of the political great powers as a great power. That can only happen through Prussia. Prussia cannot thrive without Germany nor Germany without Prussia.'

In sharp contrast to the deep divisions revealed in the debates on the bill of rights and the constitution was the emotional unity of the majority of the deputies in the shared joy of asserting historic nationalism and resisting the claims of non-German minorities to pieces of German territory. The artificial world of the Paulskirche, the former church in which the parliament met, acted as a kind of forcing-house, turning patriotism, pride in German achievement, into bombastic chauvinism. Speakers sought to outbid one another in the grandioseness of their vision. The lack of reality was seen in plans for a German navy, which, it was said, would enable Germany to wrest control of the seas from Britain. Germany was to become overnight a great world power, playing its full part in commerce and colonization and spreading its civilization far and wide. A naval victory by the Schleswig-Holstein fleet over the Danes off Eckernförde in 1849, in which the Danish flagship was destroyed, was the occasion for great rejoicing. The debates became increasingly bellicose, with calls for a great re-drawing of the borders of Europe to restore long-lost German lands, such as Alsace-Lorraine and the Low Countries, regardless of the wishes of the inhabitants. In long debates on the future of Schleswig and Posen, language was invoked by some as a rational criterion for the determination of national frontiers but the majority of the Liberal nationalists, following what Wilhelm Jordan defined as 'healthy national egoism', rejected this if it meant the loss of land historically German because a majority of the inhabitants did not speak German. In the debate on basic rights on 4 July 1848 Jordan said 'All who live in Germany are German, even if not German by birth and language'. An Austrian deputy of the Left Liberals, who supported Polish claims in Posen, was less sympathetic to minorities in Austria: 'a great nation needs space in order to fulfil its world vocation and I would prefer to die a thousand times than see Trieste taken from us, although some Italians live there.' Austrian victories over Italian insurrectionists in Lombardy and Venetia and over the Czechs in Prague were hailed as German victories. Supporters of *Kleindeutschland*, who urged Austria to turn her back on Germany, spoke of her as the agent of a German civilizing mission in the Balkans and of one day seeing the Habsburg eagle floating over the Hagia Sophia mosque in Istanbul. Many took the view that the inhabitants of Posen, Schleswig and Bohemia should welcome Germanization because of the manifest innate superiority of German culture. Learned historians proved that, throughout history, there had been dominant and subordinate peoples and that the Germans, like the ancient Greeks and Romans, belonged to the former group. Though the Radicals were usually more consistent in their support of national self-determination, even Struve's planned federal German republic was to include Czech, Polish and Danish minorities. The 1849 constitution eventually included a geographical rather than ethnic definition of Germany: Article 131 stated 'The German nation (*Volk*) consists of the members of the states which form the German *Reich*', that is, all who lived within the borders of Germany, as designated, were Germans. It guaranteed non-German minorities the use of their languages in churches, education, justice and local administration but more comprehensive guarantees of national minority rights were rejected after debates.

1848 saw the first attempt by the Germans to solve the 'German question' without foreign involvement since the Thirty Years' War. The fact that they failed cannot be attributed to the lack of foreign support, though this lack had a damaging effect on the morale of the Parliament. It became clear very quickly that the creation of a strong Germany was as little in the interests of her neighbours in 1848 as it had been in 1815. Even the Liberal regime in France had the same interest in the preservation of particularism in Germany as had Louis XIV and signed a defensive alliance with Russia to meet the threat of German aggression. The aggressiveness of German nationalism in 1848 alienated many. British Liberal opinion, initially sympathetic, changed to support of the Danes in the Schleswig-Holstein affair, though other considerations, especially strategic, played a part in this. The Dutch, who in the 1830s had seriously considered joining the Confederation in the hope of gaining economic advantages from association with the *Zollverein*, dropped such plans after 1848.[36]

The causes of the failure lay within Germany. The Liberals were unable to build any mass support, especially among the groups who had, indirectly, given them power, the peasants and urban artisans. The latter were beginning to organize nationally and articulate their demands at a series of all-German congresses, such as that held in Frankfurt in July 1848. It is interesting that its demands were economic rather than national-political. Whereas the Liberals sought progressive change, the peasants and artisans were often reactionary in their desires. The Parliament received large numbers of petitions, in particular from organized artisan groups, calling for a minimum wage, the restoration of guild restrictions, organized social welfare systems and state guarantees of employment. Discussed at length in the Economic Committee of the Parliament, such demands were rejected as 'making war on progress'. The debates revealed that there were very wide divisions of opinion on economic matters in the Parliament. It proved impossible to reach agreement even on a common tariff for Germany and other measures of economic unification. (German chambers of commerce did not come together in a single organization until 1861.) Full-blooded *laissez-faire* Liberals were in a minority at Frankfurt, as were businessmen and entrepreneurs, and there was a fear among the so-called Social Liberals that unrestricted competition would be a source of disorder among a rootless proletariat prey to radical appeals. Many of the Catholic clergy elected to the Parliament also supported social reform.[37] The Liberals were hampered by their fundamental mistrust of the masses and unwillingness to mobilize them in support of Liberal aspirations. They refused to see themselves or their fellow Germans in class terms, regarding the notion of class as a variant of the orders of the despised old regime or a dangerous tenet of Socialism. They continued to view

[36]F.G. Weber, 'Palmerston and Prussian Liberalism 1848', *JMH* 35 (1963), pp. 125–36.
[37]D. Rohr, *The Origins of Social Liberalism in Germany* (Chicago, 1963).

society as a collection of individuals from whom, in a system of equal opportunities and a free economy, natural leaders would emerge to join the middle class and, therefore, become qualified to exercise political power. Before 1848 Liberals had supported night-schools, savings banks and educational societies as the means by which such social elevation might be achieved. They had earlier had a strong belief that there was nothing to fear from educated men (in contrast to the conservative fear of the educated proletariat) but this faith began to slip in 1848, when many Liberals began to share Metternich's fear of the masses being led astray by educated scribblers and agitators. The Liberals also very quickly discovered a common interest with the old ruling class in defence of property, especially when more extreme political groups began to emerge. Significantly one of the earliest acts of Liberal administrations in individual states was the establishment of civic guards to protect property. The revolution removed all controls on the expression of opinion and this new freedom after years of enforced restraint allowed a swarm of extremist groups to appear.

The Liberals were seriously worried by the activities of the Radicals, a weak but noisy group particularly active in Baden, Saxony and the Rhineland. Memories of the swing to extremism in the French revolution in 1793 were very much alive in 1848. There is a danger in attaching a single label to these groups, because it suggests that they formed a cohesive whole and that they were completely separate from the Liberals. In fact the Radicals encompassed a wide range of different opinions and there was a considerable overlapping between the two movements. An attempt was made in the autumn of 1848, by the establishment of the *Central-märzverein*, to create an umbrella organization for almost a thousand groups but it fell apart from March 1849 in reaction to the king of Prussia's refusal of the imperial crown. Fatherland Societies and Workers' Societies set up in 1848 were also short-lived. Only a small extreme minority had genuinely revolutionary aims. Radicals proclaimed a German democratic republic three times, in April and September 1848 and in April 1849. A 'German Legion' of students and gymnasts invaded Baden from Alsace in April 1848 to support the democratic republic proclaimed by Hecker. Although they were easily defeated, the prospect of a return visit frightened men of property. As time passed the Radicals became more extreme, calling for community of property and other horrors. The Radical leaders were very good at delivering marrow-withering speeches against the bourgeoisie and were able to cash in briefly on the grievances of the artisans, which the liberals had refused to deal with, and a brief wave of national outrage following the Parliament's apparent failure to secure Schleswig-Holstein for

Germany, which culminated in serious riots in Frankfurt on 18 September. The parliamentarians had to rely on Prussian and Austrian troops to rescue them and two were killed by the mob. The Radicals were also prominent in the so-called Second Revolution of April and May 1849, sparked off by the king of Prussia's refusal of the imperial crown and the apparent failure of the constitution and threatened return to pre-revolutionary conditions. This suggested that national aims were still seen by some Germans as a means of achieving something desirable. The violence was most serious in the Saxon cities, the Rhineland and Westphalia, Franconia and, above all, Baden, where the Radicals took over the government and much of the army. Deep divisions in the leadership were again revealed and the risings were suppressed, often very brutally, mainly by Prussian troops, who went into action without waiting for invitations from the governments concerned. The king of Saxony was very unhappy about Prussian intervention but it was seen as the lesser of two evils. Only in Baden was the suppression difficult, though the Badenese rising was dominated by progressive Liberals rather than Radicals. Struve was not elected to the Badenese assembly in June 1849 and the programme of the Badenese revolutionary government of May 1849 was very moderate, with no mention of a republic. The Radicals' support was essentially ephemeral; the Liberals considerably exaggerated the threat they represented but behaved in accordance with their fears rather then the reality.

Even weaker but even more terrible to the moderate Liberals was the extreme or Socialist Left.[38] The *Trierer Zeitung* of 11 February 1848 stated: 'Day by day it is becoming more painfully evident that there are two conflicting classes in society, capital and the proletariat.' If referring to Germany, this was certainly a gross oversimplification. The working-class movements which appeared during the revolution varied widely in their political positions. Socialist and Communist groups existed but they were small and scattered and they did not all follow the same ideology. Many of the leaders of the Left, Wilhelm Weitling, Karl Marx and Friedrich Engels, were anti-nationalist, taking the view that the proletariat had no fatherland and supporting instead the unity of the oppressed of all nations. A more real and more radical workers' movement, one which did not distinguish between guild and non-guild workers, was beginning to appear under the influence of Germans who had experienced developments in France and Switzerland. At the *Handwerker* Congress in July 1848 the arrogance of the masters pushed many journeymen and apprentices towards alliance with

[38]O.J. Hammen, 'The Spectre of Communism in the 1840s', *J.Hist.Id.* 14 (1963), pp. 404–20.

the non-guild workers, a movement symbolized in the growth of Stefan Born's Brotherhood of Workers (*Arbeiterverbrüderung*), an attempt to create an organization for all workers. Its success was limited. A General German Workers' Congress held in Berlin in 1848 demanded free movement for workers but not a unitary German republic. The activities of the extreme Left in France and events such as the demonstration in Cologne on 3 March 1848, including members of Andreas Gottschalk's Communist League carrying red flags, convinced many that the Red Peril was real. A movement which did not seek to join the middle class but had contempt for it was profoundly worrying to Liberals and, faced with a society which threatened to become anarchic, they increasingly identified with the *Rechtstaat* and looked to a strong state as a bulwark of order.

The Parliament also failed to win the support of the German Churches. The Protestant Church came out firmly against the Liberals and nationalists. Ironically, the first all-German Protestant congress in Wittenberg in 1848 favoured an extension of charitable work and social reform but strongly condemned the revolution and the Frankfurt Parliament.[39] The first all-German Catholic Congress at Mainz in October was very ambivalent and more concerned with defending Catholic rights than building a New Germany.

The final passing of the economic crisis, from late 1848, with a good harvest and the opening of Californian gold resources, revealed the inherent weaknesses of the German Liberal nationalists, who owed their brief power in Germany to the special circumstances of 1848. The counter-revolution found it very easy to win back power. In the event, the Conservatives proved to have a much more astute appreciation of political reality in Germany. Prussia was a typical example. Had the king kept his nerve in March 1848 there would probably have been no revolution. He was a victim of his own illusions; the king was convinced that the troubles in Berlin were the beginning of a great conflagration engineered by Metternich's bogeymen, foreign agitators. His withdrawal of the troops from Berlin on 19 March after serious clashes with rioters and his subsequent public appearances wearing the tricolour and declarations of support for German unity demolished the Conservative forces and handed power to the Liberals. The army remained a centre of Conservative power. The new government failed to win the support of the peasantry, from whom the bulk of the army was drawn, and the *Landwehr*, on which Liberals had placed great hopes, did not become the guardian of constitutional liberties

[39]W.O. Shanahan, *German Protestants Face the Social Question* I: 1815–71 (Notre Dame, 1954).

against tyranny, except in the Rhineland during the risings of April 1849, when it had to be put down by the regular army. The elections to the Prussian parliament, which also called itself a national assembly, in May 1848 produced an impractical radical majority which lingered on until December but became increasingly divorced from reality. Deep divisions among the Liberals and increasing violence in Berlin gave the growing counter-revolutionary forces ammunition. On 5 December the king dissolved the Assembly and announced a new moderately Liberal constitution. A new parliament was elected but this too was dissolved in May 1849. Apart from sporadic violence in Berlin, there was no opposition to this.

The Austrian Conservatives similarly found it easy to regain their authority.[40] On 15 May the Emperor and his family moved from Vienna to Innsbruck, leaving the city increasingly isolated and unrepresentative as more extreme groups dominated by students and artisans took over. The elected all-Austrian imperial diet, which met in July, contained no Hungarian delegates and was numerically dominated by the Slavs. One of its earliest acts was to abolish all remaining feudal obligations on land, with the state taking over the cost of compensating the owners of these rights. All the propaganda benefit from this accrued to the Emperor, in whose name it was promulgated. The diet was deeply divided in its attitude to the Hungarian revolution taking place simultaneously, with which the Left and many German nationalists were sympathetic. Attempts by the government to use military force against the Hungarians led in October to serious rioting in Vienna, in the course of which the war minister was lynched. As a result the Emperor and government again left the city. Attempts by the Frankfurt Parliament to take control of events came to nothing. After imperial troops had taken the city on 31 October the authority of the central government was restored. As in Italy and Bohemia, military force was to bring to an end the revolution among the Austrian Germans. Although the imperial diet continued to sit in Kremsier in Moravia and eventually produced a new constitution, its work was increasingly irrelevant. The new Emperor Francis Joseph who took over on 2 December after the abdication of Ferdinand I was committed to the maintenance of the Austrian state intact and opposed to the merging of part of it in a new German state. He dissolved the diet on 4 March and issued a new unitary constitution for the whole Empire. Only in Hungary did the revolution linger on until put down by Russian troops, sent on the invitation of Francis Joseph.

[40]R.J. Rath, *The Viennese Revolution of 1848* (Arlington, 1957).

When the counter-revolution came, in most states it was moderate and the rulers, when restored to full power, followed Bismarck's maxim, borrowed from the Chinese, of building golden bridges for their enemies to make it easy for the Liberals, already seriously worried by mob violence and the activities of the Radicals, to reconcile themselves to the return of order, even if it was the old order. There was no widespread White Terror. Only in Baden and Vienna was the suppression of the revolution followed by courts martial and large-scale executions. An estimated 80,000 refugees fled from Baden. There was another large wave of emigration, including many Radicals, after 1851 as much because of dashed hopes and economic factors as political persecution. The events of 1848 reinforced the trend, already apparent among Conservatives before the revolution, to offer intellectual justification for their creed, seen in the work of the Berlin law professor Friedrich Julius Stahl, whose *Monarchical Principle* (1845) put forward a modernized version of paternalistic monarchy founded on Christian principles combined with constitutionalism. The Conservatives quickly learned the value of organization and propaganda. In Prussia the *Neue Preussische Zeitung*, known as the *Kreuzzeitung* (Cross Newspaper), founded in May 1848, became an important vehicle for Conservative views and the summer of 1848 saw the first steps in the creation of a Conservative political movement. A Society for Guaranteeing the Interests of Landowners was set up in August 1848, which attempted to spread its influence more widely especially in rural areas through the Prussia Society movement (*Preussenvereine*). Many intelligent reform Conservatives, known in Prussia after their newspaper as the *Wochenblattpartei*, were ready to accept political and economic progress provided the basic structures of the state and society were not damaged and saw in the British system something which could be imported with profit into Prussia.[41]

Although the situation varied from state to state, many of the Liberal governments and the reforms of 1848, for example judicial reforms and fairer taxation systems, remained intact. Economic growth returned quickly and in most parts of Germany the thing which the Liberals regarded as their main enemy, 'feudalism', did not survive 1848–50. The aristocracy were not all privileged drones but played a major role in government and the economy. Landowners remained the predominant social group in the majority of German states but the opportunities of the middle class to join them were multiplying after 1848. Political influence was not beyond the reach of the middle class: constitutions survived in most states

[41]J. Weiss, *Conservatism in Europe 1700–1945* (1977).

after the revolution, though the Prussian constitution of 1850, which remained in force until 1918, was considerably less liberal than that of 1848. On the other hand, the divisions among the Liberals shown up in 1848–9 continued to weaken them and they remained essentially a class party without mass backing. All-German consciousness and links were considerably strengthened by the events of 1848–9 and lived on in enlarged musical and cultural groups and the more political National Societies and Fatherland Societies, where they were allowed to survive. Many saw their suspicion of state welfare schemes confirmed and the boom of the 1850s seemed to support those who argued that a little social distress was an unavoidable accompaniment to a free and growing economy. The Conservatives, in so far as they were able to satisfy the aspirations of the peasants, enjoyed far more mass support after 1848. If later these same peasants migrated to the towns, they were as likely to vote Socialist or Catholic as Liberal. Some Liberals sought an answer in the concept of the *Mittelstand*, the middle Estate as the independent heart of the nation, above partial and party interests. There was, however, no avoiding the conclusion that Germany had again avoided having a real revolution and that little had been done to advance the political education of the German people, though embryonic political parties which were to be important for the rest of the century had emerged in 1848–9, Conservatives, Clericalists, Socialists, Progressives and Liberals.

Whatever consolation Liberals could draw from the failure of 1848, a united Germany seemed no nearer. Germany remained a 'delayed nation'. After 1848 the Liberal nationalists realized that any solution to the German problem would have to take fuller account of the German states and their rulers. They needed strong states to protect them and to achieve unity. The Liberals had watched with approval as princely armies rescued them from mobs in Frankfurt, rioting after the Parliament approved the Malmö armistice and again in May 1849, after the king of Prussia refused the imperial crown. Princely armies also put down the Radical 'Second Revolution' in Saxony, Baden and the Rhineland.

It can be argued that the failed revolution produced among Germans a reinforcement of the already strong belief that progress was not something which could be seized by the people through insurrection against authority but something which would be handed down to a grateful people by an all-wise all-seeing state. Their confidence dented and deeply anxious about the way German society seemed to be evolving, the Liberals returned to their earlier strategy of working to liberalize individual states, seeing in Prussia especially a possible future leader of unification. During the 1850s the Liberals again began to advance in the south German states and Baden in particular became a centre of Liberal nationalism. In spite of the growth of this 'realistic policy' (*Realpolitik*, a word coined in 1853 by a former Liberal, Ludwig von Rochau), the Liberals continued to believe that the forces of reaction would in the end be defeated and to see themselves as the party of the future. Although overt political activities were difficult in the immediate aftermath of the revolution, a Liberal substructure remained in existence in the form of professional bodies, chambers of commerce, clubs and academic associations. A close connection between Liberalism and German nationalism remained into the 1850s and 1860s.

5

The Partition of the Nation
1850–1871

In tracing the development of German nationalism, the events culminating in the creation of the *Reich* of 1871 must be considered, though not in great detail.[1] Nationalism played a marginal role in the process and was more a consequence than a cause of unification. The unification of Germany was very different in character from that of Italy, lacking the element of popular participation in the form of plebiscites and Garibaldi's volunteer movement. A number of general points should be borne in mind as background. Traditionally excessive emphasis has been placed on the role of Prussia and Bismarck, who has been portrayed as a great manipulator. In fact many of the initiatives which eventually led to the unification came from Austria and other powers. The role of Napoleon III of France has been underestimated. Insufficient emphasis has been given to the 'Southern problem', the part to be played within Germany by the substantial south German states, especially Bavaria.

Bismarck was no innovator. He simply pursued well-established Prussian policies with greater vigour than his more reticent predecessors, whose actions were restrained by a feeling of conservative solidarity with Austria and other German states. The basic policy, which had been pursued since 1815 or earlier, was to persuade or force Austria to accept Prussia as an equal in German affairs. Bismarck pursued this aim with such energy that his achievement has been described as a revolution in Prussian foreign policy, though a revolution from above. Before he came into power, he had condemned what he saw as Prussia's passive and spineless attitude towards Austria: she had done nothing but remove stones thrown into her garden by others; she had been the anvil when she could have been the hammer.[2] At the same time he preserved

[1]Basic works on the unification: H. Friedjung, *The Struggle for Supremacy in Germany 1859–1866* (1935); O. Pflanze, *Bismarck and the Development of Germany* i (Princeton, 1963); T.S. Hamerow, *The Social Foundations of German Unification* (2 vols., Princeton, 1969–72); R. Austensen, 'Austria and the Struggle for Supremacy in Germany 1848–64', *JMH* 52 (1980), pp. 195–225; J.J. Sheehan, 'What is German History? Reflections on the Role of the *Nation* in German History and Historiography', *JMH* 53 (1981), pp. 1–23; E. Kraehe, 'Austria and the Problem of Reform in the German Confederation 1851–1863', *Am.H.R.* 56 (1950–1), pp. 276–94, and 'Practical Politics in the German Confederation: Bismarck and the Commercial Code', *JMH* 25 (1953), 13–24; R.M. Berdahl, 'New Thoughts on German Nationalism', *Am.H.R.* 77 (1972), pp. 65–80.
[2]F. Gundolf (ed.), *Otto von Bismarck, Mensch und Staat. Aus den Briefen. Reden und Schriften* (Munich, 1956): letters to Leopold von Gerlach, Frankfurt, 2 and 30 May 1857, pp. 88–97.

the traditional political and social structures in Prussia against the threat of a revitalized Liberalism. Although Bismarck claimed to have despised Napoleon III of France, during his period as Prussian ambassador in Paris he was much influenced by the French Emperor, who seemed to have squared the circle by building a repressive conservative regime, on the basis of universal male suffrage and managed elections, while at the same time embarking on an adventurous foreign policy aimed at overturning the 1815 settlement of Europe. If Bismarck wished to assert Prussian power in Germany, he too had to dismantle the Vienna settlement, which had given Austria informal hegemony in Central Europe. It was never Bismarck's wish or intention to unify Germany in the way he did in 1871. He was pushed into it by forces beyond his control inside and outside Germany. The settlement he eventually achieved was only one possibility among many available. Germany did not grow together but was forced together. Arguably 1871 saw not the unification of Germany but its partition and colonization by Prussia and Bismarck ensured that the settlement was both non-national and non-Liberal. The manner of unification was of importance to the subsequent development of nationalism: in 1870 mass nationalism was brought to fever pitch and then frustrated.

Traditionally too much attention has been given to the events of the 1860s and not enough to the 1850s, which saw very important developments. If a date has to be found for the beginning of the process leading to German unification, it should be 1854. The outbreak of the Crimean War broke the 1815 settlement and began the dismantling of its central structures, which earlier breaches, like Greek and Belgian independence, had left intact. This, plus defeats in Italy in 1859 and 1860, represented a major blow to Austria's position in Europe, which unsettled her internal political balance and made her more determined to recover her prestige in Germany. She chose to attempt this by three methods, a challenge to Prussia's economic power, a political campaign to reform the *Bund* and, ultimately, a war against Prussia.

The first steps in this process were taken before the 1848 revolution had run its course. With the restoration of order in Austria-Hungary, a new government under Prince Felix von Schwarzenberg was installed in November 1848.[3] A skilled and vigorous administrator and politician, he was very close to the new Emperor Francis Joseph and his premature death in 1852 robbed Austria of a leader of talent. His policy rested on one basic principle, that the unity of the Austrian state was to be preserved. He based his government

---

[3] A. Schwarzenberg, *Prince Felix zu Schwarzenberg* (New York, 1946).

on a centralized and modernized autocracy, with efficiency and economic growth as its aims. He realized that the traditional basis of Austrian government, the aristocracy, was no longer adequate to meet these aims and he was ready to work with the middle class and moderate Liberals. His Interior and Justice Ministers, Stadion and Bach, were leading Liberals. The work of economic reform was largely in the hands of Karl von Bruck, a Liberal member of the Frankfurt Parliament, and was designed as much to enable Austria to catch up with Prussia economically as to bolster Austria's position as a European great power.

Schwarzenberg was eager to reassert Austrian power in Germany. In March 1849 he floated a scheme for the amalgamation of Germany and the whole Austrian Empire, the so-called Seventy-Million *Reich*, under a presidency alternating annually between the king of Prussia and the Austrian Emperor. By May it was clear that the constitution produced by the Frankfurt Parliament would not come into operation and Schwarzenberg began to take the first steps leading to a *restoratio in integrum* of the old Confederation. This was based on the legal fiction that the Frankfurt Parliament was itself a continuation of the old Confederate Diet: when in May the rump of the Parliament tried to sack the Administrator they were informed that his authority derived not only from them but from the 39 German governments. At the same time Schwarzenberg rejected a Prussian proposal for the creation of a *kleindeutsch* confederation of the German states, with a parliament elected under a very narrow franchise, in a close alliance with a separate Austria.

Simultaneously Prussia was making a bid for leadership in German affairs by the creation of the Erfurt Union. This was to lead to the so-called Humiliation of Olmütz of 29 November 1850, an event of a significance sometimes not recognized.[4] Although Frederick William IV had refused the imperial crown offered by the Frankfurt parliament, Prussia was not averse to taking advantage of the brief surge of nationalism in Germany associated with the Schleswig-Holstein affair and of Austria's preoccupation with risings in Italy and Hungary to improve her position in Germany. This period saw a battle for influence in the Prussian court between the reactionary 'Camarilla' party and the conservative Romantic Joseph Maria von Radowitz and the Liberals. The last two gained a temporary ascendancy over the king and this resulted in the creation of the Union, a Prussian-led alliance of mainly north German states with its own army and an elected assembly at Erfurt. In November 1847 Radowitz had put forward a plan for a small

[4] The description of the treaty as a humiliation is a sign of the potency of the Borussian legend in traditional historiography.

Prussian-led league within the Confederation if Austria rejected reform plans. After the failure of Frankfurt and while Austria was still involved in suppressing internal troubles, Germany was in a kind of limbo without any political framework and Prussian diplomacy played on the nervousness of governments to win them over for the Union. The whole thing was in reality an exercise in conservative nationalism, the exploitation of lingering hopes for unity for the enhancement of Prussian state power. The plan was approved by a meeting of moderate Liberals, the remains of the *kleindeutsch* party in the Frankfurt Parliament, in Gotha in July following the promise that the constitution of the Union would be worked out in co-operation between an elected parliament and the 26 member governments. There were still hopes of rescuing political gains from the ruins of the dream of national unity.

From the outset Schwarzenberg worked to undermine the plan, using diplomatic pressure and deep suspicion of Prussia in south Germany, especially Bavaria. His success was shown when, at a meeting of the heads of the member states, 12 of the 26 original members refused to ratify the Union constitution. Prussia collaborated with Austria in the restoration of the Confederation in the hope of buying Austrian acquiescence in the Union but in February 1850 Bavaria, Württemberg, Hanover and Saxony agreed to co-operate with Austria in ending the Union and restoring the Confederation. On 1 May 1850 the Austrian Emperor formally invited the German states to appoint delegates to a restored Confederate Diet. Eventually, after Germany had come close to war between the restored Confederation and the Union, Prussia, with no hope of help from Russia, backed down and agreed at Olmütz to the dissolution of the Union. Informal hegemony in the north had been Prussia's aim since 1815 and it was now to be the basis of Bismarck's German policy.

On this occasion, Bismarck drew attention to himself by a speech in the Prussian diet on 3 December 1850 supporting the abandonment of the Union on the grounds that any other policy would lead to war between Prussia, Austria and Russia, from which only the revolutionaries would benefit.[5] This confirmed his reputation as an extreme and uncompromising reactionary, gained at the time of his emergence into politics in the Prussian diet in 1847 and during the events of 1848. His opinions were not shared by a majority of his fellow Conservatives. Shortly afterwards he was sent as Prussian representative to the confederate assembly in Frankfurt, where his apparently pro-Austrian views would be useful. His experiences there formed another important stage in his

[5]Gundolf, pp. 68–70; L. Gall, *Bismarck. The White Revolutionary* I (1986), pp. 79–80.

political learning process. He quickly became disillusioned with the pettiness of the assembly and began to pursue a tough anti-Austrian line, though he was not supported by his government. During these years the main lines of Bismarck's policy began to harden: in an age of industrialization and mechanized warfare Prussia could not maintain her status as a European power and a barrier against the dangerous forces at work in Germany, including nationalism, unless she had access to German manpower and resources beyond her borders. Otherwise she was too small for the roles she was trying to fulfil. The predatory recruiting policies and looting of neighbouring territories which had sustained Prussia in the age of Frederick the Great were no longer available. Austria needed these same resources in order to maintain her status. Germany therefore had to be controlled by one or other of its two great powers; it was too small for both.

Austria's intentions were soon made clear. In the early 1850s, building on her victory at Olmütz, she began an offensive against Prussian economic influence in Germany, putting forward a scheme for a wider economic union to replace the *Zollverein*.[6] As early as 1832 Metternich, well aware of the dangers to Austrian influence which the *Zollverein* represented, had negotiated for an Austrian customs union with the south German states. He pressed for Austrian membership of the *Zollverein* again in 1841 but others in the Austrian government refused to see the matter as urgent. This changed after 1850. Bruck had a plan for a giant Central European Customs Union of the Confederation and the rest of the Austrian lands. The earlier ambivalence about Austria's German role, based on the assumption that Austria was a great power in her own right and did not need Germany, changed. Austria now moved towards a more definite involvement in German affairs and began to take measures to facilitate economic union. A German postal and telegraph union was agreed in 1850. Monetary union was established in 1857 with agreed harmonization between the *Zollverein* and Austrian currencies. Major rail links between Germany and Austria, of great symbolic importance, were built in the 1850s and a system of chambers of commerce, long in existence in many German states, was established. An Austro-Prussian treaty was signed on 19 February 1853, which contained an undertaking for a customs treaty between them but this was never realized. In 1853, when the *Zollverein* treaties came up for renewal, all the members chose to rejoin rather than support the Austrian alternative. The

[6]H. Böhme (ed.), *The Foundation of the German Empire. Select Documents* (Oxford, 1971); F. Stern, *Gold and Iron. Bismarck, Blechröder and the Building of the German Empire* (1977) p. 20ff.

economic interdependence of Germany had grown since the foundation of the *Zollverein*, though there is a danger in exaggerating this.[7] Ernest Renan, author of the famous phrase about the nation as a daily plebiscite, also said 'A customs union is not a fatherland'. The mechanisms for achieving harmonization and co-operation between states touchy about their sovereignty were slow and awkward. Although the *Zollverein* brought benefits, Prussian dominance of it was mistrusted, especially by Bavaria, Hanover and Saxony. Prussia sold most of her iron and sugar in Bavaria. Prussia was the best market for Saxon textile manufactures, which drew the bulk of their yarn from Bavaria, which, in turn, bought Saxon coal. The Prussian east was the main source of foodstuffs for the growing industrial areas of the south and west. Mobility of capital in the customs union was also important, as Prussia replaced France as the main source of investment capital in Germany. The union continued to grow with the accession of Hanover, long an opponent of Prussia, and Oldenburg in 1854. The advantages of the customs union were shown even more clearly when Central Europe was struck by a minor economic depression in 1857, in which Austria suffered badly. Austria was still too backward to replace the economic benefits the *Zollverein* offered, though politically the smaller German states would have been happier had both Austria and Prussia been members.

Although Prussia was ruled in the 1850s by the Manteuffel-Westphalen *Camarilla*, ultra-conservative and committed to solidarity with Austria in the fight against the revolution and Jacobinism, especially as there was a Bonaparte on the French throne, the government was ready to resist Austrian attempts to take over the economic leadership in Germany. Beneath a surface of unbroken restoration calm, reflected in the regular meetings of German rulers (*Fürstentage*) held in the 1850s and early 1860s, there were serious strains in the relations of the two states. So long as Prussia did nothing to undermine Austria's position politically, the Conservatives in the government could reason to themselves that they were not threatening the established order in Germany, but the mid 1850s saw an economic war between the two states. During this period the economic growth of Prussia continued apace, as the state, having no great foreign policy commitments, allowed the army to stagnate and devoted its resources increasingly to economic expansion. Between 1821 and 1866 the percentage of state

[7]The extent of the economic growing together of the *Zollverein* states in the 1850s and 1860s is questionable. While some developments were working in favour of greater unity, others were working against it. There was no obvious trend towards unification at the economic and social levels: G.G. Windell, 'The Bismarckian Empire as a Federal State 1866–1880: A Chronicle of Failure', *Cent.Eur.H.* 2 (1969), pp. 291–311, esp. p. 249 n.10.

spending devoted to the economy rose from 16 to 31 per cent. Austria, in contrast, experienced serious difficulties in the 1850s. In particular, the need to maintain expensive military establishments in Hungary and Italy restricted the amount of money available for economic modernization and she could not afford to lower her tariffs without risking a flood of cheap foreign imports. Prussia, by far the most advanced economy in Germany, could move towards freer trade.

The traditional view of post-1848 Prussia as totally reactionary is now changing. For many people of progressive views, Prussia was the hope of Germany. Technical and scientific progress was impressive and the Prussian universities began to expand after a period of stagnation since about 1830. For Protestant academics in Germany a university post in Prussia was the highest goal. The *Gründerzeit* (The Time of Foundations) was a period of internal peace and social harmony.[8] The constitution of 1850, although under it ministers were still appointed by the crown without reference to the parliamentary situation and promises of further liberalization were not fulfilled, and the introduction of a progressive income tax in 1851 helped to reconcile the middle classes to the regime. The lower house of the parliament was elected under the three-class electoral system. The adult male population was divided into three classes, each paying a third of the total amount of direct taxes paid in each constituency. Each class chose one third of the electors, who in turn chose deputies. About 5 per cent of the electorate were in Class I, about 13 per cent in Class II and the rest in Class III. In rural areas this guaranteed overwhelming influence to the landowners but in expanding urban areas the middle class found its electoral weight increasing. The elections of 1852 and 1855 were real contests, though divisions of principle were played down, and saw slow Liberal gains. The parliament met in cramped quarters for only some three months a year, there was gerrymandering in the conservative interest and interference in elections by the crown's agents. Sixty-one per cent of the parliament elected in 1855 were state employees and they were subject to considerable official pressure. Fifty per cent of the government's revenue continued to be derived from indirect taxation. Noble powers, police and judicial, remained strong in the countryside. There were, therefore, many things for the Liberals to fight against without directly challenging the established order. In 1858 a Chamber of Trade was established, which quickly became a Liberal-dominated pressure group working for freer trade. Two leading elements in

---

[8]The *Gründerzeit* was so called because it saw the foundation of the *Reich* and the establishment of a large number of firms.

the economy, commercial groups and large-scale farmers, were moving together into an alliance, which was further cemented by increasing exchange of capital between the two, symbolized by middle-class purchases of noble land and noble investment in railway construction. Only the iron manufacturers, afraid of Belgian and British competition, opposed Free Trade. Such divisions of opinion did not seriously weaken Prussia's economic growth.

In 1860 Austria resumed an economic offensive in Germany, made even more urgent following her defeat in Italy. Her aim was either to join the *Zollverein* or replace it with a rival union, the *Steuerverein*, and lure the German states into it. This struggle reached its high point in the campaign by Prussia to effect a commercial treaty between France and the *Zollverein*, eventually signed in March 1862. This involved mutual tariff reductions, which made Austria's accommodation in the German customs union even more difficult. Austria's offensive was strongly resisted by the Prussian foreign minister, Albrecht von Bernstorff, whose more assertive policy was to be inherited by Bismarck later. These events were accompanied by a revival of nationalist agitation as a political factor in Germany, which gave rise to a rash of schemes for reform of the *Bund*, originating both from governments and political groups, and by serious political crises inside the two leading German states, which affected their German policies. In particular, in order to understand the process leading to the unification of 1871, it is essential to understand the Prussian Army Crisis.

This major constitutional and political crisis of the early 1860s had a number of important effects on the subsequent development of Prussia and Germany, which have led one historian to describe it as the most significant event in the domestic history of Germany in the nineteenth century.[9] It brought Bismarck to power as prime minister of Prussia. It accelerated the process leading to the unification of 1871: once installed in power, Bismarck, in order to remain there and solve the constitutional problem, chose the strategy of a vigorous foreign policy in Germany. The crisis guaranteed the continuation of the special position of the Prussian army, which lasted until after the First World War. It brought about a massive defeat of the Prussian Liberal Party, which had developed into the strongest Liberal party in Germany but which was denied any decisive say in the manner and form of Germany's unification. In the course of the crisis the Prussian bureaucracy suffered its first major purge, involving the exclusion of the Liberal and progressive elements, which had carried the legacy of the Reform period and

---

[9]C. Schmitt, *Staatsgefüge und Zusammenbruch des zweiten Reiches* (Berlin, 1934), p. 10.

had been responsible for important reforms, especially in the economic sphere, in the first half of the century.[10] The Crisis also revealed how the nature of political life in Prussia and other German states had changed since 1848 with the beginning of mass parties and the end of the old exclusive *Honoratiorenpolitik* (the politics of the upper classes). The readership of newspapers expanded sharply in the 1860s and a distinct ideological tone began to enter political life.

Detailed narratives of the Army Crisis are available and this account will concentrate on certain aspects.[11] It is sometimes difficult to appreciate from textbooks the emotion and bitterness which accompanied the crisis. To many Liberals in Prussia and the rest of Germany it seemed as if the country was about to be fundamentally transformed from an absolutist into a Liberal parliamentary state. In the course of the 1850s Liberal attitudes had changed. The great optimism which had at once sustained and weakened the German Liberals before 1848 was increasingly replaced by greater realism and a recognition that ideas and ideals were not enough to bring about lasting political change. It was now thought necessary to come to terms with the existing order and pursue realistic policies. Liberals increasingly placed their hopes for Germany in a modernized and economically vital Liberal state. Prussia seemed about to be converted into such a state and it was increasingly seen as the only means of achieving the material, spiritual and moral progress which, for the Liberals, was an essential element in unification. A fundamental transformation of Prussia was, however, quite unacceptable to the Prussian Conservatives. Therefore, the basic issue in the Army Crisis concerned the nature of Prussia and its role in Germany. It was also accompanied by serious social tension. Prussia had experienced rapid economic growth which had produced large-scale internal migration and urbanization, especially in Berlin, Danzig, Breslau and the Rhineland. There was growing radicalization and the beginnings of Socialism. Urban attitudes were spreading into the surrounding rural areas, a phenomenon commented on by contemporaries. Since the mid 1850s the Conservatives had come to believe that the tide was running in favour of Liberalism and a movement of moderate reform Conservatives had grown up with a skeletal party

[10] J.R. Gillis, *The Prussian Bureaucracy in Crisis 1840—1860* (Stanford, 1971), pp. 168—88.
[11] G.A. Craig, *The Politics of the Prussian Army* (Stanford, 1964), pp. 136—79; E.N. Anderson, *The Social and Political Conflict in Prussia 1858—64* (Lincoln, Neb., 1954); G. Ritter, *The Sword and the Sceptre. The Problem of Militarism in Germany* i (Coral Gables, Fla., 1969), pp. 21—59; J.J. Sheehan, *German Liberalism in the Nineteenth century* (Chicago, 1978), pp. 95—119; G. Grünthal, 'Crown and Parliament in Prussia 1848—66', in *Parliaments, Estates and Representation* v (1985), pp. 165—74.

organization. Expectations of change had been roused. The onset of the Crisis was preceded by a sharp economic recession, which brought a wave of distress and it was this which helped to give the Liberals a majority in the lower house of the Prussian parliament in 1858.

Liberal nationalist hopes were further raised when in the autumn of 1858 King Frederick William IV became irretrievably mad and was replaced by his brother and heir presumptive, Crown Prince William, first as regent and eventually as king. As heir presumptive William had suffered from the crown prince syndrome, showing increasing impatience with the passive foreign policy of his brother's government. As governor of the Rhineland province he had acquired a mildly Liberal reputation. Although he was more flexible than his brother he was no Liberal. From the outset the regent/king and the Liberals completely misunderstood one another's basic aims. Wishful thinking produced among the Liberals a simplistic but growing conviction that the missing magic ingredient, a Liberal king, the lack of which had ruined their cause in 1848, was at last available. Such convictions increased when, on his accession as regent, William announced a New Era in Prussia and promised a more forward German policy, social unity at home and firmer action against Napoleonic France, a good nationalistic policy. He sacked some of his brother's more reactionary ministers and installed a few moderate Liberals in ministerial posts. Briefly the constitutional form of government, made possible under the 1850 constitution, actually worked. In 1861 he pushed a progressive reform of the land tax through a recalcitrant upper house by the threat of a massive creation of new Liberal peers. It was, in reality, the only Liberal action he took, but it was sufficient to encourage Prussian and German Liberals in their illusions about him.

This quickly became obvious over the issue of army reform, the thing dearest to the king's soldierly heart. When he spoke of making 'moral conquests' in Germany for Prussia, he did not, as the Liberals imagined, intend a Prussian-led unification. He pursued the traditional policy of achieving equality with Austria in Germany and a recognition of Prussia's informal hegemony in the north and believed that a modern Prussia, in which the middle classes were allowed a share of political power, would exercise greater attraction on the other German states. In order to achieve greater weight and defend Prussia, the army, long neglected, would have to be modernized and enlarged. Prussia had enjoyed peace since 1815 and the annual intake of conscripts had been maintained at the same level, in spite of a rising population. From 1825 conscripts were selected by lot. Doubts were also raised about the wisdom of maintaining a conscript army when most of Prussia's neighbours had long-serving veteran armies on the French model. Spending on the army had fallen as more resources were diverted to other things. The resulting deficiencies in the army were shown up clearly during the Franco-Austrian war of 1859–60. Although Prussia remained neutral, the Prussian army mobilized to defend the Rhine frontier against a possible French invasion. This involved the call-up of thousands of half-trained conscripts and the result was a shambles. The new war minister Roon proposed an enlargement of the army, with the creation of new units and a lengthening of the period of military service, increasing the military budget by about a third. The Liberals were not opposed to the reforms *per se* as they too wanted a stronger Prussia to take the lead in German unification. Their interest in power had grown since 1848, as expressed in the famous statement of Julius Fröbel in 1859 to the effect that the German nation was 'no longer satisfied with principles and doctrines, literary greatness and a theoretical existence' but wanted 'power, power and more power'. They saw the proposed army reform as the issue on which they could fight and, if successful, liberalize Prussia, a goal they now believed winnable with a small effort. They chose the wrong issue. Among Conservatives there was a long-standing emotionally held belief that Prussia had been created by its army, that it had saved the state from extinction more than once and that it alone, as a bulwark against the Jacobin tendencies of the age, stood between Prussia and anarchy, as in 1848. They continued to identify Liberalism with mob-rule, Jacobinism, Jews, Freemasons and the French. In order to fulfil its functions, they believed, the king's control of the army had to remain total and undiluted. In reply to the question whether the royal right of command could be subject to civilian control, the Conservatives gave a decisive no while the Liberals saw it as essential if Prussia was to become a thoroughly modern state.[12]

The single reform on which the Liberals took their stand was the proposed amalgamation of the militia (*Landwehr*) with the regular reserve. The *Landwehr* was seen by Liberals as a symbol of the Reform Era, a constitutional army under middle-class officers which, if necessary, would defend the constitution against tyranny. If the Liberals genuinely believed this, they were living in a world of total illusion: in 1848 most units of the *Landwehr* had fallen over themselves to send addresses of loyalty to the Crown. It made useful propaganda to portray the proposed enlargement of the army as part of a conspiracy to create a gigantic anti-Liberal machine, with more barracks, backwoods *Junker* officers and brutal NCOs designed to convert the sons of citizens into automata

[12]M. Howard, *The Franco-Prussian War* (1962), pp. 18–29.

ready to shoot down their relatives at the whim of tyrants. Memories of the brutal military suppression of the 1849 troubles in some Rhineland towns were very real. More likely, the Liberals chose this as an emotionally attractive issue when their opposition was as much to the tax increases they suspected the army reform would make necessary, and which, they feared, might lose them votes.

Certainly, after muted beginnings, the crisis quickly escalated and became very emotional. In January 1861 William became king. He came increasingly under the influence of the chief of his military cabinet, Edwin von Manteuffel, a strong reactionary, who urged him to carry out a military *coup*. This remained a distinct possibility and some commentators have argued that a civil war was possible.

In June 1861 the German Progressive Party was formed from the more radical elements in the Liberal party, though it remained, like the Liberals proper, a party of *Bildung und Besitz*. This became the model for *kleindeutsch* Liberal parties in other German states, calling for internal reform and a Prussian-led unification of Germany. In other states, as in Prussia, they benefited from property franchises and urbanization. Ironically, while the Prussian government was fighting the Progressives at home, it was supporting the Progressives in other states, with money and in other ways, as vehicles of its political influence. The foundation of the Prussian party illustrated the fissiparous tendencies of German Liberalism, a problem which afflicted the movement into the twentieth century and produced a dangerous weakness in the middle of the political spectrum. In 1861, however, the Progressives seemed on the verge of total success. In the election of December of that year they won a large majority in the lower house and adopted a still more intransigent attitude on the army issue. In March 1862 they won an even larger majority and the same was to happen in every election until 1866, in spite of election-rigging and appeals to patriotism by the Conservative interest. The electoral system was the Prussian Liberals' worst enemy: time and again they were able to win deceptively strong majorities in the lower house of parliament in elections held under a property franchise. Such results were not an accurate reflection of public opinion and they gave the Liberals no genuine power, as the government and administration remained dominated by their opponents. The iceberg below the surface remained very conservative, as Bismarck was to show. Political apathy, even at the height of the crisis, was widespread, as reflected in the low turn-out at elections (it hovered around one third), especially in the Third Class, which contained the mass of lower-class voters. For a state with high literacy levels, the newspaper readership was also small. The Liberals and Progressives had no strong power base in local and provincial government. In spite of this, they remained attached to the property franchise, though it protected them against neither monarchical absolutism nor Socialism, a growing movement in Prussia in the early 1860s. In 1863 Ferdinand Lassalle's General German Worker's Association was set up but the Liberals refused to abandon their attachment to self-help as the answer to social problems and made no serious attempt to win over working-class support. Worse, in the 1860s the Liberals were to lose much of what lower-class support they had and this was one factor in causing the emergence of organized Socialist movements in Germany earlier than in other states. This split between the Liberals and the working class was to help Conservative forces to keep their power in Prussia and, later, in Germany. The nationalist movement remained overwhelmingly middle-class and this is one reason why it did not become a movement of genuine social emancipation. This was in spite of the fact that Lassalle's movement shared the Liberals' vision of German unification under Prussian auspices, seeing Austria as the main barrier to progressive change. Although the Socialists did not become part of the nationalist movement, some of them had excessively high hopes of what a national state might achieve. Some had an idealized vision of a 'nation state of comrades'. Clause 1 of the 1867 party programme of the Lassalleans called for the abolition of the federative organization of Germany and the union of all the German 'tribes' (*Stämme*) in a single unit: 'through unity to freedom'. The Social Democratic Marxist wing of the movement was also not opposed to a *kleindeutsch* federal union if it was democratic.[13]

The Army Crisis quickly developed into a stalemate. There was no provision in the constitution for the impeachment of ministers and no provision for the situation in which the three elements in the constitution, king, ministers and parliament, could not agree. The Prussian Liberals were unwilling to break the constitution, which, they feared, the king was only waiting for an excuse to annul. The king, for his part, was equally unwilling to break his oath to observe the constitution. There appeared no way out.

When in 1863 the lower house rejected the whole budget, the government invoked the 'gap theory' (*Lückentheorie*), the idea that there was a hole in the constitution which enabled the government, in the absence of a budget, to continue to take taxes under the previous budget. It also raised loans and increased its income from state enterprises and indirect taxes thanks to an economic

[13]R.W. Reichard, *Crippled from Birth. German Social Democracy 1844—1870* (Ames, Iowa, 1969).

boom, building up a substantial surplus. At this point Roon advised the king to bring in his friend Bismarck, the Prussian ambassador in Paris, to take over the campaign against the parliament.

Bismarck's appointment as prime minister of Prussia was a sign of how desperate William I was to solve the Army Crisis. The king threatened that he would abdicate if his new prime minister failed. Bismarck was feared by the Liberals as a reactionary and mistrusted by more orthodox Conservatives as an unpredictable wild man, a view which Bismarck fostered as part of his psychological warfare against the Prussian parliament. He was seen as a hard-line defender of *Junker* interests but in reality his views were flexible and individual. He worked hard during his political career and in his memoirs, written in the bitterness of his enforced retirement, to create his own legend as an iron superman and the supreme juggler and manipulator of kings, parties and whole populations when in reality he was a flexible, versatile and resourceful politician. He viewed the great majority of his fellow men with contempt and his political behaviour reflected this. As he aged, his view of politics became more twisted and wilful. The Bismarck legend was reinforced after 1890, when a Bismarck cult became popular, especially among academic youth, as seen in the hundreds of statues and Bismarck towers erected after his fall.[14]

His prime aim was to maintain the power of the crown in Prussia, to defend the interests of the class to which he belonged, to improve Prussia's German and international position and to consolidate his own power. He was initially very vulnerable, having no party behind him and enjoying only half-hearted support from the king. He needed success in order to survive. He saw the constitutional crisis as a barrier to Prussian greatness and he adopted a combined strategy of attack and diversion to defeat the Prussian Liberals. He feared Liberal nationalism as a dangerous movement which threatened not only to submerge Prussia in a Liberal Germany but to subvert Prussia by liberalizing her government and making her the spearhead of the unification movement. At first Bismarck attempted to achieve a compromise. In a speech to the budget committee of the lower house on 30 September 1862 he attempted to win over the Progressives by emphasizing Prussia's German role. In the course of the speech he produced an olive twig, picked in France, as a symbol of his desire for compromise but he also used the phrase which became almost his motto: 'the

[14]L. Gall's two-volume *Bismarck: The White Revolutionary* (1986–7) is the most up-to-date biography. E. Crankshaw, *Bismarck* (1981) brings out the dark side of Bismarck's character and emphasizes the blighting effect he had on German political life, though Crankshaw's characterization of him as a nihilist of genius seems to overlook the core of principle and religious belief at the centre of his political credo. See also B. Waller, *Bismarck* (1985).

great issues of the age are not decided by speeches and majority decisions ... but by blood and iron'. The impact of this was the exact opposite of what Bismarck had intended: in Prussian and German Liberal circles it was seen as proof that he was a black reactionary and all hope of compromise disappeared. Early in 1863 he began to take strong measures, including another dissolution of parliament, a new press edict giving the government wide powers of censorship, the sacking or demotion of civil servants with pro-Liberal sympathies and even actions against the Crown Prince Frederick who, married to Queen Victoria's daughter, had vaguely Liberal views. Bismarck considered the abolition of the three-class electoral system, which favoured the Liberals, and the introduction of universal male suffrage on the same lines as Napoleon III in France. He held 'secret' conversations with the Socialist leader Lassalle, knowing that news of this would frighten the Liberals, and made vague promises of social reform. Interestingly, Engels warned Lassalle that universal suffrage, superficially attractive, might prove a trap if the Prussian peasantry remained outside the proletarian movement. Bismarck certainly made the same calculation.

The other strand of Bismarck's policy was a new assertive policy in Germany, a more muscular revival of the policies of his predecessor, von Bernstorff. In his view, the main weakness of Prussian policy in the past had been that 'we have been Liberal in Prussia and conservative abroad, we have held the rights of our king too cheap and those of foreign princes too dear ... Only by a change of direction in our foreign policy can the position of the crown in Prussia be relieved of the pressure on it'.[15] This revolution from above in Prussian foreign policy has produced the characterization of Bismarck as a 'white (i.e. counter-) revolutionary'. It coincided with Austria's attempt to reassert her power in Germany after defeat in Italy. Austria also seemed to be moving towards a Liberal government; in 1861 the first Liberal ministry since 1848 took over under prime minister Schmerling and it at once began to institute constitutional reform.[16] This Austrian constitutionalism could have provided an alternative pole of attraction for German Liberals, which would have been dangerous to Bismarck.

At the same time German nationalism as an organized force was reappearing, initially incoherent but of mounting significance. The 1850s and 1860s saw growing discussion in intellectual circles of how a German national state could be established. The 'national question' was also discussed at meetings and conferences of a large number of non-political groups, gymnasts, sharp-shooters

[15]Letter to von Roon, St. Petersburg 2 July 1861, Gundolf, pp. 106—8.
[16]Schmerling in 1848 had been prime minister of the German provisional government.

and singing circles, through which the views of the educated middle class percolated downwards in society. The centenary of Schiller's birth in November 1859 and the festivities surrounding the fiftieth anniversary of the Battle of Leipzig in 1863 were the occasions for many such meetings. As in the 1840s, there is some danger in exaggerating the significance of these movements, which were not always progressive and often the home of idealistic but unfocused youthful enthusiasm, but they played a part in the 'national awakening' of the 1860s. The numbers involved were certainly growing. Before 1860 there were about 240 gymnastic societies; by 1863 there were 1,300 with some 135,000 members. Professional groups also acted as vehicles for the discussion of German affairs. In 1856 the Association of German Engineers was established, in 1858 the first all-German economists' congress was held and in 1860 the first all-German lawyers' congress. The first meeting of the German Commercial Diet (*Deutscher Handelstag*), an organization of chambers of commerce, took place in Heidelberg in 1861. The majority of the delegates were *grossdeutsch*, favouring measures of economic unity but not at the cost of states' rights, and their main concern was economic not political. Events like the Prussian Army Crisis and the Hesse-Cassel constitutional crisis of the 1850s, caused by the unilateral alteration of the 1831 constitution by the Hessian government, aroused avid interest in political circles in the rest of Germany. There is irony in the fact that the Prussian government, at the height of the Army Crisis, actively supported the Hessian Liberals in the Confederate Diet, which in 1862 voted in favour of a restoration of the 1831 constitution.

The idea that Prussia had a mission to unify and regenerate Germany was winning growing support as she was regarded as more modern and more German than Austria. There was growing realism among Liberal nationalists as more of them came to accept that there could be no unity including Austria. Such ideas were given concrete expression by the National Society (*Nationalverein*), established in September 1859 in imitation of the Italian National Society. Its Eisenach Declaration called for the establishment of a strong central government for Germany with an elected all-German parliament and looked to Prussia to play the part of the German Piedmont in achieving these aims. In the early 1860s the *kleindeutsch* idea was at its height, though it never enjoyed mass support in Germany. The *Nationalverein* was a very middle-class association. When established it had some 600 members, of which 133 were lawyers, 75 businessmen and 87 manufacturers. At its greatest it had only 25,000 members though political involvement in general remained a minority activity in most German states and all the parties and movements involved in the national debate were small. The substantial pamphlet literature on the issue in the years 1859—66 should not be taken as evidence of mass involvement. There was no provision in the rules of the *Nationalverein* for the payment of subscription by instalment, a sure sign that it had no desire to attract mass support, and it openly boasted that it was a movement of *Bildung und Besitz*. Its main aim was to spread propaganda in favour of German unification under Prussian auspices and to act as an umbrella organization for *kleindeutsch* movements throughout Germany. It offered its services to the Prussian government but the offer was turned down. The *Nationalverein* was banned in many states and frowned on in others and the Confederate Assembly debated but rejected a motion to ban it throughout Germany.

In 1862 a rival *Reformverein* was set up to promote *Grossdeutschland*, a reform of the Confederation including Austria.[17] It never achieved the coherence and effectiveness of the *Nationalverein*. It lasted a bare two years and its main effort was devoted not to the issue of German unity but to fighting the growth of Liberalism, increasingly identified with Prussian influence, in individual states. Of more lasting significance was the Prussian People's Association (*Preussische Volksverein*), established in 1861. Its aim was to achieve *grossdeutsch* unity through a reform of the Confederation carried out by governments, while preserving the power of the states, especially Prussia, and without a central German parliament. The *grossdeutsch* movement was hindered from the beginning by deep divisons between its conservative, clericalist and democratic republican wings. Among the last, the political heirs of the Radicals of 1848—9, there were some who rejected both Prussia and Austria and placed their hopes in a great popular rising to unite Germany. The *grossdeutsch* Conservatives took their stand on the preservation of states' rights in any reform of the Confederation and found their strongest support in rural areas, especially in backward states like Hesse-Cassel, and among vested interests who feared the victory of Liberalism, like the clergy, aristocracy and guild masters. Where they were able to mobilize anti-Prussian feeling and state loyalty, they were able to attract a short-lived popular following. To Roman Catholics the prospect of Prussia doing in Germany what Piedmont had done in Italy was dreadful. They feared *Kleindeutschland*, in which they would be a minority of only some 35 per cent (they were a majority in the Confederation), and saw a powerful Austria not only as a guarantee of their status but also as a defender of the papacy. When Prussia officially recognized the

[17]N.M. Hope, *The Alternative to German Unification* (Wiesbaden, 1973).

new Italian state in July 1862 there was a wave of outrage among German Conservatives and Catholics.

Neither Prussia nor Austria could afford to ignore a movement which might be of use in their campaigns to win influence in Germany. Austria's policy was again to try to undermine the *Zollverein* and at the same time to outbid Prussia as the leader of German feeling by putting forward schemes for reform of the Confederation. Austria's German mission was also emphasized in propaganda. For example, in 1863 the Austrian Emperor commissioned a magnificently produced work on the crown jewels of the Holy Roman Empire, kept in the Treasury of the Vienna Hofburg. Again the lines of Bismarck's policy were clearly laid down when he took power. In December 1861 Prussia rejected a Saxon reform plan. In August 1862 Austria and other leading states proposed a German assembly drawn from the assemblies of the states. Prussia blocked it. In October 1862 an Austrian motion in the confederate diet condemning the Franco-Prussian commercial treaty of that year was defeated. In August 1863 Francis Joseph called a conference of all the German rulers (*Fürstentag*) to Frankfurt to discuss reforms but Bismarck was able to sabotage this by persuading William I not to attend, in spite of a personal invitation from the Emperor and a second personal visit by the king of Saxony on behalf of his fellow rulers.[18] The refusal of the king to take part saved Bismarck from serious difficulties, as the proposed congress of princes aroused great interest and a wave of *grossdeutsch* enthusiasm in Germany.

In the economic disputes Bismarck deliberately used nationalism as a moral weapon against other German rulers to prevent their leaving the *Zollverein*. The frequently quoted statement by J.M. Keynes to the effect that Germany was united more by coal and iron than blood and iron is, however, incorrect. Without Austro-Prussian rivalry and power politics, economic change would never been enough to unify Germany politically. Bismarck was not resolved on a total breach with Austria from the outset and he attempted to cajole or bully her into making concessions in the years 1864—6. Realistically, he foresaw the eventual clash. Germany was too small for both Prussia and Austria, as he had realized early. Bismarck's analysis of the German question was outlined in his Baden-Baden or Rheinfeld memorandum of July and October 1861.[19] He urged William I to pursue a much more active policy in Ger-

[18]B. Rowland and J.C. Easton, 'The Assembly of German Princes of 1863', *JMH* 14 (1942), pp. 480—99.
[19]The July or Baden-Baden draft of the memorandum is in Gundolf, pp. 108—113, and the later revised Rheinfeld version is described in Gall i, p. 164ff.

many in order to force Austria to accept Prussia as an equal. He attributed the troubles of the 1830s and late 1840s to the removal of the French threat, which had made Germans intolerant of the petty jealousies of the little states, which often produced unnecessary barriers and bad government. Germany needed more unity but only in defence and economic matters, to be achieved, in his view, by a reform of the *Bund*, a common defence system and internal free movement, which would not be unacceptable to Conservatives. He saw value in an indirectly elected national assembly alongside a federal authority as a counterweight to dynastic particularism. Prussia resented being expected to defend half of Germany while Austria continued to treat her as a petty principality. An effective means of precipitating the desired changes would be a threat of Prussian secession from the *Bund* and the unilateral floating of a reform plan. At the time his views were seen as too extreme but they were not completely out of line with the king's opinions.

The situation became more heated with the reappearance of the Schleswig-Holstein issue after years of quiet. With it reappeared anti-foreign mass nationalism, of which there had been a brief outbreak in the form of pro-Austrian feeling during the Italian war of 1859—60. Both Austria and Prussia tried to cash in on this, using nationalism as a weapon in their struggle for influence in Germany. The issue also roused Liberal interest, as the German candidate for the duchies was the duke of Augustenburg, who enjoyed a reputation as a Liberal. The German victory over the Danes in 1864 stoked up nationalism more; it was seen as the first German victory since 1815 and revenge for the humiliation of 1848. Austria's abandonment of Augustenburg, in support of whom the Confederate Assembly approved military action against Denmark, alienated many of her supporters in the Third Germany. The uneasy co-operation of Austria and Prussia in the Schleswig-Holstein affair only postponed the showdown between them. The final blow to Austria came in 1866 when the *Zollverein* treaties came up for renewal. Austria's efforts to lure the members into her rival *Steuerverein* were revealed as a failure; the economic benefits of the Prussian-led union were too great to be abandoned, especially after a commercial treaty with France in 1865 gave members access to the British and Belgian markets. Eighteen sixty-six also saw the establishment of the Toll Parliament, made up of members of the parliaments of the *Zollverein* member states, to discuss economic issues. This was later to be directly elected and was seen by some as the embryo of an all-German parliament without Austria. Bismarck's motive for establishing it probably had little to do with German unification. More likely, he feared the creation of a more genuinely federal system which would lead to greater unity but might endanger Prussian control of the customs union.

Throughout all this manoeuvering Bismarck risked losing the initiative to Austria which, by the summer of 1866, saw war as the only means left to rescue her position in Germany. Bismarck's careful diplomatic preparations, especially his negotiations with the French, caused hostile comment in Germany. In May 1866 an Association for the Protection of the Left Bank of the Rhine was set up in the southern Palatinate to oppose Prussia's supposed intention to cede the area to France. In early June the duke of Coburg toured southern Germany on behalf of the Prussian government and reported mounting anti-Prussian feeling arising from the conviction that Prussia was about to buy off the French with German territory. To meet this Bismarck issued two pieces of propaganda, a Prussian plan for reform of the Confederation to exclude Austria and give joint control to Prussia and Bavaria on 10 June and a proclamation to the German people on 16 June, two days after the outbreak of war with Austria, stating Prussia's mission to lead Germany. Bismarck precipitated war by engineering a breakdown of relations over the Austrian administration of Holstein, where popular support for Augustenburg remained strong. He did this in order to pre-empt an Austrian declaration of war, which Francis Joseph, with great misgivings, had decided was unavoidable. Austria used her influence to convert her war into a confederate execution against Prussia and she was followed in this by the majority of the German states. Prussia, supported only by a few north German states who had little choice, won a surprisingly rapid victory not only over Austria but over the other leading states. Some historians see the war of 1866 as a German civil war and it was later to be known as the 'War of Brothers' (*Brüderkrieg*). In reality it was a cabinet war between states to resolve the question of which of them would dominate the Germanic space.

Prussia's victory led to a radical reorganization of the German political system. The whole thing was settled quickly without foreign interference, which Bismarck feared. The *Bund* was abolished and Austria was excluded from Germany. As a result there was again no political framework embracing the whole German nation. Massive annexations, without plebiscites, of Hanover, Hesse-Cassel, Nassau, Frankfurt and Schleswig-Holstein, removed all rivals to Prussian dominance in the north. The elimination of Hesse-Cassel was strategically important as it cut deeply into Prussia from its border on the Main. Schleswig-Holstein was also strategically valuable, controlling as it did the 'Baltic Dardanelles'. Frankfurt was a major financial centre and an outpost of Austrian influence in Germany. The North German Confederation was established, in which Prussia enjoyed total control. Hesse-Darmstadt voluntarily joined the North German Confederation for its territories north of the Main, probably to avoid their annexation by Prussia, which had already seized parts of the state in the cause of geographical neatness. The bonds linking the *Zollverein* states were tightened and the Toll Parliament was to be directly elected. A joint commission including members from the four south German states was established to complete measures of economic unification between north and south. After further extensions of the *Zollverein* in 1867 only the commercial cities of Hamburg and Bremen were left outside it.[20] Tight military alliances bound north and south together. Southern Germany was an informal colony of Prussia, which now had access to the economic and military resources of the whole of Germany outside Austria.

The victory of 1866 also solved the constitutional crisis in Prussia. The winter of 1865—6 had seen a brief period of economic troubles which had produced strikes, riots, marches and anti-conscription demonstrations, renewing the Liberals' fear of the mob. Economic growth resumed in the spring of 1866. An election to the Lower House in July 1866, before news of the great Prussian victory at Sadowa arrived, showed a massive swing to the Conservatives, achieved partly by appeals to patriotism in wartime, the vigorous use of state employees and landowners as unofficial pro-government election agents and the introduction of a scheme of state loans to small farmers to help them buy land. It also reflected disillusionment with the Liberals' lack of achievement and revealed the conservative sentiments of the mass of the peasantry, which the government had succeeded in mobilizing on this occasion. The Liberals also did badly in the Prussian elections to the North German constituent assembly in February 1867.[21] The Conservatives were to retain their majority in the Prussian parliament until 1918. Bismarck's foreign policy triumph completed the defeat of the Liberals. In the autumn of 1866 the Progressive Party split. Part of it joined the Liberals to form the National Liberal Party to support what they imagined was Bismarck's intention to complete the unification of Germany. They remained his supporters until 1879. In the hope of seeing unity achieved quickly, they were prepared to shelve their Liberal aspirations until later. Their capitulation

[20]They joined in 1888.
[21]T.S. Hamerow, 'The Origins of Mass Politics in Germany 1866—7', in I. Geiss and B.J. Wendt (eds.), *Deutschland in der Weltpolitik des neunzehnten und zwanzigsten Jahrhunderts* (Düsseldorf, 1973), pp. 105—20.

was symbolized most clearly in their support for the Indemnity Act of 3 September 1866, which forgave Bismarck for actions performed during the Army Crisis, which he admitted were illegal and unconstitutional. To the unifier of Germany, all things were forgiveable. In return the government agreed to a more restrictive budget law, which increased the parliament's financial control. In reality Bismarck needed the National Liberals as much as they thought they needed him. His German policy, culminating in the dispossession of several crowned heads, outraged the majority of the Prussian Conservatives and they deserted him. They had never backed him with much enthusiasm and Bismarck was not a party man. During the army crisis several of his conservative ministerial colleagues came close to losing their nerve and he had had to bully them into following him. In 1866 a minority of the Conservatives, mainly Reform Conservatives and industrialists, formed the Free Conservative Party, after 1871 the *Reichspartei*, and continued to support him. The agrarian majority in the Conservative party saw him as a traitor.

The settlement of 1867 was highly satisfactory to Bismarck. It gave Prussia effective control of Germany and produced internal stability. The monarchical order in Prussia was no longer threatened. It also guaranteed his personal power. His policy was to promote free trade and economic growth and, on this basis, to allow a slow extension of unity. To the Liberals' fury, he had no intention of forcing the pace and being rushed into further measures of unification, knowing that it might strengthen the Liberals or lead to the growth of an uncontrollable nationalist movement in Germany. He also feared that any further growth of Prussian power in Germany might well prove unacceptable to other European powers and might attract unwelcome foreign attention. It was remarkable, in view of the deep European interest in German affairs from the seventeenth century onwards, that the German 'settlement' of 1864—1871 was carried through without foreign involvement, due to Bismarck's careful diplomatic preparation and the rapid victories of the Prussian army.

As Bismarck informed the Liberals in the North German diet in 1869, when they tried to force the government's hand by threatening to withhold tax grants, one cannot ripen fruit by holding a candle under it. Rather he planned, as he said, to put Germany into the saddle and she would know how to ride. He envisaged a slow organic growing together of the German states for practical purposes. He regarded the sentimental nationalism of the Liberals as totally unsuitable in Germany, where, because of her history, real nationalism consisted in the individual German's loyalty to his ruling prince. A closer union between north and south was, in his view, undesirable, as the southern states contained too much Catholicism, Liberalism and age-old anti-Prussianism. Bismarck's hostility to the south was deep. In the Prussian parliament in 1848 he had spoken strongly against the Prussian monarchy 'sinking into the rotting fermentation of south German indiscipline'.

Why then did Bismarck proceed to further unification only three years later? The answer is: fear. It was not the result of 'blood and iron', aggressively pursued intent, but was essentially defensive. Bismarck responded to initiatives taken by others. Developments between 1867 and 1870 inside and outside Germany seriously threatened what he had achieved. The events of 1866–7 were profoundly disturbing to France, Austria and the south German states. French public opinion regarded the growth of Prussian power in Germany as a blow to France. After a period of neutralism, French opinion was becoming bellicose. The Bonapartist regime became the main target of these frustrations and was accused of allowing national honour to be slighted. The government's proposal to increase conscription was unpopular. Earlier the French had viewed German and Italian nationalism in the same patronizing manner, that is as movements which could safely be supported as a means of spreading French influence and enhancing the prestige of Napoleon III's regime. There was also the pleasing prospect of territorial gains for France. In the case of Germany, the rivalry between Prussia and Austria, two bastions of the Vienna settlement, could only be welcome. Napoleon III had made this clear in a well-reported speech at Auxerre on 6 May 1866, in which he attacked the 1815 settlement and implied support for Prussian expansion in Germany. In the summer of 1866, however, the whole thing had turned very sour.[22] Napoleon had hoped to see the two German states fight themselves to a standstill, providing a chance for France to step in as mediator and claim the Rhineland as a reward. The rapidity of the Prussian victory destroyed these hopes. The French Liberals' traditional view of the Germans as a nation of poets and thinkers was changing to growing criticism of Prussian militarism.[23] The collapse of the French-sponsored Mexican Empire in 1868 did nothing to strengthen Napoleon III's standing among the French. As a result of these factors, French policy became less cautious after 1866.

In Austria the defeat of 1866 precipitated a major constitutional crisis, the main results of which were that Francis Joseph had to

[22]On reactions in France see G. Wright, 'Public Opinion and Conscription in France 1866–70', *JMH* 14 (1942), pp. 26–45.
[23]A similar change of view was also visible in British Liberal circles: J. Mander, *Our German Cousins. Anglo-German Relations in the 19th and 20th Centuries* (1974), p. 188f.; P.M. Kennedy, *The Rise of the Anglo-German Antagonism 1860–1914* (1980), p. 13.

agree to the *Ausgleich*, the grant of autonomy to the Hungarians, and to make substantial concessions to the Liberals in the Austrian part of his Monarchy. The Austrian government did not accept the verdict of 1866 as the final word on the German question and quickly began conversations with the French in preparation for a joint attack on Prussia.[24] Economic and military co-operation between them grew. Eventually a plan for a combined offensive was drawn up between the two general staffs, envisaging a joint invasion of Prussia, culminating in a last great battle near Berlin, after which Prussia would be detroyed. France would take the Rhineland and Austria Silesia. More Prussian territory would be given to a restored and enlarged Hanover. A new German confederation and a new economic union would be created under Austrian control and the *Ausgleich* would be abolished.[25] In the autumn of 1869 French and Austrian diplomats were working hard in St Petersburg to detach Russia from its alliance with Prussia. Austria also began to approach the south German states in the hope of luring them out of their connection with the north. The *Trias* policy, the reorganization of Germany into three blocs, Austria, Prussia and the 'Third Germany', was refloated. Discussions were held about the creation of a Southern Confederation (*Südbund*) but they came to nothing. Such plans were encouraged by state elections in the southern states and the first elections to the Toll Parliament in January 1868. These showed that the *grossdeutsch* idea was attracting a mass following as a reaction to Prussia's expansionism. There was an anti-Prussian landslide in Bavaria, where this was the first election held under universal male suffrage. In the election campaign the clergy campaigned actively for anti-Prussian candidates and slogans summed up the Bavarian popular view of conditions in Prussia: 'Join the army, pay your taxes, shut your gob'. The use of the abusive *Saupreiss* (Prussian pig) was common in Bavaria, including on public platforms, and this continued long after the unification. Anti-Prussian parties also did well in Württemberg and Hesse-Darmstadt. Although National Liberals held their own in Baden, a centre of vocal nationalism in the late 1860s, and the Protestant part of Bavaria, south Germany's rejection of

[24]H.A. Schmitt, 'Count Beust and Germany 1866–1870. Reconquest, Realignment or Resignation?', *Cent. Eur. H.* 1 (1968) and R.B. Elrod, 'Bernhard von Rechberg and the Metternichian Tradition: The Dilemma of Conservative Statecraft', *JMH* 56 (1984), pp. 430–55.
[25]There had been a foretaste of this in earlier conversations between the Austrian ambassador in Paris and the French monarchs regarding a great restructuring of Europe, including the resumption by Austria and France of Silesia and the Rhineland respectively and the recreation of an independent Polish state. Ironically, under this scheme Prussia was to be compensated for her losses of Polish land by being allowed to make large-scale annexations in north Germany.

closer links between north and south was a blow to Bismarck's hopes of untroubled informal Prussian control of Germany and made it easier for the Bavarian government to be less co-operative in the work of economic and military unification. Also worrying to Bismarck was the emergence of strong anti-Prussian movements in the states annexed in 1867, Hanover, Frankfurt, Nassau and Hesse-Cassel, where it had been necessary to introduce strict censorship after the annexation.[26]

Against this background Bismarck, well-aware of the threat to the 1867 settlement, launched a pre-emptive strike and engineered war with France in July 1870. An earlier attempt to provoke France into war over the Spanish marriage business failed, when the king of Prussia withdrew the candidacy for the Spanish throne of a member of the Catholic south German branch of his family. The new French Liberal government under Ollivier needed a prestige-boosting foreign-policy success[27] and this led to the clumsy diplomacy which enabled Bismarck to doctor the Ems telegramme to make it appear that French national honour had suffered an unacceptable affront, pushing France into a declaration of war. Prussia therefore appeared as the victim of aggression. Bismarck was not totally confident that foreign interference would be avoided and that the German states would fulfil their military obligations to the North German Confederation without quibbles. He was still concerned that Prussia's hold on Germany was weak and, in order to legitimize the war and put pressure on Bavaria, which was pro-French and might be inclined to neutrality, he deliberately stirred up anti-French feeling through the press. After the victories of 1866 Bismarck had used part of the captured fortune of the Hanoverian royal family, the so-called Welf funds, which were at the disposal of the government without reference to parliament, to buy newspapers to carry Prussian government propaganda. These newspapers were in July 1870 salted with articles produced in the Prussian Foreign Office designed to stir up the anti-French resentment deeply felt by most Germans. In August 1870 news of the first German victories in the war, at Vionville-Mars le Tour and Gravelotte, arrived and Germany was swept by a wave of spontaneous chauvinistic nationalism far more intense than similar outbreaks earlier in the century and far greater than Bismarck had planned. The German victories, an historically rare event, were seen as revenge for centuries of indignities inflicted on Germany by the French and final proof of the innate moral superiority of the

[26]S.A. Stechlin, *Bismarck and the Guelph Problem 1866–1890. A Study in Particularist Opposition to National Unity* (The Hague, 1973).
[27]T. Zeldin, *Emile Ollivier and the Liberal Empire of Napoleon III* (Oxford, 1963), pp. 171–8.

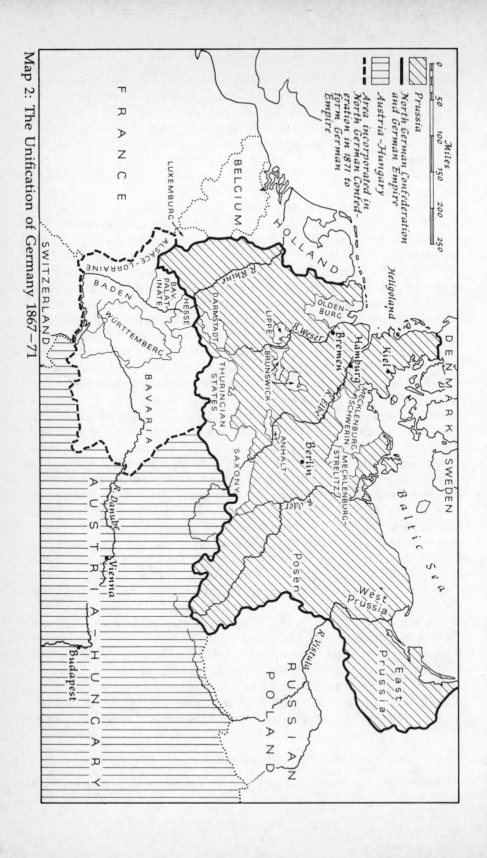

Map 2: The Unification of Germany 1867–71

Prussia

North German Confederation
and German Empire

Austria–Hungary

Area incorporated in
North German Confed-
eration in 1871 to
form German
Empire

Miles
0   50   100   150   200   250

FRANCE

LUXEMBURG

BELGIUM

HOLLAND

Heligoland

DENMARK

SWEDEN

Baltic Sea

ALSACE-LORRAINE

SWITZERLAND

BADEN

WÜRTTEMBERG

BAV.
PALAT-
INATE

HESSE

DARMSTADT

R. Rhine

OLDEN-
BURG

LIPPE

R. Weser

Hamburg

Bremen

BRUNSWICK

Kiel

MECKLENBURG-
SCHWERIN

MECKLENBURG-
STRELITZ

BAVARIA

THURINGIAN
STATES

SAXONY

ANHALT

Berlin

R. Elbe

R. Oder

Posen

West
Prussia

East
Prussia

AUSTRIA–HUNGARY

R. Danube

Vienna

Budapest

Posen

R. Vistula

RUSSIAN
POLAND

Germans compared to the trivial light-weight inhabitants of the 'New Babylon'.[28] Bismarck, faced with a flood of nationalism when he wanted only a gentle trickle, had good cause to fear it; the National Liberals saw it as a chance to seize the initiative out of Bismarck's hands. They at once sought to capitalize on the national euphoria before it died away in order to put pressure on the German governments to proceed to a real unification of Germany. Public opinion in favour of unification was strong, not as the result of a popularization of the Liberal nationalist programme but of anti-French feeling. From all parts of Germany came reports of manifestations of popular joy and the despatch of messages of congratulation to German rulers, calling on them to give the German people the fruits of victory, Alsace-Lorraine, the unity of Germany, a German parliament and the military strength to defend Germany against future aggression. There was talk of a revival of *Kyffhäusersehnsucht*, yearning for the return of a mystical Emperor sleeping under a mountain. South German governments, especially that of Baden, also began to pressurize Bismarck for national unity. Bismarck was also concerned about attempts by Austria to assemble a League of Neutrals, including Britain, Russia and Italy, to mediate in the war and ensure that south Germany remained independent. Only in November 1870 did the Austrian government change direction and accept that a *kleindeutsch* state was to be created. Bismarck made this more palatable by hinting at the possibility of German support for Austrian expansion in the Balkans and denying any desire to include the Austrian Germans in his new state.

Bismarck was therefore compelled to unify Germany by forces beyond his control but he did this in a manner least dangerous to his political principles. The unification of Germany was a damage-limitation exercise. The unification process was quickly taken out of the hands of nationalists and took the form of diplomatic negotiations between German governments carried on at Versailles, the headquarters of the Prussian government during the siege of Paris. Attempts by the North German parliament to have a say in the settlement during debates in December 1870 were firmly rejected. The main problems were with Bavarian and Württemberg separatism but Bismarck won them over by minor concessions and by bribing the king of Bavaria, Ludwig II, with money from the Welf funds to enable him to build more fairy-tale castles.[29] The letter in which Ludwig offered the imperial title to William I, dated 30

[28]A.J. Hoover, *The Gospel of Nationalism* (Stuttgart, 1986), pp. 128—31.
[29]Stern, *Gold and Iron*, p. 133 and 'Gold and Iron: The Collaboration of Gerson Bleichröder and Otto von Bismarck', *Am.H.R.* 75 (1969), pp. 37—46.

November 1870, was written for him by Bismarck. It stated: 'The German tribes, led to victory by Prussia's heroic king, united for centuries in language and customs, science and arts, now can celebrate a brotherhood of arms, which gives glowing witness of the power of a united Germany.' The wording was significant. The final settlement was completely non-nationalist, the only concessions to nationalist sentiment being the use of the words *Reich* and *Kaiser* rather than *Bund* and president to describe the new confederation and its head. In the proclamation of the Empire on 18 January 1871 there were specific references to the end of the old *Reich* in 1806 and only 65 years separated the two events. This deliberate linking of the new German state to the Holy Roman Empire was not welcome to everyone as some commentators believed that the old *Reich* had a negative and Roman Catholic image. To make the title acceptable to the king of Bavaria, Bismarck, according to his memoirs, agreed to the formula 'German Emperor' rather than 'Emperor of Germany or of the Germans'. He also reassured Ludwig II by pointing out how powerless the Emperor had been in the old Empire. The constitution mentioned 'Germany' very little and in the purely geographical sense of the borders of 1871 not as a nation. The *Reich* of 1871 was a perpetual alliance of sovereigns and governments, who devolved some of their powers upwards to a federal government consisting of the Emperor and the chancellor. In reality the *Reich* was no more than an extended version of the economic and military unity already in existence before 1870, with the addition of a common foreign policy and a supreme court. Decisions on major aspects of government affecting the daily lives of Germans remained with the individual state governments. The unification seems to have roused indifference among the Germans. No euphoria attended its creation and only 51 per cent of eligible voters turned out for the first elections to the new *Reichstag* on 3 March 1871. Equally it seems to have aroused little hostility. A few Bavarian patriots left for Austria and Switzerland rather than live under Prussian rule but the numbers were very small.[30]

For years the *Reich* lacked symbols like a national flag or national anthem, which might have provided a focus for popular sentiment. The *Reich's* official arms were the Prussian eagle with the arms of the Hohenzollern house and an imperial crown, a symbol of the unification as a Prussian colonization of Germany. In 1892 a black white and red tricolour, the Prussian colours, was adopted

---

[30]A number of leading *grossdeutsch* activists like the historian Onno Klopp, Beust, the Saxon prime minister and later Austrian foreign minister, and Heinrich von Gagern had gone into exile in Austria after 1866.

as a national flag but it was not widely used. A national anthem, *Deutschland über alles*, was not adopted until 1922. The Empire's unofficial national day was the anniversary of the battle of Sedan, marking the French defeat, not the proclamation of the *Reich*, and this was the result of private rather than government initiatives. Sedan Day symbolized the division rather than the unity of the German people and its importance declined in the later years of the Empire. The anniversary of the proclamation of the *Reich* only became significant for some Germans after 1918, when its observance symbolized a rejection of the democratic Weimar Republic.

The basic economic structure of the *Reich* was created in the years 1867−73, when a German common market was established with free movement of goods, capital and labour, free enterprise, a common credit market, easy company formation, standard weights and measures, common posts and telegraph systems, common patent and commercial law, a common gold-standard currency, a federal consular service and central financial institutions. In this process the political unification was irrelevant.

Bismarck was forced to make concessions to Liberal demands. Although the constitution contained no bill of rights, the Empire was a state based on law (*Rechtsstaat*). The new *Reichstag* was given wider legislative and budget powers than he had originally intended and he accepted Liberal demands for inviolability of the mails, personal immunity for *Reichstag* deputies and the publication of *Reichstag* debates. He also agreed that the whole house could debate all matters, dropping an earlier proposal that the delegates of states not involved in a matter under debate would leave.[31] These minor sops did nothing to create a genuine parliamentary government for Germany. Bismarck in 1871 therefore succeeded in creating a Germany which was neither united nor Liberal nor national. In reality, as was quickly to become clear, he had partitioned Germany.

[31]H.W. Koch, *A Constitutional History of Germany* (1984), pp. 122−34.

6

The Fractured Nation: Germany 1871–1914[1]

German and other historians sometimes complain that judgements on German history are distorted because the concept of historical progress is interpreted in an exclusively Anglo-Saxon light. They urge that Germany's development should be judged in the light of German not British conditions. For example, they object to the notion that Germany was 'going wrong' in the late nineteenth century because it was not, apparently, evolving towards a liberal parliamentary system on the British model and attack, in particular, the concept of a German 'special road' (*Sonderweg*), a unique and unsound political and social development leading, by implication, to National Socialism. Exponents of the *Sonderweg* argue that it resulted from four causes, the lateness of the achievement of national unity, the lateness of the industrial revolution, the lack of a successful middle-class revolution and the weakness of the parliamentary tradition in Germany. This far from unique combination of circumstances would seem to place Germany in the same category as many European states. What differentiated Germany from most of its neighbours was the size of its population and resources, its location, with open borders to East and West, in the centre of Europe, its military and economic power and the advanced standards of its scientific and technical education.[2]

Whatever view is taken of the *Sonderweg* controversy, it could

[1]General works on the *Kaiserreich*: A. Rosenberg, *The Birth of the German Republic* (1931, reissued in 1970 as *Imperial Germany*); E. Eyck, *Bismarck and the German Empire* (3rd edn, 1968); J.C.G. Röhl, *Germany without Bismarck. The Crisis of Government in the Second Reich* (1967); F. Fischer, *From Kaiserreich to Third Reich* (1986); M. Balfour, *The Kaiser and his Times* (1964); V.R. Berghahn, *Germany and the Approach of War in 1914* (1972); H.-U. Wehler, *The German Empire* (Leamington Spa, 1985). There are several valuable collections of articles: F. Stern, *The Failure of Illiberalism* (1973); R.J. Evans (ed.), *Society and Politics in Wilhelmine Germany* (New York, 1978); J.J. Sheehan (ed.), *Imperial Germany* (New York, 1976); G. Iggers (ed.), *The Social History of Politics* (Leamington Spa, 1985); G. Eley, *From Unification to Nazism* (1986).
[2]There has been a long dispute between the followers of E. Kehr, a German historian writing in the 1930s, and his opponents on the nature of the *Reich*: E. Kehr, *Economic Interest, Militarism and Foreign Policy* (Berkeley, 1977). See D. Blackbourn and G. Eley, *The Pecularities of German History* (Oxford, 1984) for an analysis of the debate on the notion of a German *Sonderweg* and a cogent demolition of the whole concept. The authors argue that Germany experienced a 'silent bourgeois revolution' in the form of economic modernization and the establishment of the *Rechtsstaat*. They also emphasize the importance of the rise of spontaneous popular political movements in the 1880s and 1890s.

be maintained that it was the unification of 1871 which was a radical departure from earlier trends in German history. Before 1871 there was no irresistible trend towards the creation of a *kleindeutsch* state and the unification was carried out to solve Prussia's internal political difficulties not the German problem. The *Reich* was artificial and unnatural and its creation perverted Germany's development and set it on a *Sonderweg*. The unresolved issues of the Prussian Army Conflict were transferred into the *Reich*. There are also deep disagreements among historians about the nature of the German Empire and its constitution. Whatever else it was, it was a deeply divided society and the divisions were made worse by the government's policies. Germany's international position was not improved by the unification. Under the Confederation, arguably, Germany was growing into a giant Switzerland at the heart of Europe; after 1871 its very existence was seen as threatening the Continent.

It was Germany's misfortune that the unification was followed closely by the onset of the Great Depression or Great Deflation, a period of economic stagnation usually held to have lasted from 1873 to 1896. The era when the main standard-bearers of German nationalism were the Liberals ended, ironically, in 1871–3. A combination of circumstances gave rise in the last quarter of the nineteenth century to the first mass nationalist movement in German history, as distinct from the brief and essentially negative xenophobic waves seen earlier. This new nationalism was based on disappointment, resentment and frustration and it was to leave a deep imprint on Germany.

The significance once attributed to the Great Depression is now held to be exaggerated but it did have important effects on Germany's economic and political development.[3] The period of the unification was marked by great optimism, a belief that everything could be achieved by industry and manufacturing, the products of common effort, and that they could overcome particularism and social divisions. After 1873 this gave way to scepticism and a sharp reaction against individualism and materialism, the core of the Liberal creed. Overproduction was held by many to be the cause of Germany's economic and other problems and it was seen as a cause of unrest and a serious threat to the established social order. There was growing disillusionment with a materialistic

[3]H. Rosenberg, 'The Political and Social Consequences of the Great Depression of 1873–1896 in Central Europe', in Sheehan, *Imperial Germany*, pp. 39–60; S.B. Saul, *The Myth of the Great Depression 1873–1896* (1969); Stern, *Gold and Iron*, pp. 182–3; 'The crash and ensuing depression had a profound effect on German society. It dramatized, as nothing before had, the changed nature of that society: it demonstrated that Germany had become a capitalistic country despite the precapitalistic ethos which still prevailed.'

money-grubbing society becoming visibly less German and more like the rest of Western Europe. The frantic speculation of the *Gründerzeit* produced a reaction against the free economy long promoted by Liberals as a solution to all society's problems. There were claims that the fruits of honest German toil were being filched from solid hard-working citizens into the pockets of stock-jobbers, finance swindlers and speculating captains of industry through the stock exchange. German agriculture was badly hit by the Depression, with falling prices for the products of the large farmers of eastern Prussia and growing pressure from cheap imports in the late 1870s and early 1880s. This had important political results. It contributed to an ambivalent attitude towards industrialization and a growing suspicion that it was dangerous to 'healthy national life' (*gesundes Volksleben*), something interpreted in a way increasingly unrealistic, folkloric, picturesque and nostalgic. This was important in creating a new image of the ideal Germany.

A period of political instability in Germany after 1873 culminated in the so-called Second Founding of the *Reich* in 1879, when Bismarck abandoned his alliance with the National Liberals. This ended the temporary community of interest between the Prussian state and middle-class nationalism which had attended the foundation of the *Reich*. It also precipitated a split in the party and the effective end of German Liberalism as a major force.[4] The rather simplistic argument that they gave up freedom for unity is not tenable; to the majority of German Liberals the second was an essential precondition for the first. The *Reich* was a first step and, although it was not founded on Liberal principles, it was acceptable as a temporary stage in the creation of a Liberal Germany. To Bismarck it was final, complete and permanent. When it became obvious that Liberal hopes were groundless, Liberal nationalism lost its vigour and its supporters consoled themselves in enjoying the economic freedom, which Bismarck offered as an alternative to political freedom, and sunning themselves in the reflected glory of German power. The National Liberal Party became part of the pro-government Establishment.[5]

The waning of Liberal nationalism opened the way for the revival of the other main strand of nationalism, the Romantic version,

---

[4] J.J. Sheehan, *German Liberalism in the Nineteenth Century* (Chicago, 1978), pp. 181–218.
[5] The change was symbolized in the family magazine *Die Gartenlaube* (The Summer House), studied by H. Gruppe, *'Volk' zwischen Politik und Idylle in der Gartenlaube 1853–1914* (Frankfurt, 1976). From its foundation until 1871 the magazine consistently supported the Progressive Party. It then backed the National Liberals and by the 1880s had become the mouthpiece of the government and a vehicle for government-sponsored nationalist propaganda.

based on the idea that the main criteria of nationality were culture, language and blood and not devoted to the achievement of national unity as a means of political emancipation, as normally understood. From the beginning this movement showed a tendency to spawn irrational and metaphysical attitudes. After 1873 it was to feed on growing frustration and disappointment and the economic and social discontents of the past-unification period, eventually emerging as a mass movement known by the name *völkisch* nationalism.[6] This was to remain the most spectacular manifestation of German nationalism into the twentieth century. It was active nationalism in that it was based on gross dissatisfaction with prevailing conditions in Germany and sought to bring about fundamental changes. This differentiated it clearly from the passive nationalism or patriotism which simultaneously came to affect almost all groups in German society.

The *Reich* of 1871 was not a nation state but after 1871 the German government found it necessary, for reasons to be described later, to begin a campaign to create German national feeling by artificial means. The German Conservatives soon lost their fear of nationalism and came to recognize its value in combating international movements like Liberalism and Socialism. Nationalism was available to be manipulated by conservative forces as a weapon against the extension of democracy and in the service of imperialist, anti-democratic and authoritarian regimes. Once national power became the highest political goal, all effort was devoted to the maintenance of what Germany's rulers defined as national interests and everything else was subordinated to this. Of course, it was not only in Germany that nationalism was mobilized in support of imperialism or to help maintain a threatened social, political and economic order; France, Italy, Britain and the USA all experienced similar developments but in other mature industrial societies it did not have the same consequences it did in Germany.

The period also saw the rise within Germany of a wide range of different forms of nationalism, including agrarian, Socialist, Catholic and democratic forms. As a result, many different and conflicting visions of the ideal Germany of the future existed side by side, which added to the polarization of society. After 1880 there were broadly three groups, those favouring the maintenance of the *status quo*, those favouring a democratization of German society and those who wanted neither, the *völkisch* nationalists.

---

[6]The German word is difficult to translate as the closest English equivalent, 'folkish', does not sufficiently express the racial element which quickly became central to *völkisch* nationalism.

All this represented just one of many problems facing Wilhelmine Germany in the years before 1914. The establishment of a powerful state and its simultaneous rapid modernization in themselves created new problems and unleashed new forces in Germany, which any government would have found it hard to deal with. The problem was worse in Germany, where the position of the government was in some respects artificial and the constitution represented an element of rigidity and limited the government's freedom of action. This has led one German historian, Michael Stürmer, to describe it as 'the restless *Reich*'.[7] Bismarck and the government he headed were able to live off the great bank of prestige built up during the unification process but, from the beginning, the Bismarckian state gave the impression that it was artificial and provisional. Some have concluded that it was fundamentally unworkable. It is, however, wrong to take an excessively unfavourable view of Wilhelmine Germany and to exaggerate the decomposition of German social and political life. Germany was not seriously threatened by civil war or violent revolution, its administrators were not corrupt and it was technically advanced and culturally lively. The standard of living of its citizens improved measurably between 1871 and 1914. It was a *Rechtsstaat*, in which basic civil rights were defended. On the other hand, the police had wide powers and were a strong and visible presence on public occasions. Trade unions were only freed from direct police surveillance in 1908. In Prussia and other states the government had sweeping emergency powers and farm labourers in Prussia's eastern provinces were subject to extremely unfavourable contracts backed by law.[8] There were in addition basic structural flaws built into the constitution and the political system and ideological divisions within German society were deepening over time. At first the problems remained hidden but they appeared in full flower under William II, who came to the throne in 1888. It has been argued that many of Germany's problems stemmed from the Kaiser's egregious personality and the premature death of his father, Frederick III, after a reign of only a hundred days, has been seen as a great lost opportunity. Frederick's Liberal reputation has been exaggerated. William II was prone to 'oratorical derailments', inane public statements, and his advisers lived in constant fear of the next blunder. His profuse marginal notes on official documents reveal his great

[7]M. Stürmer, *Das Ruhelose Reich: Deutschland 1866–1918* (Berlin, 1983). See D. Schoenbaum, *Zabern 1913. Consensus Politics in Imperial Germany* (1982), chapters 1 to 3 for a very good brief description of the Wilhelmine Empire.
[8]For an attempt at a balanced view see G. Eley, 'Capitalism and the Wilhelmine State', *H.J.* 21 (1978), pp. 737–50, and *From Unification to Nazism*, pp. 42–58.

knowledge but almost total lack of common sense. His behaviour certainly made matters worse but many of Germany's problems were structural and rooted in the constitution.[9]

The political framework of the *Reich* was already outdated in 1871. The constitution drawn up by Bismarck was a monstrosity designed to satisfy his immediate political objectives.[10] It combined elements of the old Holy Roman Empire, the Confederation of 1815 and the 1849 constitution and was, in reality, a system of checks and balances carefully designed to prevent any one element in the political system from becoming too strong. It was part of the damage-limitation exercise which was the unification of Germany. There is dispute among historians regarding the nature of the constitution: some argue that it was an autocratic monarchy disguised as a democracy, others that it was a limited constitutional monarchy with potential for development into a genuine parliamentary democracy. The former view seems more accurate as the Bismarckian system denied the *Reichstag* any control of affairs and any real change in the distribution of power within the system would have required the capitulation of the Prussian ruling class and the abandonment of the principles upon which Bismarck had established the Empire. From the outset that class set its face firmly against any change and this was one of the causes of the political crisis of the *Reich*. Many employers persisted in the 'lord and master' (*Herr-im-Haus*) approach to their workers and they expected the government to adopt the same attitude towards the subject. There was also no place in Bismarck's scheme for political parties, especially mass parties, and he had a naïve faith in the power of governments to manipulate and control the opinions of the masses.

Originally Bismarck had intended to give the federal council (*Bundesrat*) more power and to use its committees as federal government departments but this idea was quickly abandoned. Instead all imperial functions of government were under the control of the chancellor, the sole imperial minister, and his civil service officials. The system was intended to preserve political power in the hands of those who traditionally exercised it while leaving an open door for ambitious men who made money to join this élite, through

[9]J.C.G. Röhl and N. Sombart (eds.), *Kaiser Wilhelm II. New Interpretations* (Cambridge, 1982) (a collection which somewhat plays down the importance of the Kaiser's personality); L. Cecil, *Albert Ballin. Business and Politics in Imperial Germany 1888–1918* (Princeton, 1967); I.V. Hull, *The Entourage of Kaiser William II 1889–1918* (Cambridge, 1982); J. van der Kiste, *Frederick III: German Emperor 1888* (1981).
[10]H.W. Koch, *A Constitutional History of Germany* (1984), p. 122ff; G.G. Windell, 'The Bismarckian Empire as a Federal State 1866–1880: A Chronicle of Failure', *Cent.Eur.H.* 2 (1969), pp. 291–311.

ennoblement and involvement in court ceremonial for example, provided they accepted the attitudes of the élite. By the end of the nineteenth century traditional upper-middle-class values, thrift, self-help, an unostentatious life-style and so on, were losing their appeal. As members of this group were accepted as worthy of presentation at court (*hoffähig*) and fitted, at low positions, into the official hierarchy of precedence, they began to adopt the values and life-style of the aristocracy.[11]

Faced with a crisis, two basic weaknesses of the system appeared. There was an inbuilt rigidity in the constitution which made it very difficult for it to be changed to adapt to new circumstances. Also, power within the *Reich* was diffused among too many individuals and institutions: the Emperor, the German rulers, the parliaments and governments of the individual states, the civil service and the army, with the chancellor supposedly holding all the strings in his hands.

The position of the Emperor in the constitution, in particular in relation to the other German monarchs, was ambivalent. William II boasted that he did not know the constitution and had never read it. He had not been properly trained for government but had an exalted view of his own ability and dangerously rigid opinions. Before his accession he was very critical of his parents, whom he regarded as too Liberal. More dangerous was William's inconsistency. During the period of his so-called personal rule, 1894–1908, he did not, in fact, rule but interfered in government business in a haphazard and unpredictable manner. He suffered from a butterfly mind, an inability to concentrate consistently for a long period on one thing. Also, he spent so much time with civil and military ceremonial and in travelling that he did not have enough left over for government business. His blustering manner intimidated those who came into contact with him and very few dared to stand up to him. Under William II the problem of the diffusion of power was made worse by his habit of appointing favourites like Bülow, Tirpitz and Philip Eulenberg to positions of authority and influence.

The power of the army grew after Bismarck's fall.[12] The Prussian/imperial court had a strong military tone and the army was regarded as a model of organization. The army also had a strong effect on German society rather than being an accurate reflection of it. Officers were selected from an extremely narrow section of society and were schooled to regard themselves as guardians of the throne against internal as well as external enemies. This bred in many the mentality of occupiers in a hostile country. They were

[11]L. Cecil, 'The Creation of Nobles in Prussia 1871–1918', *Am.H.R.* 75 (1970), pp. 757–95.
[12]M. Kitchen, *The German Officer Corps 1890–1914* (Oxford, 1968).

also afraid of parliamentary 'encroachment' on the military sphere. The army had highly developed plans for action against a Socialist rising involving the carefully maintained veterans' associations, which acted as a channel of influence between the army and public opinion. These had been set up in the 1830s but expanded rapidly in the 1860s. Reserve officer status was an effective means of bringing members of the middle class into touch with military values and attitudes. The army was effectively beyond parliamentary control and maintained what amounted to a shadow government in the Military Cabinet. Its ability to get away with acts of blatant illegality was illustrated by the Zabern affair of 1913.[13]

Bismarck's successors as chancellor may have lacked his talents but, even before his fall in 1890, the government faced growing problems from political parties, national minorities and economic interest groups. Severe strains were beginning to appear and Bismarck was seriously suggesting a *coup d'etat* as the only solution to the *Reich's* problems. Serious divisions and polarization in German society were a major result of the unification of Germany. The more the German economy grew — and by 1914 it was second in the world after that of the USA — the more artificial became the position of the ruling élite, an alliance between the traditional aristocracy and the upper middle class. After the unification, this ruling class actually strengthened its hold on the decision-making process, in the universities, the civil service[14] and the officer corps, and on the controlling heights of the economy, where their power was enhanced by the process of cartelization encouraged by the government. The landed aristocracy became increasingly dependent on state subsidization, either directly in the form of protective tariffs or through privileged access to state employment. Power in Prussia was in too few hands and it was from Prussia that the bulk of the German ruling class was drawn. As a result the governing body did not in any way reflect the pluralistic nature of German society. This was shown by persistence of the three-class electoral system in Prussia and other forms of fancy franchises in many other states, though there was growing democratization in some states, particularly the southern. There is some danger of exaggerating the narrowness of the German political system and in particular one should beware of descriptions of the German ruling class as 'feudal' or 'pre-capitalist' élites or the view that Germany

---

[13]For a full account see Schoenbaum, *Zabern*.
[14]J.J. Sheehan, 'Conflict and Cohesion among German Elites in the 19th Century', in Sheehan, *Imperial Germany*, pp. 62–92; L. Cecil, *The German Diplomatic Service 1871–1914* (Princeton, 1977); J.C.G. Röhl, 'Higher Civil Servants in Germany 1890–1900'; and F.K. Ringer, 'Higher Education in Germany in the Nineteenth Century', *J.Cont.H.* 2 (1967), pp. 101–21 and 123–38.

contained two economies and two societies, pre-capitalist and capitalist, side-by-side but with little overlapping between the two. Germany was ruled by a conglomerate ruling class, in which the middle classes had an important role in administration and the economy while the traditional aristocracy set the social and political tone and it remained the ambition of the middle class to join it. Agriculture remained a more important sector in the economy than in late-nineteenth-century Britain but the whole structure was thoroughly capitalist. The ruling class, described graphically as a 'cartel of fear' or 'class war from above', was held together largely by negative forces, especially fear of the rising appeal of the Socialists, seen not just as a political opponent but as an enemy of civilization. Their view of Socialism was coloured by memories of the Paris *Commune* and the activities of Russian terrorists: the workers' movement was seen as threatening the cataclysmic overturning of everything, the *Umsturz*.

The political parties did not develop into national parties but remained defensive and sectional interest-group movements, a situation described as 'the economization of politics'. The government was prepared to allow the operation of a kind of informal corporatism, which permitted group opinions to make themselves heard in high places, provided the real bases of its power were not threatened. Politics did not revolve around principle or ideology but concentrated on persuading the government to act for the benefit of one group rather than another. The rise of pressure groups which sought to bring influence to bear directly on the government, by-passing parliament, was significant. Some represented economic interest groups such as the farmers and white-collar workers, while others were overtly political. Economic pressure groups like the Farmers' League (*Bund der Landwirte*) exerted an influence out of all proportion to the number of their members or their share of the economy. The government was anxious to preserve a strong agricultural sector in order to balance, at least symbolically, industrialization of the economy, with all its unpleasant consequences. The *Junkers*, the large-scale agrarians of the eastern provinces of Prussia, were regarded as particularly important as traditional pillars of the Prussian state, whose preservation was vital to society as a whole. In the early 1890s they moved to protect their privileged position through the Farmers' League.[15] The League, dominated by these large farmers of the

[15]R.M. Berdahl, 'Conservative politics and aristocratic landowners in Bismarckian Germany', in *JMH* 44 (1972), pp. 1–20; H.J. Puhle, 'Lords and Peasants in the Kaiserreich'; and I. Farr, 'Peasant Protest in the Empire – The Bavarian Example', in R.G. Moeller (ed.), *Peasants and Lords in Modern Germany* (1986), pp. 81–109 and 110–139.

Prussian East, also exercised tight control over small- and middle-sized farmers in the rest of Germany on the basis of the myth that their interests were identical. Spontaneous small-farmers' movements, such as anti-Semitic outbreaks in Franconia in the 1880s and 1890s, happened where the League had not established its authority. The League, in alliance with traditional heavy industry, was able to persuade the government to take action to protect it at the cost of the interest of export industries, small farmers and consumers.

Different in aims but symptomatic of the same weakness of the political system were groups like the Army League, the Colonial Society and the Navy League, which wished to push the government into adopting certain defence or colonial policies. The *Hekatisten* and the Society for Promoting Germandom in the Eastern Marches, set up in 1894, wished to strengthen the German presence in the eastern provinces of Prussia with Polish populations. The aims of the Imperial League against Social Democracy were evident in its name. The Pan-German League (*Alldeutscher Verband*), established in 1891, and the Society for Germandom Overseas were ultra-nationalist. Their aim was to support German nationalist movements wherever they existed and to unite all the Germanic elements on the globe to this end. For its members the creation of the *Reich* of 1871 was only the first step in the realization of the Germanic destiny. There was a marked racist element in the League, which envisaged the purging of the non-German elements from Germany and the eventual creation of *Grossdeutschland*. The movement found growing support in the National Liberal Party in the 1890s.[16] Some of these groups enjoyed backing from the government or the army. All organized meetings, social events, trips, exhibitions, publicity campaigns and, after 1900, film-shows to mobilize popular support for their particular campaigns. They did not see themselves as sectional but as fulfilling a national mission and they attracted many *völkisch* enthusiasts. Germany was not unique in this respect as similar groups were appearing in other states at the same time, including Britain,[17] France, Russia and the USA, but they had a much greater following in Germany. The

[16]M.S. Wertheimer, *The Pan-German League 1890–1914* (New York, 1924); G. Eley, *Reshaping the German Right. Radical Nationalism and Political Change after Bismarck* (Yale, 1979); R. Chickering, *We Men who Feel Most German* (1984); Hannah Arendt, *The Origins of Totalitarianism* (5th edn., New York, 1973). The appeal of such groups can be seen as evidence of a kind of national inferiority complex, a classical sign of which was seen in campaigns to purify the German language by purging foreign words: see Eduard Engels, *Sprich Deutsch! Ein Buch zur Entwelschung* [Speak German. A Defrenchifying Book] (Leipzig, 1917).

[17]J.A. Mangan, 'The Grit of Our Forefathers: invented traditions, propaganda and imperialism', in J.M. MacKenzie (ed.), *Imperialism and Popular Culture* (Manchester, 1986).

great influence of such groups was a sign of the perceived weakness of legitimate political institutions and they sometimes embarrassed the authorities, for example with their shrill attacks on Slavs, Jews and Socialists and their sharp criticism of the Emperor during the *Daily Telegraph* Affair of 1908. They agitated on behalf of suffering members of the German diaspora in Russia, Bohemia and Hungary, about which Bismarck and his successors and most German citizens cared very little: so much for national solidarity. In 1912 the leader of the Pan-Germans, Heinrich Class, published under a pseudonym *If I were the Emperor (Wenn ich der Kaiser wär')*, a strongly-worded attack on the government and a call for a leader (*Führer*) to carry through radical changes inside Germany, including a ruthless fight against democratization and anti-Semitic measures, and for strong action against the ring of jealous enemies hampering Germany's growth. The Pan-Germans were not representative but their sabre-rattling roused fears among Germany's neighbours.

The government faced the growing problem of building alliances of 'reliable' parties in the *Reichstag* against the threat of Liberalism and, later, Social Democracy. The easiest way was to buy support by making concessions to special interests but this was an essentially short-term device. Coalitions like Bismarck's *Kartell*, Miguel's *Sammlung* and Bülow's *Block* did not last and were very unstable and difficult to hold together. In spite of difficulties such as harrassment by the authorities, the refusal of government to change the constituency boundaries set up in 1871 to take account of population changes and the electoral system (*Stichwahlsystem*),[18] which at first favoured the Right, opposition parties were able to increase their representation in the imperial diet. As a result, the government's options narrowed. It was ironic that the very groups which favoured expansionist policies abroad in order to preserve their power inside Germany seemed ready to ignore the fact that these made necessary a great industrial base, with more cities and workers, which strengthened Socialism. Such policies also led to an expansion in the functions of the *Reich* government, which Bismarck had deliberately restricted, and required larger grants of taxes from the *Reichstag*, for example to finance colonization and the construction of a powerful navy, which only enhanced opportunities for an institution increasingly difficult to manage to make a nuisance of itself. After reaching a peak of 70 per cent in the 1887 election, the pro-government (i.e. Conservative, National Liberal and Centre party) vote fell steadily to 43 per cent in 1912. At the same time the strength of the Left or 'anti-national' parties (Social

---

[18]Under this system a second run-off election was held if one candidate failed to win an absolute majority on the first ballot. This normally favoured the parties of the Right.

Democrats, Progressives and national minority parties) rose. In the 1912 election the SPD became the largest party in the *Reichstag*.

Along with all European states, Germany faced serious financial problems after 1900 as a result of greater armaments spending. Tirpitz's claim that the fleet would be funded from increasing economic prosperity was wrong and the cost of it was much greater than predicted. As the functions of the *Reich* expanded, the government was forced to look for new sources of income as an alternative to increasing the power of the *Reichstag*, creating a serious threat to the unity between the different groups, on which it relied for support. A major reform of the finances of the *Reich*, long overdue, was carried out in 1906 but by 1908 the problem was as acute as before. Land-owning interests condemned proposed inheritance taxes as the death-knell of their class while some manufacturers predicted that higher indirect taxes would undermine the competitiveness of German exports. In spite of its spectacular successes the German economy was a strange mixture of strength and vulnerability. The economy grew in the years after 1873 but the growth was uneven with periods of expansion punctuated by intervals of stagnation.

The lack of an overseas empire and the country's late arrival as an economic power increased feelings of inferiority and produced among its symptoms the formation, with government encouragement, of cartels of firms, which divided the home market between them, the better to be able to compete with foreigners abroad. Germany also mounted an aggressive export drive in the Balkans, the Turkish empire and South America, which worried its rivals.[19] Around 1900 a growing obsession with overseas empires appeared among all the great powers. It was held that any state without colonies was doomed to second-class status and that it was the duty of every nation to spread its culture over the globe. Imperialism also had an important internal function. It would make possible a constant expansion of the economy without causing social problems in Germany. The ruling class viewed German society as a boiler with pressure building up inside it: overseas expansion would provide a much-needed safety valve. A dynamic and growing economy expanding overseas would therefore produce a static political and social order in Germany. This was an extension to the world of the approach which Bismarck had applied to German politics in the 1860s to solve Prussia's internal problems. Unfortunately it did not have the results expected of it. Commercial

[19]E. Feis, *Europe the World's Banker 1870—1914* (Yale, 1931), chap. 3; E. Maschke, 'Outline of the History of German Cartels from 1873 to 1914', in F. Crouzet (ed.), *Essays in European Economic History 1789—1914* (1969), pp. 226—58.

interests and the more modern and export-orientated branches of manufacturing, such as chemicals and electrical products, increasingly resented a system under which the prices of food and other goods were kept artificially high for political reasons, thus increasing labour costs and strengthening the appeal of Socialism, especially as the development of government-led social welfare schemes ended just when social tensions were again becoming serious after 1900. These divisions, symbolized in rival pressure groups like the Farmers' League (*Bund der Landwirte*) and the *Hansabund*, respectively favouring Protectionism and tariff reductions, represented a dangerous split in the ruling class. After 1911 politics became reduced to a series of day-to-day expedients. Long-term planning was very difficult and there appeared to be no clear vision on the part of the government as to the direction Germany was moving in.[20] On the eve of the First World War a 'Cartel of Creative Estates', an alliance of parties to support the government, was set up but it proved to be very fragile and difficult to hold together on either a negative or positive basis. Total paralysis of the German political system seemed imminent.

The rise of *völkisch* nationalism was another symptom of the problems of German society. It grew out of Romantic nationalism and added to the perversion of the philosophies of the early nineteenth century a distortion of the scientific theories of the later decades of the century, especially those of Darwin. Important contributors to its ideology were Paul de Lagarde (1827–91), Julius Langbehn (1851–1907) and Houston Stewart Chamberlain (1855–1927). Lagarde, a Göttingen academic, in 1881 launched an attack on the *Reich* as insufficiently German and destructive of *gesundes Volksleben* and called for the elimination of Jewish influence and the creation of a German national religion. Langbehn was the anonymous author of *Rembrandt as Educator* (*Rembrandt als Erzieher*) (1890), a meandering work on art, philosophy and German national qualities. It contained a great deal on the superiority of German blood and on the German destiny to rule the world. H.S. Chamberlain's *The Foundations of the Nineteenth Century* (*Die Grundlagen des neunzehnten Jahrhunderts*) (1899), an attack on democracy and a justification of anti-Semitism, became very popular when word spread that the Emperor was a supporter of the author's ideas.[21] The appeal of such ideas was at first limited to sections of

[20]B. Heckart, *From Bassermann to Bebel. The Grand Bloc's Quest for Reform in the Kaiserreich 1900–1914* (Yale, 1974).
[21]An English edition of Chamberlain's work appeared in 1910 under the title *Foundations of the Nineteenth Century*. G.C. Field, *Evangelist of Race. The Germanic vision of Houston Stewart Chamberlain* (New York, 1981); M. Woodroffe, 'Racial Theories of History and Politics: The Example of H.S. Chamberlain', in P.M. Kennedy and A. Nicholls (eds.), *Nationalist and Racialist Movements in Great Britain and Germany* (London, 1981), pp. 143–153.

academic and literary opinion but it gradually spread until, by the end of the century, they had become the accepted ideology of a large section of the German people. Middle-class youth was strongly influenced.[22] Many studies deal mainly with the intellectual origins of *völkisch* ideas and there is certain danger in this because, in order to understand the phenomenon and to appreciate why such ideas were so appealing to many Germans, it is not sufficient to analyse intellectual or pseudo-intellectual attitudes. Ideas in a vacuum would not have had such an impact. Group psychology must also be understood, in particular why increasing numbers of Germans became profoundly dissatisfied with the situation prevailing in their country. Essentially, the *völkisch* movement resulted from the crisis produced by industrialization combined with frustrated nationalism.[23] After the creation of the *Reich* there was among a growing number of Germans a search for unity in idealized spiritual forms, an attempt to replace by imagination what did not exist in reality. The 'unification' of 1871 produced a kind of reversion to attitudes seen before 1815, a belief in the impregnable '*Reich* of the spirit', in which culture was more important than politics. Many Germans seem to have seen 'this secret something' as missing from the *Reich*,[24] where pure *Kultur* was seen as being sacrificed to materialistic *Zivilisation*.[25]

The main characteristics of *völkisch* nationalism were: adoration of heroes and soldiers, the idealization of the rural way of life, romanticization of the past, an irrational rejection of modernity, deep pessimism about the future and a total rejection of foreigners

[22]G.L. Mosse, *The Crisis of German Ideology. Intellectual Origins of the Third Reich* (1966); F. Stern, *The Politics of Cultural Despair* (Berkeley, 1961); R. Stackelberg, *Idealism Debased. From völkisch Ideology to National Socialism* (Kent, Oh., 1981); D. Glaser, *The Cultural Roots of National Socialism* (1978); A. Mitzman, 'Tönnies and German Society 1887–1914: From Cultural Pessimism to Celebration of the *Volksgemeinschaft*', *J.Hist.Id.* 32 (1971), pp. 507–24; A. Lees, 'Critics of urban society in Germany 1854–1914', *J.Hist.Id.* 40 (1979), pp. 61–83; P.G.J. Pulzer, *The Rise of Political Anti-Semitism in Germany and Austria 1867–1938* (1964); P. Gay, *Freud, Jews and other Germans. Masters and Victims in Modernist Culture* (Oxford, 1978); G.D. Stark, *Entrepreneurs of Ideology. Neo-Conservative Publishers in Germany 1890–1933* (Chapel Hill, 1981); W.Z. Laqueur, *Young Germany* (1962); P.D. Stachura, *The German Youth Movement 1900–1945* (1981); K.H. Jarausch, *Students, Society and Politics in Imperial Germany. The Rise of Academic Illiberalism* (Princeton, 1982).
[23]M.D. Biddiss, *The Age of the Masses. Ideas and Society in Europe since 1870* (1977), p. 29ff.
[24]Ranke in *Politisches Gespräch* (*A Political Conversation*, first published 1836) (Munich, 1924), p. 35: 'Our fatherland is not just the place where we are comfortable. Our fatherland is with us. Germany lives in us .... We are derived from it in the beginning and cannot emancipate ourselves from it. This secret something, which fills the lowest as well as the highest, this spiritual air which we breathe in and out, takes precedence over every constitution and vitalizes and fills all constitutional forms.'
[25]This has been investigated in relation to technology in early-twentieth-century Germany: J. Herf, 'The Engineers as Ideologue: Reactionary Modernists in Weimar and Nazi Germany', *J.Cont.H.* 19 (1984), pp. 631–48 and *Reactionary Modernism. Technology, Culture and Politics in Weimar and the Third Reich* (Cambridge, 1984).

and foreign ideas. It mixed reactionary and Utopian elements. Whereas the Liberals and later the Socialists offered a Utopia of the future, the new nationalism promised the recreation of a perfect society which was held to have existed at some time in the past. *Völkisch* nationalism was 'back to the future'. Germany was regarded as a 'belated nation', united too late and confined in the centre of Europe with no obvious possibilities of growth and expansion. The unification of 1871 seemed a pointless step if it did not lead to a clear assertion and demonstration of German power. Bismarck had stated in 1871 that Germany was a 'satiated nation' in order to reassure the rest of Europe that the creation of the *Reich* represented no threat to the established states system and that it had no designs on its neighbours' land, including the parts of Austria with German populations. If this was the case, if a united Germany was not going to behave like a great power, what was the point of unifying it? This was a question explicitly asked by many, including the Liberal imperialist Max Weber in his much-quoted inaugural lecture at Freiburg in 1895, when he said that the unification should have been left undone if it did not lead to a German world power policy. For Bismarck the achievement of 1871 may have been enough but many Germans did not feel satiated by it.

For many, the new Germany created in 1871 quickly turned sour as it seemed to be devoted to strengthening those aspects of the modern world which Romantic nationalists believed were corroding the essential and distinct Germanness of Germany. One of the more famous individuals affected in this way was Richard Wagner, who at first welcomed the establishment of the *Reich* as a source of new national strength which would oust French culture from its position of usurped predominance. He soon became disillusioned, perhaps partly because the new *Reich* did not wish to foster his grandiose artistic plans, and expressed the belief that a united Germany had been created at the cost of the German spirit, showing a pessimism shared by many. Bismarck carried out a severely practical unification designed to foster military strength and economic growth. It offered nothing spiritual, nothing to feed inflamed national enthusiasm. Germany was becoming more industrialized and urbanized and quickly acquired political parties seeking radical change, especially the Social Democrats, whose internationalism was seen as a threat to German values and whose following swarmed in the cities which the Romantic nationalists loathed.

The alienation of these nationalists was made worse by the rapid economic and social changes which occurred at the same time as the unification, the most spectacular of which was probably the great internal migration from countryside to towns, which began in the 1880s and, by 1907, left only about a third of Germans still living in the place of their birth. Also important was the fact that from the 1860s the real incomes of industrial workers rose, narrowing or eliminating the material gap between them and many of the lower middle class. This tendency was made much more acute by the Depression. Such fears were strengthened by a growing conviction in some sections of the German people that the *Reich* of 1871 was a fragile and precarious structure, threatened from outside by jealous neighbours and from inside by 'un-German' forces. After the unification, groups of Germans began to view other groups of Germans as agents of foreign ideas and therefore their enemies: this was a further sign of the division rather than unity brought about by the creation of the *Reich* in 1871. The bonds holding it together were perceived as becoming weaker. The answer for *völkisch* nationalists was to reject totally notions of progress and modernization, as both were seen as destructive of German virtues. Instead, extreme nationalists increasingly sought a 'German way' in politics, economics and social organization and a German or national revolution, a complete restructuring of society leading to a spiritual regeneration of the German people, the recreation of a Germany of peasants and small-town craftsmen, properly rooted in the pre-industrial past, and the elimination of all artificial divisions of class, party and religion which sundered the *Volk*.

This vision came to be known as the folk community (*Volksgemeinschaft*), a concept which was to become very potent and acquire a quasi-religious following, especially as the appeal of conventional religion declined. *Völkisch* nationalism was a consciously anti-intellectual movement and it interpreted man's place in the world in an irrational and emotional manner. It rejected the world as it existed and desired to replace it with something vague, ill-defined and very appealing. Individuals who could not identify with the mass world in which they lived and felt alienated from it were offered the chance to retreat from an unreal and artificial society and to find a new identity by submerging themselves in a greater whole or community, the mystic *Volk*, which alone represented true reality. Reality was the universe, the cosmos, from which radiated life forces; the individual could only achieve union with these forces through an organic living body, the *Volk*. There was a large element of pantheism in *völkisch* nationalism. Only in the German landscape could the *Volk* find its roots, in the rivers, mountains, and, above all, the forests of Germany. In the city a layer of asphalt cut the German off from the soil in which true Germanness resided. Cities also made possible the vice and unnatural sexual practices which were sapping the vitality of the nation.[26] Back-to-Nature movements were not unique to Germany; in the face of industrialization most Western European states experienced an idealization of the rural way of life. In Germany many of its manifestations were harmless, such as the youth hiking groups, the *Wandervogel, rus in urbe* allotment movements or the nudist *Naturmenschen*. It produced growing interest in ethnography and folklore, especially regional customs and peasant costumes, and a search for 'closed cultural regions' (*geschlossene Kulturlandschaften*), untouched by railways, remote from towns and unvisited by tourists. In its most extreme form, in *völkisch* nationalism, it turned into the 'blood and soil' (*Blut und Boden* or *Blubo*) ideology, which saw in the peasantry the germ-cell of the *Volk*, which could consist only of those rooted in the landscape. The countryside was seen as the repository of a genuine German popular culture, essentially unchanged since pre-Christian times, while urban life was being swamped in un-German or anti-German uniformity.

To such feelings *völkisch* nationalism offered an answer. It made no attempt to deal with the problems caused by industrialization and urbanization but offered a Germany without such developments. Many of its ideas appear in retrospect to have been quite ridiculous, deriving from a gross distortion of German history and of science and philosophy. Its basic roots lay in the old view of the uniqueness and innate superiority of the German *Volk* developed by Arndt, Jahn and others at the beginning of the nineteenth century. As these notions developed in the later nineteenth century, they became the basis of the ideas and attitudes of National Socialism. There was nothing new in the ideology of Nazism when the party emerged after 1918; its main tenets were already respectable and well-accepted before 1914. The supporters of these ideas rejected the existing and traditional political systems, including the state based on law (*Rechtsstaat*), the basis of the Liberal ideology. Instead they searched for a Utopian solution to all Germany's problems involving the rejection of all alien ideas.

In other respects the new nationalism also produced a radical narrowing of the criteria of nationality, no longer held to be determined by language or blood alone but by attitudes. Cast out as traitors to the nation were those who followed alien and international movements. Such were the deracine urban workers, who followed Socialism, the non-German minorities inside the *Reich*,

---

[26]K. Barkin, 'Adolf Wagner and German Industrial Development', *JMH* 41 (1969), pp. 144−59 and H. Lebovics, '"Agrarians" versus "Industrialists". Social Conservative Resistance to Industrialism and Capitalism in Late Nineteenth-Century Germany', *International Review of Social History* 12 (1967), pp. 31−65 on agrarian nostalgia in the *Reich*, G.L. Mosse, 'Nationalism and Respectability: Normal and Abnormal Sexuality in the Nineteenth Century', *J.Cont.H.* 17 (1982), pp. 227−8.

Roman Catholics, Freemasons, large-scale capitalists and, above all, the Jews. The rise of *völkisch* nationalism concided with the appearance of a new racism in Europe, signalled in A. de Gobineau's *Essay on the Inequality of Races* (1854).[27] The older religious, economic and salon anti-Semitism remained but it was now reinforced by pseudo-scientific arguments. There is danger in exaggerating the appeal of anti-Semitism in late-nineteenth-century Germany but it certainly found followers among sections of the middle class who feared descent into the proletariat and for whom the Jew became a perfect anti-model to idealized Germanness.[28] There was a powerful belief that, if these various enemies of the German nation were eliminated, the *Volk* would bloom anew in the *Volksgemeinschaft*, the superiority of the German would be made manifest in the world and a stable and truly unified *Reich* would come into being.

Such half-baked Romantic mysticism found a ready hearing among a growing number of Germans. Initially espoused by some academics,[29] *völkisch* nationalism by the turn of the century had acquired mass support from the peculiarly Central European lower-middle-class group known as the *Mittelstand*.[30] Because it played a part in the rise of National Socialism in the 1920s, there is a danger of attributing too much importance to the *Mittelstand* movement in the period before 1914, but it has a place in a study of German nationalism. This group had been a factor in German politics throughout the period we have been examining. In the early nineteenth century the inability of its members, in spite of all their efforts, to rise into the élites had led them towards Liberalism. Now the same emotions were to lead some of them to extreme nationalism. For the sake of convenience this group is usually divided into the 'old' and 'new' *Mittelstand*, the former made up of the 'little men' of the economy, self-employed artisans, small farmers, shop-keepers and the like, the latter of the rapidly expanding white-collar workforce of clerks, shop-assistants and minor civil servants. The various elements were too variegated to be able to form a single movement, though in the 1890s they were beginning to organize into pressure groups and white-collar unions.

[27]M.D. Biddiss, *Comte Gobineau: Selected Political Writings* (1970).

[28]Stern, *Gold and Iron*, especially chap. 18.

[29]Stern, *Politics of Cultural Despair*, pp. 291–2.

[30]J. Kocka, 'Class formation, interest articulation and public policy. The origins of the German white-collar class in the late 19th and early 20th centuries', in S. Berger (ed.), *Organising Interests in Western Europe* (Cambridge, 1981), pp. 63–81; R. Gellately, *The Politics of Economic Despair: Shopkeepers and German Politics 1890–1914* (1974); S. Volkov, *The Rise of Popular Anti-Modernism in Germany 1873–93. The Urban Master Artisans* (Princeton, 1978); A.J. Mayer, 'The Lower Middle Class as Historical Problem', JMH 47 (1975), pp. 409–36.

Their disunity was one of the reasons why they found the alternative vision of a national community so attractive. Although many of them were indistinguishable from industrial workers in material terms, the SPD made little headway among them, especially in rural areas. Craft workers saw themselves as superior to and distinct from industrial workers and this perceived social gulf became more important to the guild members as the material gap between them and factory workers disappeared. This attitude was symbolized in, for example, resistance to intermarriage between the groups and the refusal of the *Mittelstand* to join industrial workers' unions and co-operative movements.

For the *Mittelstand*, life in the last quarter of the nineteenth century seemed to be one long crisis and, after the resignation of Bismarck in 1890, the *Reich* itself seemed to face grave problems. The *Mittelstand* became deeply pessimistic about their own place in a Germany which seemed to offer them no future except a descent into the proletariat they despised. In fact the *Mittelstand* was more resilient than its members feared. Some sections were able to modernize their activities and the small self-employed remained an important element in the German economy. This was not, however, widely appreciated. Increasingly they identified their own fate as a class with the fate of Germany, seeing themselves as the only stable and truly German element in society. Motivated by the 'politics of resentment', they turned their hostility against Socialism and capitalism, both too easily subsumed in anti-Semitism. They supported the ultra-nationalist pressure groups like the Navy League in what has been described as 'political self-mobilization from below' and 'a participation revolution'. Numerically they represented a substantial section of German society and no government could ignore them. In the 1890s guild rights were reinforced by legislation, though this was of symbolic rather than real significance. Some of the political parties also found it advisable to pander to *Mittelstand* prejudices: in its Tivoli Programme of 1892 the Conservative Party adopted *völkisch* attitudes, including anti-Semitism and ultra-nationalism. The Roman Catholic Centre Party founded in 1870 was also affected.[31] Parties whose only platform was anti-Semitism flourished briefly but came to nothing; there was no need for them as their attitudes were taken over, in a more muted form, by others.

In addition to the growing appeal of *völkisch* nationalism to some Germans, another form of nationalism came to affect the whole of society during the same period. This is Benedict

[31]D. Blackburn, 'Roman Catholics, the Centre Party and anti-Semitism in Imperial Germany', in Kennedy and Nicholls, *Nationalist and Racialist Movements*, pp. 106–29.

Anderson's 'official nationalism': 'an anticipatory strategy adopted by dominant groups who are threatened [or, one could say, *feel* threatened] with marginalization or exclusion from an emerging nationally-imagined community', in other words loss of power, status and property.[32] G.L. Mosse describes the same phenomenon as 'the nationalization of the masses'.[33] It was ironic that Bismarck, a convinced opponent of nationalism, should have achieved the conversion of the German élites and a substantial section of the German people to that ideology. It became a deliberately adopted policy of the German government to persuade all Germans to identify with the nation and involve themselves in its struggles. One motive for this was to divert attention from the problems of the new *Reich* and concentrate the people's eyes on Germany's struggles against her internal and external enemies.[34]

The policy took many forms. The young were an obvious target and the education system was widely used to teach desirable attitudes and 'correct' views.[35] School teachers had long been an important element in the national movement. Friedrich Diesterweg, a teacher and educationist, in 1851 produced a scheme for German National Education to combat the excessive cosmopolitanism still present in traditional systems: 'The spirit of world history has called the people of this country to take possession of all the greatness and sublimity of the earth and from here to spread itself out in all directions. It represents in the body of Europe the heart, pumping nourishing blood to the furthest parts'. The function of the education system, he believed, was to create German national conviction,' by which I mean essentially the inner feeling of affection for all who speak German, live on German soil ... with which is united hatred of all things foreign.' Often teachers needed little prompting from the government to spread the nationalist message to their charges. The General German School Union (*Allgemeine Deutsche Schulverein*) was established in 1881, an alliance

---

[32]B. Anderson, *Imagined Communities* (1983), p. 80ff.

[33]G.L. Mosse, *The Nationalization of the Masses* (New York, 1975) and 'Mass Politics and the Political Liturgy of Nationalism', in E. Kamenka (ed.) *Nationalism. The Nature and Evolution of an Idea* (1976), pp. 38–54.

[34]V.R. Berghahn, *Germany and the Approach of War in 1914* (1973); H.-U. Wehler, 'Bismarck's Imperialism 1862–90' *P. and P.* 48 (1970), pp. 119–55 and *The Germans Empire*, p. 176ff. For the debate on the 'manipulative strategies' of the German government: G. Eley, 'Defining Social Imperialism. Use and Abuse of an Idea', in *Social History* 1 (1976), pp. 165–90 and *Reshaping the German Right*; P.M. Kennedy, 'German Colonial Expansion. Has the "Manipulated Social Imperialism" been Ante-Dated?', *P. and P.* 54 (1972), pp. 134–141; H. Medick's review of H.-U. Wehler, *Bismarck und der Imperialismus* (Cologne, 1969) in *History and Theory* 10 (1971), pp., 228–239.

[35]W.C. Langsam, 'Nationalism and history in the Prussian elementary schools under William II', in E.M. Earle (ed.), *Nationalism and Internationalism* (New York, 1950), pp. 241–61; E.N. Anderson, 'The Prussian *Volksschule* in the Nineteenth Century', in G.A. Ritter (ed.), *Entstehung und Wandel der modernen Gesellschaft* (Berlin, 1970), pp. 261–79.

of academics and educationalists, to promote the German language and culture inside and outside Germany. Many of its leaders were later active in the Pan-German League. After 1890, according to one headmaster, the main aim of schools was to teach 'love of German customs, the German language, German art and science, a partiality and preference for all things German, even with the risk of injustice and error, for love has the inalienable right to be blind.' History was the subject most favoured by those anxious to foster nationalist opinions in children. A Prussian royal edict of 1889 laid down that school history text books were to be subject to stronger state influence and were to be written in a manner more supportive of the existing order. This seemed superfluous, as most authors of such books and most high-school teachers seemed to need little prompting to blow the national trumpet. Very few resisted, a notable exception being the Socialist historian Franz Mehring. It is interesting that disputes over school history books revived after 1918, when some state governments tried to get rid of the old favourites, an attempt which met fierce opposition from teachers.

The teaching of *Landesgeschichte* (the history of the individual states) in high schools was gradually replaced with German history and by 1900 the transformation was complete even in Bavaria. The Germans were portrayed as an *Urvolk*, bearers of a high civilization passed to them by the Greeks and Romans, and a chosen people, the ideal bearers of Christianity. The innate superiority of the Germans was emphasized, as was their pure blood and spirituality, in contrast to the vice and craftiness of foreigners, especially the ultimate foreigner, the Jew. Men like Heinrich von Treitschke, in the early 1860s a vocal critic of Bismarck and then won over to become an admirer, were responsible for a deliberate perversion of Germany's history designed to portray it as unbroken progress towards the Prussian-led creation of *Kleindeutschland* in 1871. Great emphasis was placed on the identity between 'Prussian' and 'German'; the part played by Austria in Germany's history was consistently denigrated until the Third *Reich*. The Borussian legend might have gone from scientific historiography after 1890 but it lingered on in the popular consciousness. Treitschke's *German History* remained a widely read book.[36] The role in that history of martial power and hero figures like Bismarck, Krupp, Arminius, Charlemagne, Luther, Frederick the Great, Prince Eugene and Emperors William I and II was elevated while Liberal and democratic movements in German history were consistently belittled. 1848

[36]H. von Treitschke, *Deutsche Geschichte im neunzehnten Jahrhundert* (new edn, 5 vols., Leipzig, 1927).

was taught in terms of the actions of Frederick William IV and the Archduke John and the democratic and revolutionary aspects were played down. The poet and writer of popular history books Felix Dahn (1834—1912) urged his readers to look back with pride to their forefathers, Alaric the Goth, Attila the Hun and Hagen, the anti-hero of the *Nibelung* saga. Schools also made lavish use of the works of Emanuel Geibel (1815—84), the author of dreadful chauvinistic verse.

The identity of the imperial dynasty and the nation was strongly emphasized under William II. His grandfather refused to abandon specifically Prussian symbols and ceremonies, retaining to the end of his life a deep mistruct of the whole imperial business. He introduced the ceremony of personal oath-taking in Berlin for recruits to the army but, significantly, separate oaths were administered not only to men of different faiths but to the citizens of the different German states. This changed under William II. Ceremonials such as openings of buildings, dedications of war memorials and annual festivals of remembrance were employed as occasions to bang the German national drum, a revival of E.M. Arndt's tactic of using festivals and monuments to create a national spirit.[37] In the last decades of the nineteenth century there was a government-sponsored renaissance of Jahn's reputation in the form of great National Festivals (*Volksfeste*) of marksmen and gymnasts, for example the annual Federal Shoot (*Bundesschiessen*), as vehicles for nationalist and pro-government rhetoric and propaganda. These 'festivals of German brotherhood' (*Deutsche Verbrüderungsfeste*) were openly employed before 1914 to spread an anti-Socialist message. Benedict Anderson sees war memorials and cenotaphs as very powerful symbols of national unity.[38] In the case of Germany they were as much instruments designed to create national sentiment as expressions of pre-existing sentiment. Certain symbols became common, the eagle, oak leaves, laurel wreaths, winged Victory and the martial Germania figure. The government put a lot of effort into promoting their use in applied art to create a kind of national style or national image, to be displayed in museums, schools and public buildings. Patriotic paintings were commissioned for schools, town halls and railway stations, creating a kind of national iconography. The stated aim was to display the heroes of Classical antiquity and great deeds of history to children and the public in a colourful and attractive form. They also often made explicit references to Germany's place in the world and the social divisions within Germany. For example, works of 'social realism' depicting

[37]Mosse, *Nationalization of the Masses*, chap. 4.
[38]Anderson, *Imagined Communities* , p. 17.

ordinary workers were designed to romanticize work and discredit Socialism. Prestige projects like the refurbishing of the eleventh-century imperial palace (*Kaiserpfalz*) at Goslar in 1879 provided splendid opportunities for this sort of thing. The Classical style favoured earlier in the century gave way to Romanesque architecture as a reminder of the Old Empire at the time of its greatness, though municipalities preferred Gothic or German Renaissance as a reminder of the imperial free cities at their height of their medieval prosperity. When the new *Reichstag* (1894) was built in Italian Renaissance style, nationalists saw this as a sign of the baleful influence of the Catholic Centre Party.

A number of huge monuments were built as symbols of German national pride. These included the Arminius or Hermann memorial (1875) near Detmold commemorating the destruction of Roman legions in AD 9 by a Teutonic chieftain, collections for which began in the 1840s, the Niederwald monument on the Rhine, Germania crowning herself, to commemorate the founding of the *Reich* (1883), the Kyffhäuser Monument on the site of Barbarossa's castle in the Harz (1896), also to commemorate national unity, and a victory memorial in Leipzig, completed in 1913. The initiatives for these came from patriotic groups, who raised funds for them, but government agencies played a full part in the attendant ceremonials. These monuments became the site of regular National Festivals. Under William II there was a concerted campaign to create a William the Great cult around the Emperor's grandfather. Public subscriptions led to the erection of hundreds of statues. Only in Bavaria and the Hanseatic cities was the response less than enthusiastic. By 1900 imperial German pageantry was displacing the older ceremonial associated with the individual German states. In 1913, William II's silver jubilee and the centenary of the victory over Napoleon at Leipzig, the so-called Battle of the Nations, a whole year of celebrations centred on the consecration of the new memorial at Leipzig.

The idea of a German mission and a belief that Germany merited a prominent role in world affairs were promoted. After 1888 William II was deliberately put forward as a figurehead in a new populist campaign to unite the nation behind *Weltpolitik*, Germany's attempt to become a naval and colonial power with a world role. The youthful and vigorous Kaiser combined in his person the traditional Prussian martial values and the modern technological world of science, railways and industry. In 1909 he inaugurated the Kaiser Wilhelm Society to promote scientific research. A nationalist tone was also heard here: Berlin was actively promoted as the intellectual capital of Germany and scientists were frequently reminded that Germany could not be allowed to fall behind in research or it would risk losing its power. Nicknamed the *Reise-*

kaiser (travelling Emperor), he made frequent journeys all over Germany in his special imperial train, inspecting, dedicating and performing opening ceremonies. He probably overegged the pudding as his too frequent appearances provoked some reaction against him, seen in the Bismarck cult after 1898, which led to the building of numerous statues and Bismarck towers. The excessive ceremonial around the Emperor upset the middle classes, most of whom were not admitted to it, and alienated many of the old nobility, who saw it as a further regrettable dilution of Prussian principles.[39]

The policy of distraction and manipulation was only a partial success and substantial sections of the German people were neither fully integrated nor won over to support the prevailing order. Polarization in society was increased by Bismarck's techniques of political management, which produced permanent 'ins' and permanent 'outs'. He habitually labelled his political opponents as disloyal or 'enemies of the state' (*Reichsfeinde*). He mounted concerted attacks on the Roman Catholics, the Socialists and the national minorities to provide targets against which the rest of the nation could unite, the technique of secondary integration. The *Kulturkampf* of 1874–80, a concerted attack on the position of the Roman Catholic Church in Prussia, imitated in some other states, was typical. Bismarck was worried at Liberal successes in elections to the *Reichstag* and some state parliaments: in 1872 in Hesse-Darmstadt the Progressives won 41 out of 50 seats. The attack on the Church was designed to divert the Liberals' attention from criticism of other aspects of the constitution by offering them the Catholic clergy as a target. The device worked as many Liberals had looked to unification as an opportunity to destroy the influence of an obscurantist clergy over the minds of Germans. In launching the *Kulturkampf* Bismarck deliberately played on nationalism by reviving memories of the medieval Investiture Dispute, for example in his *Reichstag* speeches in April 1873. It achieved its aim but left German Catholics feeling more vulnerable than they had since 1815, outsiders and a persecuted minority, and encouraged them to form their own institutions in defence. There was something of a Protestant state for a Protestant people about the *Reich*: its north German Protestant character was emphasized at different times by Bismarck, Bülow and the National Liberals and its ruling class was overwhelmingly Protestant.[40]

[39]I. Hull in C. Fink *et al.* (eds.), *German Nationalism and the European Response* (Norman, Okl., 1985).
[40]*European Studies Review* 12, part 3 (1982) is devoted to 'Religion and Society in Germany'; D. Blackbourn, *Class, Religion and Local Politics in Wilhelmine Germany* (New Haven, 1980); R.J. Ross, *Beleaguered Tower: The Dilemma of Political Catholicism in Wilhelmine Germany* (Notre Dame, 1976) and 'Enforcing the *Kulturkampf* in the Bismarckian State and the Limits of Coercion in Imperial Germany', *JMH* 56 (1984), pp. 456–82.

Similar tactics were used against the Socialists under the Anti-Socialist laws (1878–90). Even after the lifting of the ban in 1890 the SPD was subject to harrassment in the form of a strong police presence at meetings, prosecutions of members on catch-all charges like threatening public order and insulting behaviour, provocative use of troops during strikes, house searches and the like. Mourners attending Socialist funerals were likely to have their wreaths inspected by the police to ensure that nothing inflammatory was written on them. In 1896 the franchise for elections to the Saxon state parliament was changed to make it more restrictive and reduce the representation of the Socialists, the biggest party since 1877.[41]

The Polish, Danish and French minorities in the Empire were also easy targets.[42] There was a vigorous debate on the position of the 10 per cent of the population of the *Reich* who were not German, mainly on the question of language rights. Prussia was a miniature version of the multi-national empires of eastern Europe and had long contained non-German minorities but a pragmatic policy on language use had prevailed. As a result the various linguistic minorities had remained loyal subjects. A sign of changing attitudes came in 1861, when the Prussian census contained questions on language use for the first time, and there had been clear signs of Germanization policies against the Poles even earlier in the 1830s. German attitudes towards the Poles had long been ambivalent. Sympathy for the Poles among Liberals in the early nineteenth century was mixed with a belief that they were culturally inferior and that Germans had a missionary duty to Germanize them for their own good. There was a tendency to regard the Poles as would-be Germans who happened, temporarily, to speak Polish. The National Liberals strongly supported enforced Germanization measures after 1872. Bismarck's anti-Polish prejudice was deep and visible from his emergence into politics in the 1840s. He saw the Poles as an anarchic and revolutionary people, dangerous to the stability of their neighbours. His achievement in February

[41]V.L. Lidtke, *The Outlawed Party. Social Democracy in Germany 1878–90* (Princeton, 1966); A. Hall, *Scandal, Sensation and Social Democracy* (Cambridge, 1977); G. Roth, *The Social Democrats in Imperial Germany* (New York, 1979); W.L. Guttsman, *The German Social Democratic Party 1875–1933* (1981); S. Miller and K. Potthoff, *A History of the SPD* (Leamington Spa, 1986); P. Gay, *The Dilemma of Democratic Socialism. Eduard Bernstein's Challenge to Marx* (new edn, New York, 1962); C.E. Schorske, *German Social Democracy 1905–17. The Development of the Great Schism* (1972); R. Fletcher, *Revisionism and Empire. Socialist Imperialism in Germany 1897–1914* (1984); P. Nettl, 'The German Social Democratic Party 1890–1914 as a political model', in *P. and P.* 30 (1965), pp. 65–95; S.W. Armstrong, 'The Social Democrats and the Unification of Germany 1863–71', *JMH* 12 (1940), pp. 485–509; D. Groh, 'The "Unpatriotic Socialists" and the State', *J. Cont. H.* I/4 (1966), pp. 151–77.
[42]See: W.W. Hagen, *Germans, Poles and Jews. The Nationality Conflict in the Prussian East 1772–1914* (Chicago, 1980); R. Blanke, 'Bismarck and the Prussian Polish Politics of 1886', *JMH* 45 (1973), pp. 211–39.

1863 of the convention with Russia, negotiated by General Alvensleben, for co-operation between Prussia and Russia in dealing with a rising in Russian Poland was an important factor in obtaining Russian consent to the major changes about to take place in Germany. Anti-Polish feeling was an element in the *Kulturkampf* and Bismarck was one of the initiators of anti-Polish policies adopted in the 1870s and 1880s, including enforced use of German, restrictions on the use of the Polish language and government measures to Germanize the soil by encouraging settlement by Germans in Polish areas. He seems initially to have believed that the mass of the ordinary peasants could be won over to loyalty to Germany if the influence of the clergy and nobility was removed and he supported the enforced use of German not from German nationalist motives but because he believed it was vital for state purposes. This proved as vain a hope as his idea of using universal suffrage to mobilize the masses against middle-class Liberalism. Instead, anti-German Polish mass nationalism was created, the very problem the Germanization measures were supposedly designed to remove.

These policies made life difficult for the government in other ways. In 1908 it planned a new law on associations including sharp restrictions on the use of any language except German in public meetings. This was strongly opposed by the Progressive Party, an important element in the pro-government coalition, which was threatened as a result. Such measures were also used against the Danish minority in Schleswig and the French-speakers of Alsace-Lorraine, with the same results.[43] In the Prussian elections to the first north German *Reichstag* in February 1867 there was a very heavy turn-out in areas with Polish populations: the Poles were voting against a German national state. Representatives of the Poles and Danes, and later the Alsatians, in the north German diet and the *Reichstag* left no doubt that they did not wish to be German. They saw themselves as unwelcome guests at the German national birthday party. In the treaty of Prague North Schleswig had been promised a referendum to decide if it should belong to Denmark or Prussia but this was not carried out. In 1870 the Posen Poles made no secret of their desire for a French victory in the war. Many German-speaking Alsatians, much to the disgust of the *Reichstag*, regarded themselves as French and pro-French feeling grew in strength after the annexation of the provinces. Some inhabitants reconciled themselves to being part of Germany but

[43]L.M. Larson, 'Prussianism in N. Schleswig', *Am. H.R* 24 (1918—19), pp. 227—52; Schoenbaum, *Zabern*; D.P. Silverman, *Reluctant Union. Alsace-Lorraine and Imperial Germany* (Philadephia, 1972).

supported wider autonomy or *Land* status rather than the semi-colonial relationship between Germany and Alsace-Lorraine. Germany was, again, not unique in pursuing such policies. One reason for growing anti-Slav feeling in Germany was to be found in the Russification policies being pursued in Russia in the last years of the nineteenth century, including restrictions on the use of German in schools in the Baltic provinces and in 1893 the closure of the long-established German-speaking university at Dorpat. These measures caused great complaint among the Pan-Germans but the government refused to take action which might be internationally embarrassing.

Official nationalism was a failure. It may have helped temporarily to consolidate the alliance of the 'ins' but it had the effect of alienating other groups. The effectiveness of indoctrination in primary schools, with classes of over 60 in some cases, is questionable, especially as Socialists and Catholics organized to counter government propaganda. Government attempts to push German national feeling to the front of Germans' consciousness came up against powerful older loyalties, the ties of family, religion, region and, increasingly, class. Dynastic and state loyalty certainly declined after 1871 but it was a slow process and state rulers, governments and parliaments remained for a long time more immediate to the daily lives of Germans than the remote *Reich*. Thus there were within Germany widely differing and incompatible visions of the country's future and bitter disputes about the exact nature of German national traditions rooted in starkly different versions of German history. Such divisions became worse in the 1890s as the working class, the *Mittelstand* and the peasantry were beginning to organize themselves and to enter the political arena as serious forces. Other forms of nationalism continued to co-exist with the *völkisch* and the state-created forms. Alternatives to the *kleindeutsch* unification disappeared remarkably quickly after 1871. An attempt in 1892 to revive an organized *grossdeutsch* movement by the creation of a States' Rights party to unite anti-Prussian groups in various states and then secure the admission of German Austria to the *Reich* came to nothing. The Catholic Centre Party remained the leading federalist movement devoted to the preservation of states' rights but it eventually found a *modus vivendi* with the *Reich*. A new generation of party leaders was emerging before 1914, whose views had not been formed in the *Kulturkampf*. They worked for the full integration of Catholics in German society but the legacy of the past was hard to overcome. The Roman Catholics, Socialists and Liberals retained their own anniversaries and special celebrations alongside those sponsored by the state, for example the anniversaries of the 1848 revolutions, May Day and the Day of the

Commune. The Socialists officially boycotted Sedan Day festivities and Socialists and Progressives publicly distanced themselves from the 'national' pageantry of 1913. These 'out' groups also maintained a lively separate association life, youth groups, sporting clubs, cultural and recreational movements and so on, often indulging in the same activities as middle-class groups but with a very different ideological motivation.[44] This polarization further symbolized the persistence of 'alternative Germanies' and the growing polarization of society, which was one of the most visible trends in post-unification Germany. In addition other government policies tended to negate the integrative effects of official nationalism.

In 1879, in a radical change of direction, Bismarck abandoned his 'alliance' with the National Liberals and refounded the *Reich* in co-operation with the Conservatives and Centre Party. This 'alliance of steel and rye', bringing together heavy industry and large-scale agriculture, was symbolized in the abandonment of Free Trade and the introduction of protective tariffs on certain foods and manufactured goods, described as 'for the protection of national work'. This healed the split in the Prussian Conservative party caused by the creation of the *Reich*, in the eyes of most Conservatives a betrayal of Prussia. The Centre Party was won over at the same time by the abandonment of the *Kulturkampf* and changes in the arrangements under which the *Reich* was financed to give, on paper, greater control to the states, the Frankenstein Clause. Although the Centre became a mass party, with strong support among Catholic workers, it remained conservative, reflecting the views of its leaders and clerical, rural and middle-class voters.[45] This alliance remained the basis of the whole political system for the remainder of the *Reich*'s existence.

One reason for the government's move to Protectionism was Bismarck's desire to end dependence on parliamentary taxation and to raise more *Reich* revenues from indirect sources. Traditionally the Prussian state had played an important part in the economy but these tariffs, introduced for political and social rather than purely economic reasons, were different in character from those of the early nineteenth century, which had been designed to protect infant industries. After 1873 Germany followed the majority of other European states in the pursuit of economic nationalism, the

[44]See: W.K. Blessing, 'The cult of monarchy and the workers' movement in imperial Germany' and G.A. Ritter, 'Workers' Culture in Imperial Germany. Problems and Points of Departure for Research', *J.Cont.H.* 13 (1978), pp. 165–89 and 357–75; H. McLeod, 'Protestantism and the Working Class in Imperial Germany', *Eur. Stud. Rev* 12 (1982), pp. 323–44; R.J. Evans, 'Politics and the Family. Social Democracy and the Working-Class Family in Theory and Practice before 1914', in R.J. Evans and W.R. Lee (eds.), *The German Family* (1981), pp. 256–88.
[45]M.L. Anderson, *Windhorst. A Political Biography* (Oxford, 1981).

belief that the economy must be isolated in order to protect it, but the German tariffs also implied that the interests of one part of German society, large farmers and traditional heavy industry, were of greater national importance than those of others and that the welfare of one group must be protected even at the cost of other groups.

The move led to a great debate on what was more in the 'national' interest, free trade or protectionism. This 'national neo-mercantilism' was important in convincing conservative groups that a powerful united Germany was of value to them and that the interests of large-scale agriculture and traditional heavy industries were the same as German national interests. It also led to a major division in the Liberal movement, which after 1881 entered a period of fragmentation and weakness. As a consequence, the organized Liberal movement became very weak.[46] In 1888 Ludwig Bamberger bewailed the fact that the national cause had been usurped by Junkers and reactionaries, 'the laughing heirs of the national movement'. Liberal nationalism did not disappear. Although some Liberals did not abandon their hopes of turning Germany into a Liberal state, increasingly they saw Germany's future in commercial expansion and the acquisition of a world empire. They wanted Germany to imitate Britain and also to offer young Germans challenge and adventure outside the army. One of the arguments put forward in favour of a German navy was that its officer corps, unlike that of the army, would be open to middle-class recruits. They found consolation in Germany's capitalist economic structure, the Navy Laws and the creation of a uniform civil law code in 1900. The Liberals' weakness should not be exaggerated. They retained a power base in municipal government and some of the states, but their freedom of action there was limited. In 1880 the more radical wing of the National Liberal Party broke away, four years later to join the Progressives in the Liberalist Party (*Deutsche Freisinnige Partei*), a very fluid and unstable coalition, while the remaining National Liberals became increasingly conservative and supported the prevailing order.

Another variant of nationalism was found in the growing German Socialist movement. Its starting point was the destruction of the Bismarckian state and its aim the building of the first Socialist state in Europe on German soil. A powerful Germany would thus become the basis for the world triumph of Socialism. The creation

[46]Sheehan, *German Liberalism*, section VI, and 'Political Leadership in the German *Reichstag* 1871–1918', *Am.H.R.* 74 (1968), pp. 511–28; S. Zucker, *Ludwig Bamberger: German Liberal Politician and Social Critic* (Pittsburgh, 1975); J.F. Harris, 'Eduard Lasker and Compromise Liberalism', *JMH* 42 (1970), pp. 342–60; G.R. Mork, 'Bismarck and the Capitulation of German Liberalism', *JMH* 43 (1971), pp. 59–75.

of the *Reich* was a great disappointment to many Socialists, who had envisaged the achievement of national unity as a progressive step. In January 1871 many leaders of the Marxist wing of the party in Prussia were in prison as subversives and the leader of the Lassallean wing, J.B. Schweitzer, resigned soon after in disgust, believing, like Bamberger, that the national cause had been usurped by reactionaries. In Socialist political writing the *Reich* was explicitly referred to as a class state run by the East Elbian *Junkers*. The Socialist working class was never integrated into the new German state. In 1875 the Lassallean and Marxist wings came together to form a single party, at first known as the Socialist Workers' Party of Germany (*Sozialistische Arbeiterpartei Deutschlands*) and later the SPD (*Sozialdemokratische Partei Deutschlands*) on the basis of the Gotha Programme. It rejected revolutionary and terrorist methods, restricting itself to parliamentary opposition, campaigning and organizing the workers, but it never accepted Bismarck's *Reich*. For them *Volk* meant the working class, not the middle class or the nation. In January 1890 William II wrote *Suggestions for the improvement of the position of the workers*, in which he concluded that the problem could be solved by charity and love of one's neighbour and that knowledge of the tenets of Christianity would stop the workers demanding things. The Kaiser's initial hopes of integrating them through the power of his personality and a welfare state, the so-called 'Social Empire', were soon abandoned and by 1895 he was publicly speaking of them as 'a mob of traitors' and a 'gang of people not worthy of the name German'. The ambivalent attitude towards the national state seen among Socialists before 1871 continued after the creation of the *Reich.* Nationalism continued to be seen as a bourgeois device to distract the workers from the pursuit of their true interests. The SPD adhered to the idea of Socialist internationalism, for example by supporting international peace efforts, opposing militarism and by a proposal, never taken seriously, that the artificial language *Volapük* should become the party language of all Socialists. At the same time the SPD accepted Germany as an economic unit, especially after the introduction of tariffs in 1879 and the beginnings of welfare-state legislation, by which Bismarck hoped to seduce the workers from Socialism. The failure of 'official nationalism' to integrate the working-class movement was obvious. The SPD supported greater centralization of government and a weakening or elimination of the states but remained ambivalent towards the national question. There were growing divisions between the reformist and radical wings of the party before 1914. Eventually the Second International postponed the solution of the national question until a Socialist revolution had cleared the decks.

In spite of their efforts, the Socialists were never able to offer an alternative political vision with the same appeal as nationalism. Other attempts were made to reconcile the workers to the new Germany. These included the Christian Social movement of the court chaplain Adolf Stöcker, set up in 1878, which tried to use anti-Semitism, and the National Social League (*Nationalsoziale Verein*), associated with the Liberal imperialist Friedrich Naumann.[47] The League offered a combination of social reform and imperial expansion as the basis for a non-Marxist national workers' party, which might give German Liberalism a new mass basis to resist domination by conservative forces. These attempts to reconcile the irreconcilable failed.

External targets could also be used in attempts to achieve national integration: Bismarck himself employed the tactic of using foreign policy crises to defuse internal problems.[48] On several occasions he deliberately created war-scares to mobilize support for the government. It was perhaps in German foreign policy that the German government's predicament was most clearly manifested. David Calleo has made the perceptive assessment that Germany was not uniquely aggressive, only uniquely inconvenient, as a corrective to the view that Germany deliberately unhinged the balance of power in Europe and planned a European war.[49] The creation of a new great power in Central Europe had an inevitable impact on the continental state system, even had Germany remained totally passive. It proved impossible to maintain Bismarck's fiction that Germany was 'satiated'. At the congresses of Berlin in 1878 and 1886 Germany could act as an honest broker, encouraging French and British expansion in Africa and Austro-Hungarian penetration of the Balkans. This was the policy of satiation at work but there was a limit to how long it could last. Even before Bismarck's resignation, the fundamental flaws in his foreign policy calculations were becoming clear. It proved impossible to keep Austria-Hungary and Russia together in an alliance as their Balkan rivalry grew. In spite of William II's pledge of 'Nibelung loyalty', the German–Austrian alliance was occasionally very stressed, for example during the Bosnian crisis of 1908, but Germany had no other reliable ally. Initially Germany had no direct interest in the

[47]M. Zimmermann, 'A Road not Taken. F. Naumann's Attempt at a Modern German Nationalism', *J. Cont. H.* 17 (1982), pp. 689–708.
[48]R. Langhorne, *The Collapse of the Concert of Europe. International Politics 1890–1914* (Basingstoke, 1981); I. Geiss, *German Foreign Policy 1871–1914* (1976); L.L. Farrar, *Arrogance and Anxiety. The Ambivalence of German Power 1848–1914* (Iowa City, 1981); W.J. Mommsen, 'Domestic Factors in German Foreign Policy before 1914', in Sheehan, *Imperial Germany*, pp. 223–68.
[49]D. Calleo, *The German Problem Reconsidered* (Cambridge, 1978), p. 56.

Balkans, as shown by Bismarck's description of Austria as a rotting galleon and the warnings of Tschirschky, the German ambassador in Vienna from 1907 to 1916, that Germany should not tie herself too closely to the decaying Habsburg Empire. After 1900, with the failure of *Weltpolitik* and the rise of *Mitteleuropa*, a scheme for a large German-dominated common market in Central Europe, Germany acquired a very real interest in the Ottoman Empire, which it saw as a valuable target for German economic and political influence.[50] After his appointment as chancellor in 1908, Bethmann-Hollweg saw Germany's future in a much stronger link with Austria-Hungary. When Germany began to seek a colonial empire for herself, the strategy of diverting French ambitions from a war of revenge against Germany to overseas expansion looked increasingly threadbare.

After Bismarck's fall Germany's foreign policy began to appear increasingly aimless and to be moving in a world of slogans rather than concrete aims.[51] Germany had no coherent foreign policy. The *Mitteleuropa* scheme was a modernized version of the Seventy-Million *Reich* of the 1840s and revived old and seductive dreams of Germany's civilizing mission in south-eastern Europe. *Weltpolitik* or social imperialism, perhaps designed to offer a counter-utopia to that promised by the Socialists, turned into a truculent, bombastic and vacillating foreign policy which seemed to have as its only aim a spectacular assertion of German power. The actual gains Germany made were tiny and resulted not from German power but from a temporary combination of circumstances in international relations. Bülow's attempts to secure better relations with Russia in the late 1890s as part of *Weltpolitik* failed, as did Bethmann's approaches to Britain when Germany returned to a more Continental strategy. Again the Emperor did not help. He was pro-Russian and anti-Russian, pro-British and anti-British by turns and was strongly influenced by anti-Russian favourites like Philip Eulenburg. It was assumed that Germany had a right to be consulted on and to participate in all great decisions from the suppression of the Boxer Rising in China to the disposition of colonies and spheres of influence in Africa, not as an 'honest broker' as under Bismarck but as a Great Power. Bülow's policy of the 'Free Hand', to make Germany the universal arbitrator, was an illusion while Germany was pursuing her own expansionist ambitions.[52]

[50]R.J. Crampton, *The Hollow Detente. Anglo-German Relations in the Balkans 1911–14* (1979), esp. chap. 2.
[51]L. Dehio, 'Thoughts on Germany's mission 1900–1918', in *Germany and World Politics in the Twentieth Century* (1959), pp. 72–108.

Many in Germany viewed a war as inevitable and desirable as they accepted the government's line that their country was surrounded by jealous enemies determined to confine her growth. It was Germany's duty to break out of this iron collar of encirclement at the time most suitable to her. Anti-foreign feeling, concentrated at different times against Britain, France and Russia,[53] was stirred up. In reality it was Germany's own blundering policy, for example in the two Moroccan crises of 1905 and 1911, which was uniting her neighbours against her. In 1911 Germany intervened in Morocco in the hope of exploding the Anglo-French entente but instead found herself isolated and her potential enemies in an even closer relationship. This was seen on the Right as a humiliating blow to German prestige and produced vocal calls for more military power to ensure that Germany woud not be pushed around again. Although it would be going too far to claim that the German government deliberately engineered the outbreak of a European war in 1914,[54] there is evidence that the crisis was not unwelcome, offering as it did the chance to shelve pressing internal problems and the possibility of a rapid victory to restore the government's prestige. The official press in the months before July 1914 took an increasingly chauvinistic line. This was part of the government's campaign to discredit the SPD but it has also been seen as psychological

[52]Calleo, *The German Problem Reconsidered*, pp. 28, 50–1 has interesting things to say about the rather blunt style of German diplomacy. Basically, it lacked the hypocrisy which enabled other expansionist powers like France and Britain to dress up their ambition in the clothes of principle. The French revolution, though it turned into imperialism, left behind a legacy of some value, and the same could be said of the British Empire. It is hard to think of anything of value left behind by the two German attempts to win world-power status.

[53]An interesting example of this, the *Deutsche Rundschau* (German Review), has been studied in R. Fuhrmann, *Die Orientalische Frage, das 'Panslawistisch-Chauvinistische Lager' und das Zuwarten auf Krieg und Revolution* (Frankfurt, 1975). This influential nationalist literary and political review was responsible for presenting a consistently hostile view of Russia to its readership in the years before 1914.

[54]J. Joll, *The Origins of the First World War* (1984), p. 119: 'A detailed examination of the political and strategic decisions taken in the crisis suggests that the motives of statesmen and generals were far less rational and well thought-out than the view that they deliberately embarked on war as a way out of their insoluble domestic political and social problems would suggest.' A lively debate on German foreign policy before 1914 was initiated by the publication in 1961 of Fritz Fischer's *Griff nach der Weltmacht*. The sharp reaction provoked by Fischer's views, including accusations of a lack of patriotism, was itself an interesting comment on the prevalence of nationalist attitudes in some sections of the German population or, perhaps, in the German press and academic Establishment. Useful accounts of this can be found in J.C.G. Röhl, *1914. Delusion or Design?* (1973); J.A. Moses, *The Politics of Illusion: the Fischer Controversy in German Historiography* (1975); P.M. Kennedy, *The Rise of the Anglo-German Antagonism* (1980); H.W. Koch (ed.), *The Origins of the First World War* (2nd edn, Basingstoke, 1984); W.J. Mommsen, 'The Debate on German War Aims', *J.Cont.H.* 1 (1966), pp. 47–72; M.R. Gordon, 'Domestic Conflict and the Origins of the First World War. The British and German Cases', *JMH* 46 (1974), pp. 191–226. Fischer's works are available in translation: *Germany's Aims in the First World War* (1967), *World Power or Decline* (New York, 1974) and *War of Illusions. German Policies from 1911 to 1914* (1975).

preparation for war.[55] The German army had long been pushing for a preemptive strike, arguing that improvements being made in the French and Russian armies would soon make it impossible for Germany to win, though in terms of planning, collaboration with Austria-Hungary, the *Reich*'s major ally, and co-ordination between the army and the navy, Germany was quite unready for war in 1914.

When war came it was welcomed by many Germans and it was accepted by many as a defensive struggle forced on Germany by jealous enemies. Speakers from most parties in the *Reichstag* debate on 4 August 1914 blamed the war on Russia and France. In spite of deep divisions in the movement, the Socialists in the *Reichstag*, with few exceptions, very reluctantly voted for war credits to support a war enforced on Germany by her enemies.[56] The party had long been moving towards a policy of *ad-hoc* co-operation with the government following the victory of revisionism and its leaders saw a demonstration of patriotism as a means of proving its reliability. Although such views were not universally shared by the rank and file of the party, the Kaiser's proclamation of the *Burgfrieden* (internal unity) in August 1914 probably reflected a more genuine national unity than had existed since 1871. Sadly, it was to prove very short-lived.

[55]Even art critics saw war as an answer to problems. Walter Schulte von Brühl in his *Reflexions on German Contemporary Painting* (Leipzig, 1881) took the view that German art was in a mess because of political divisions. The only things which might rescue Germany from the deepest abyss would be a great war of nations or a violent *coup d'état*.
[56]G. Haupt, *Socialism and the Great War: the Collapse of the Second International* (Oxford, 1972), chap. 11; J. Howorth, 'The Left in France and Germany, Internationalism and War: A Dialogue of the Deaf', in E. Cahm and C. Fisera (eds.), *Socialism and Nationalism in Contemporary Europe 1848–1945* II (Nottingham, 1978), pp. 81–100.

7

The Lost Children: German Nationalism in Austria 1866–1914

With the unification of 1871 millions of Austrian Germans found themselves excluded from the German national state. A study of German nationalism should include a brief examination of this, the largest German minority outside the *Reich*.[1] Until 1866 the Germans living in the Habsburg Monarchy regarded themselves as part of the German nation. Austria was the largest German state and the Habsburgs, with their traditional possession of the old imperial title, were seen as the leading German dynasty. The Germans were the most advanced of the nationalities in the Habsburg Monarchy and their language and way of life enjoyed high status. Many towns in otherwise non-German areas, such as Prague and Brünn/Brno, were centres of German culture and engines of Germanization. With some justification the Austrian Germans saw themselves as the *Staatsvolk*, the state nation. It was easier for men of talent to raise themselves into the aristocracy in Austria than in most other German states but the process involved a kind of de-nationalization. The ruling class outside Hungary, Dalmatia and Galicia was Germanized, the result of a long natural process by which ambitious people in many parts of the Monarchy adopted the German language and culture as a means of raising themselves. German-speakers predominated in the civil service, the officer corps and the higher ranks of the clergy, though these people

[1]General works: J.W. Mason, *The Dissolution of the Austro-Hungarian Empire 1867–1918* (1985); R. Pearson, *National Minorities in E. Europe 1848–1945* (Basingstoke, 1983); R. Okey, *Eastern Europe 1740–1980* (1982); R.A. Kann, *The Multinational Empire. Nationalism and National Reform in the Habsburg Monarchy 1848–1918* (2 vols., New York, 1950) and *A History of the Habsburg Empire* (Berkeley, 1974); C.A. Macartney, *The Habsburg Empire 1790–1918* (1969), *National States and National Minorities* (1934) and *The House of Austria. The Later Phase 1790–1918* (Edinburgh, 1978); A.J. May, *The Hapsburg Monarchy 1867–1914* (Cambridge, Mass., 1969) and *The Break-up of the Hapsburg Monarchy 1914–8* (2 vols., Philadelphia, 1966); A. Gerschenkron, *An Economic Spurt that Failed* (Princeton, 1977); E. Crankshaw, *The Fall of the House of Habsburg* (1963); S.A.M. Adshead, 'The Genesis of the Imperial Mind', in M. Francis (ed.), *The Viennese Enlightenment* (1985), pp. 15–39; K. von Klemperer, *Ignaz Seipel. Christian Statesman in a Time of Crisis* (Princeton, 1972).

On the Austro-Germans: A.F. Whiteside, *The Socialism of Fools. Georg von Schönerer and Austrian Pan-Germanism* (Berkeley, 1975); F.L. Carsten, *Fascist Movements in Austria from Schönerer to Hitler* (1977); W.H. Hubbard, 'Politics and Society in the Central European City: Graz, Austria 1861–1918', *Canadian Journal of History* 5 (1970), pp. 25–45; S.G. Konirsch, 'Constitutional Aspects of the Struggle between Czechs and Germans in the Austro-Hungarian Monarchy', *JMH* 27 (1955), pp. 231–61.

tended to see themselves as above nationality and embodied the Austrian state idea. Such attitudes were restricted to a socially very limited group, which was shrinking steadily in size in the later nineteenth century as a result of the rise of nationalism.

The Austrian Germans were in no sense a homogenous group and, although German nationalism won an increasing following among them after 1871, they remained socially and politically divided. The majority in the provinces of Vorarlberg, Tyrol, Salzburg, Upper and Lower Austria, Styria and Carinthia were conservative Catholic peasants. Provincialism was powerful and the influence of the clergy strong. There was no tradition of serfdom in Tyrol and Vorarlberg and the ending of labour services in 1848 generated great loyalty to the crown in the other provinces. In cities like Prague and Vienna the Liberal bourgeois element was predominant among the Germans, though the last quarter of the nineteenth century saw the political mobilization of the urban lower middle class and workers by Socialism and other movements. The majority of Jews in the cities saw themselves as German. In the northern parts of Bohemia another kind of German was found, urban workers in the coal-mining and textile industries. They looked towards Saxony rather than Vienna.

Before 1848 there was little to distinguish the Austrian Germans from many of their neighbours in southern Germany, sharing as they did anti-Prussian sentiments and the Catholic faith. In 1848 the first serious questions were asked about Austria's role in Germany in the course of the debate on *Kleindeutschland* and *Grossdeutschland*. As witnessed by the growing Austro-Prussian rivalry in the 1850s and 1860s, Austria clearly still regarded herself as a German state and the Austro-Germans had no need to ask searching questions about their nationality or future.

The defeat of 1866 was a terrible blow, especially to the Austro-German Liberals, further compounded by the events of 1870–1. There seemed no hope that Austria might join the new *Reich*. It is significant that, of all the nationalities in the Monarchy, the Germans were the first to produce a political party whose programme included the dissolution of the Habsburg state. Political changes in Austria resulting from the country's defeats were also very ominous to the Austrian Germans. In 1867 Francis-Joseph could no longer resist demands from the Magyars for autonomy and, by the Compromise (*Ausgleich*) of that year, total control over internal Hungarian affairs was vested in a parliament in Budapest. Only the armed forces, foreign relations and finance remained common to the whole Monarchy. All imperial protection of the non-Magyar nationalities in Hungary, which the Hungarian Liberals had refused to accept as proper nations in 1848, was abandoned. After the suppression of the Hungarian revolt in 1849 Vienna had sent in a large number of German and Czech officials, the so-called Bach Hussars, to run the country. They were very unpopular indeed and most were pensioned off after 1867. This was one reason for the increasingly oppressive policy of enforced Magyarization against the non-Magyar nationalities in Hungary after 1875 — later to become significant in the Austrian half of the Monarchy as a model for German nationalists there.

The Hungarian ruling class retained an influence in the politics of the whole Austro-Hungarian state completely disproportionate to their size for the remainder of the Monarchy's existence. They were consistently hostile to any attempt by Austria to become reinvolved in German affairs and saw the foundation of the *Reich* in 1871 as a guarantee of their position. In an attempt to place controls on the Emperor, in case he should be tempted to reverse the *Ausgleich*, the Magyars insisted that the Austrian half of the Dual Monarchy should have a constitution. Under this the powers of the parliament, the *Reichsrat*, were increased, though considerable powers remained with the Emperor and the bureaucracy. The Austrian Germans continued to believe that their language and culture were superior. This added to the resentment felt by other nationalities, which tended to identify the Germans with oppressive government conducted in the German language. The last quarter of the nineteenth century saw a general loss of German cultural influence in eastern and south-eastern Europe, where German had long been a kind of *lingua franca*, caused by events in Austria and by the German government's maltreatment of its Polish minority.

Between 1859 and 1879 the German-speaking Liberals occupied a position of growing importance in Austrian political life as the government looked to them as allies. In the 1850s a policy of promoting economic growth involved heavy government investment, the fostering of chambers of commerce and the encouragement of middle-class enterprise. Under the pressure of foreign policy defeats, political concessions had to be added and gradually the crown shifted from reliance on the nobility and the federalist 'Feudals' to the middle classes. The government's policy was based on co-operation with the 'dominant' nationalities, the Germans, Magyars, Poles and Italians (in Dalmatia) to control the 'subordinate' peoples, the Czechs, Serbs, Slovaks, Ukrainians and so on. Before 1873 the Austrian *Reichsrat* was made up of delegates from the assemblies of the various kingdoms and provinces of the Empire, in most of which the Germans, thanks to property franchises, predominated. During the period of rivalry with Prussia, it was in the government's interest to emphasize the German nature of Austria. In 1860 urban self-government and concessions to the

Jews were introduced. In 1861 Schmerling, a German Liberal, was appointed prime minister. His party, the Constitutional Party, favoured a centralized state with a strong parliament. Although there was no unity on the nationality question, a majority of the Liberals saw the whole problem as a product of backwardness, a device by which the old regime preserved its power by making the people see the Germans rather than the nobility and bureaucracy as their enemies. Economic growth, the universal acceptance of railways, gasworks and free enterprise, would, they believed, convince everyone of the virtues of the German way of life. The German language would be accepted as a vehicle of progress and improvement. Free enterprise, equality of opportunity and a few cultural concessions to the minor nationalities would, according to this view, take all the sting out of non-German nationalism.

After 1871 the Austrian Germans became a minority in a state beginning to lose its German character. Francis-Joseph embarked on a policy of juggling the various peoples of his empire in order to preserve as much freedom of action as possible for himself, especially in foreign policy. The so-called Golden Age of the Austro-German Liberals lasted until 1879. They were a brilliant class, combining business and cultural skills, but their predominance in the *Reichsrat* was maintained by a property franchise. As in Prussia in the 1860s, a fancy franchise gave them an unreal notion of their own power. Their deeply rooted anti-clericalism also made it hard to win a mass following among the strongly Catholic population of the rural areas and small towns. Austria was hit hard by the recession after 1873, which, as in Germany, damaged the Liberals' position. In reality they depended on the Emperor's support. In 1878 they made the mistake of attacking Austria-Hungary's occupation of Bosnia and Herzegovina, which brought several million more Slavs into the Empire. In 1879 Francis-Joseph broke with them and constructed the government headed by Count Edward Taaffe known as the Iron Ring, which lasted until 1890.[2]

Taaffe based his government on an informal coalition of groups in the *Reichsrat*, including the German Clericals, who were anti-Liberal and opposed centralization of government at the cost of the provinces, and certain conservative Slav parties. The continued support of these groups had to be bought by concessions, some of which intensified developments in the 1880s which were profoundly worrying to the Germans. Taaffe was anxious to win the votes of the Czechs, who had returned to the *Reichsrat* in 1879 after boycotting it since 1871 when the government, under pressure from the German political leaders, withdrew a promise to give Bohemia

[2]W.A. Jenks, *Austria under the Iron Ring 1879–93* (Charlottesville, 1965).

and Moravia an *Ausgleich* on Hungarian lines. In order to secure Czech support Taaffe issued language decrees, that is ordinances without parliamentary ratification. These, in particular the ordinances of 1881, which laid down that the 'internal administration' in Bohemia must be bilingual, were seen as threatening by the Germans. The 'external administration', that is relations between government and governed, was already bilingual to cater for people who spoke only Czech or German. The new rules laid down that the internal business of the Bohemian government would be conducted in both languages. As so few Germans bothered to learn Czech and almost all educated Czechs spoke German, this meant, in effect, that Czechs would take over the government and rule Germans, an unacceptable situation. This was reinforced by new decrees in 1897 that all civil servants in Bohemia had to be bilingual. This caused outrage among the Germans and after one year the decrees were withdrawn, which outraged the Czechs. The language issue rapidly developed into a major cause of hostility between nationalities. The increasing use of Czech in the education system and the division of the university of Prague, the oldest German university, into two in 1882 were other sources of grievance.

Demographic and social changes made the Germans' predicament worse. From about 1880 they represented a declining percentage of the total population of Austria-Hungary. The economic growth of the 1860s and early 1870s led to the rise of a substantial economic middle class among the non-German nationalities, especially the Czechs. In Bohemia there was a movement of the centres of economic activity from the German fringes of what was later to be called the Sudetenland to the Czech centre. The expansion of industry produced considerable migrations of non-Germans from the countryside into urban centres previously solidly German, for example of Czechs into Prague and Slovenes into Graz. Once the trickle of immigration became a flood, assimilation of the immigrants to the German language and way of life, which had taken place for centuries, ceased. The population figures for Prague are illuminating. In 1856 there were about 73,000 Germans and 60,000 Czechs; in 1886 30,000 Germans and 150,000 Czechs; in 1910 19,000 Germans and 200,000 Czechs. As the centre of the city became Czech, the Germans moved out into the suburbs, where they were squeezed between the Czech countryside and the Czech city. They became a minority on land they had long regarded as their own. The Czech masses were quickly politicized and given political, economic and national leadership by the emerging middle class. Demands for educational and cultural concessions to take account of the new ethnic realities rapidly appeared.

The 1890s saw the emergence of mass politics in Austria, with new political parties deliberately courting a mass electorate. Continuing political instability led the government to extend the suffrage in the hope of finding a base among a peasantry believed still to be conservative and monarchist. In 1897 the property qualification was lowered to admit virtually the whole male population to the franchise and in 1906 an equal universal male suffrage was introduced, though, significantly, the seats were apportioned by nationality. The strategy was probably adopted too late as it also enfranchised the urban population, already politicized and often nationalist. A new style of politics emerged, described by Carl Schorske as 'politics in a new sharper key'.[3] The older more patrician and gentle style of Austrian politics was replaced by a strident and violent tone.[4] A new generation of political leaders used mass meetings, demonstrations and violence to put pressure on the government, including the deliberate paralysing of the *Reichsrat* by *Obstruktion*, orchestrated philibusters, interruptions and violence.

Among the Germans a pioneer of such tactics was the Pan-German Movement, which began in 1879 among students and academics and in gymnastic clubs. The first Vienna Gymnastic Association was established in 1861; its flag, in the German national colours of red, black and gold, was ritually dipped in the Baltic. In 1885 the German Gymnastic Association was established to unite the movement throughout German Austria and it became a major vehicle of German nationalism. German-speaking students and school pupils were among the earliest supporters of extreme nationalism, at least partly out of fear that their future civil-service posts would be lost to Slavs unless they learned hard 'inferior' languages. There was also resentment of Jewish students, who, as in Germany, tended to be over-represented in the faculties of law and medicine. Support among such groups for extreme German nationalism increased in spite of strongly expressed official disapproval. An organized German nationalist movement began among German-speaking Liberals after 1871, with centres in Bohemia, Vienna and Graz. In 1882 the Pan-German People's Party was organized under the leadership of Georg von Schönerer. Its policy was set out in the Linz programme of September 1882, which combined Liberal economic and social policies, including anti-clericalism, with enforced Germanization of minorities living on soil regarded as historically German. The basic point of the programme was a radical

---

[3]C.E. Schorske, 'Politics in a New Key: An Austrian Trio', in *Fin-de-Siècle Vienna* (Cambridge, 1981), pp. 116—80; W.J. McGrath, 'Student Radicalism in Vienna', *J.Cont.H.* 2 (1967), pp. 183—201 and *Dionysian Art and Populist Politics in Austria* (New Haven, 1974), part III: 'In search of a poetic politics'.
[4]Not all Austrian Germans were drawn into this: J. Baernreither, *Fragments of a Political Diary 1897—1914* (1930), the diary of a progressive Bohemian German.

reorganization of Austria-Hungary in order to preserve a closed totally German block of territory which could, in future, pass into a revived *Grossdeutschland*. This was to include Bohemia and Moravia but it was not clear what would happen to areas of the province of Carniola with large Slovene populations. It played on anti-Slav, anti-Semitic and anti-Catholic prejudices in its appeals. In 1885 a new point was added, that Jewish influence should be eliminated from all aspects of public life. Growing anti-Semitism was reflected in the foundation of a number of Reform Associations to protect German economic interests, which usually took the form of boycotts of Jewish businesses. The Austrian Pan-Germans had close links with their fellows in the German *Reich*, who tried in vain to move the German government to intervene diplomatically on their behalf. Some German diplomats around the turn of the century speculated about the dissolution of the Monarchy as a result of internal nationality disputes and discussed the possibility that Germany might take over its German areas. The councillor in the German embassy in Vienna from 1895 to 1899, Prince Lichnowsky, was sympathetic to the German minority but, in reality, the German government had no interest in acquiring some 12 million Austro-Germans, which would have produced a Catholic majority in the *Reich* and, so it was argued, threatened a revival of religious strife, as in the Holy Roman Empire. The power of the German state, not sympathy for members of the German nation, dominated policy-making. The Austro-German Dual Alliance, formed in 1879, lasted until 1918 and became the foundation of the German alliance system.[5] German interests required a strong Austria-Hungary as an ally not a state torn apart by nationality disputes. In addition, Germany was not willing to offend Emperor Francis-Joseph by giving support to extreme German nationalists.

Schönerer successfully radicalized Austrian politics but his party remained very much a minority movement and he continued to draw his main support from academic youth, among whom anti-Semitic and *völkisch* ideas became more deeply rooted than in Germany. To these was added a fierce hostility towards Slav nationalism. His movement fell apart when he was imprisoned in 1888 after involvement in a violent attack on the offices of the *Neue Wiener Tageblatt* newspaper. The role of main standard-bearer of German interests in Austria passed to Karl Lueger's Christian Social Party, founded in 1889. This differed in important ways

[5]It is interesting that Bismarck, in persuading William I to agree to the Dual Alliance, which the Emperor thought might weaken Germany's link with Russia, used a nationalist argument, claiming that the alliance would appeal to German national sensibilities: H.F. Young, *Prince Lichnowsky and the Great War* (Athens, Ga., 1977), pp. 11–16.

from Schönerer's movement. It was not an overtly nationalist movement, though it drew its main support from Germans. It was more loyal to the Habsburg dynasty and the Austrian state and did not have its roots in the Liberal movement. It was a mass Catholic party, similar in some ways to the German Centre Party, but was much later in appearing. More successfully than the Pan-German party, it combined nationalism with the exploitation of economic and social grievances. It was also able to mobilize working-class anti-Semitism, which did not exist to the same extent in Germany. Lueger avoided Schönerer's anti-Catholicism, symbolized in the motto *Los von Rom* (Away from Rome), and the proposal that the Austro-Germans should convert *en masse* to Lutheranism as a badge of their solidarity with Germany. The Christian Socials were thus able to win over the mass of Catholic German peasants in the rural provinces as well as the Viennese *Mittelstand*. A skilled populist politician, Lueger became mayor of Vienna and was responsible for important municipal improvement projects. The Christian Social Party was strong in German areas that were seen as particularly 'threatened' by alien immigration – Bohemia, Vienna and Carinthia – but it also spread to solidly German areas. In 1909 the Salzburg and Vorarlberg parliaments enacted laws making German the only legal language in the provinces, although there was no possibility of any other language striking root there. Lueger's movement strongly influenced the young Adolf Hitler, who adopted not only its anti-Semitic attitudes but also its political style, which, like Schönerer's, was based on mass mobilization.[6]

A more direct link can be demonstrated between National Socialism and working-class nationalism in Austria than in Germany. Although the Social Democratic Party retained the support of a majority of Austro-German workers, other movements won a substantial following in areas where German national interests were seen as threatened. The Social Democrats had no real solution to the nationality problem. Before the Socialist party conference of 1888 in Hainfeld, the party leaders saw the nationality problem as a matter of culture and employment, of concern only to the petty bourgeoisie or deliberately stirred up by capitalists to divide the workers and divert their attention from the class struggle. As the membership grew and became more multi-national, it became difficult to maintain this approach. In 1897 the party was federalized but nationality disputes continued. In 1905 the party was divided into six separate national sections, the only way of preventing the complete break-up of the movement on national lines. Within the

[6]There is some irony in the fact that both Schönerer and Lueger have been celebrated in an Austrian postage stamp series as pioneers of Austrian nationalism.

German-speaking sections relics of old attitudes of national superiority persisted: some continued to offer German culture and assimilation to a German way of life as a means of removing the nationality problem.

German Socialist leaders like Karl Renner and Otto Bauer made serious attempts to reconcile nationalism and Socialism. In his *The Right of National Self-Determination with Special Reference to Austria* Renner attacked nationalism in Germany and bewailed the fact that a united Germany had not become the instrument of German culture but a weapon of the *Junkers*.[7] The cultural and political ideas of the nation had been debased into racial fanaticism, Teutonism, ridiculous language-purity campaigns, Wotan worship 'and other such tasteless games'. Renner and Bauer put forward schemes for a democratic confederation of nationalities enjoying total cultural freedom, the 'United States of Greater Austria'. Unlike many Marxists, they recognized the historical validity of nation. They held that true national emancipation was possible only through Socialism. Under Socialism the working class would be admitted fully to national culture, a part of their heritage from which they had been long excluded. They made a serious attempt to reconcile nationalism and Socialism but their principle of extra-territorial personality, which saw nationality as a cultural matter, was of very limited applicability in Austria. A temporary *modus vivendi* between Czechs and Germans was found in the 1905 Moravian settlement based on clearly defined minority rights in mixed areas but it would have been difficult to apply this solution universally. It failed to appreciate the problem of two nationalities claiming the same piece of soil, as was the case in Bohemia.

Because there was a more visible enemy, the non-Germans, *völkisch* ideas had a wider following and appeared in a more virulent form in Austria than in Germany, gaining support among sections of the working class as well as the *Mittelstand*. In 1893 the German National Workers' league was founded in Eger in the German fringe of Bohemia to mobilize working-class resistance against Czech encroachments. In 1898 the League of German Employees' and Workers' Associations was established to offer the workers a combination of German nationalism, anti-Semitism, anti-Slavism and Socialism. In August 1918 it changed its name to the German National Socialist Workers' Party (DNSAP), which

[7]Renner's work was published first under a pseudonym in 1902 with the title *The Struggle of the Austrian Nations for the State*. Bauer's work, *The National Question and Social Democracy*, was published in Vienna in 1907. See also A.G. Kogan, 'The Social Democrats and the Conflict of Nationalities in the Habsburg Monarchy', *JMH* 21 (1949), pp. 204–17; J.F.N. Bradley, 'Czech Nationalism and Socialism in 1905', *American Slavic and East European Review* 19 (1960), pp 74–84.

rejected monopoly capitalism, clericalism, the Jews, Marxism and non-Germans. Among the Austro-German lower middle class such ideas found a substantial following and it was in this environment that Adolf Hitler grew up and from it that he drew many of his ideas. He was influenced by the writings of the Austrian German Jörg Lanz von Liebenfels (1874—1954), who gave up being a Cistercian monk in 1899 to found the Order of the New Temple to promote pure Aryanism. He founded and wrote for the journal *Ostara*, which became a vehicle for his ideas and had a large circulation. His crazy theories produced a pseudo-scientific justification for German superiority and anti-Semitism.[8]

Partly as a result of such movements, Austrian life and politics became increasingly polarized on national lines in the years before the outbreak of the world war. Prime minister Badeni resigned in 1898 after his attempts to solve the nationality problem by a policy of balanced concessions, especially on the language issue, had demonstrably failed. Serious nationality riots broke out in several cities in 1897, particularly Prague and Graz, involving mainly students and the lower middle class. In the same year the *Reichsrat* had to be cleared by the police after it dissolved in fist-fights. From then until 1905 it was paralysed by campaigns of *Obstruktion* mounted by the Czechs and Germans. After the 1906 elections German parties controlled 233 seats and the non-Germans 283; the electoral system disproportionately favoured the Germans, as the linguistic census on which it was based was framed in a way designed to maximize the use of the German language. There were over 30 parties in the *Reichsrat* but there was a growing tendency to vote in national blocs. In the election of 1911 the National Union (*Nationalverband*), an alliance of German parties, became the biggest party in the parliament, with only the Christian Socials and Socialists outside it. The Germans were increasingly on the defensive. In 1901 the Czechs asked for 19 Czech-medium schools in Vienna. The city and the province of Lower Austria retaliated by passing laws making German the only legal medium of instruction. Plans for an Italian section in the university of Innsbruck and for Polish courses in Silesian teacher-training colleges had to be dropped in the face of German opposition. There was a battle in mixed areas to push as many as possible of one's nationality into official posts: the civil service, long a bastion of the idea of the Austrian state above nationalities, was thus becoming nationalized. The situation was made much worse by the government's blunders, such as the Zagreb treason trials in 1909 against Slav political

[8]N. Goodrick-Clarke, *The Occult Roots of Nazism* (1986). There is danger in exaggerating the direct influence on Hitler, who had no time for the more extreme manifestations of Aryanism.

leaders, in which it was revealed that much of the state's evidence was forged. International condemnation of Austria as 'the dungeon of nationalities', often based on inadequate knowledge, mounted.[9]

Buffeted on all sides, the Austro-Hungarian government, like its German counterpart, looked increasingly to foreign policy as a means of diverting attention from internal problems. The Hungarians, faced by growing trouble from their subject nationalities, moved closer to the embattled Austro-Germans and pushed for a more assertive policy in the Balkans. When the Sarajevo assassinations happened, they provided the opportunity for a war which, as in Germany and for similar reasons, was welcome to many.[10]

[9]H. and C. Seton-Watson, *The Making of a New Europe. R.W. Seton-Watson and the Last Years of Austria-Hungary* (1981); Kann, *Habsburg Empire*, pp. 448, 457–8; W. Fest, *Peace or Partition. The Habsburg Monarchy and British Policy 1914–1918* (1978).
[10]J. Remak, 'The Healthy Invalid: How Doomed the Habsburg Empire?', *JMH* 41 (1969), pp. 127–43.

8

The Nation Betrayed: The First World War and the Revolution of 1918[1]

After 1918 many Germans looked back to the proclamation of the *Burgfrieden* in August 1914 as a moment of unparalleled national unity and the end of a period of mounting pessimism about Germany's political, economic and military future. Germany's 'brotherhood in arms' with Austria was seen in nationalist circles as a 'Greater German Community of Struggle' (*Grossdeutsche Kampfgemeinschaft*), a reunion of the nation torn apart in 1866. It was later to become the aim of some political leaders to recreate the circumstances of August 1914 on a permanent basis and to enshrine 'the ideas of 1914' in a political and social system. The unity was short-lived and began to break down from 1917. 'National unity' concealed continuing class and other antagonisms. In November 1918 Germany experienced major political changes, traditionally described as a revolution. The Emperor and the German rulers abdicated and Germany became the parliamentary Weimar Republic. The origins of the first German republic in a 'revolution' were to influence strongly the way in which different groups of Germans viewed it and to add to the deep divisions within the nation. The 1920s saw the rise of a powerful new manifestation of nationalism in Germany, the New or Radical Right, from which the National Socialist Party emerged as the most important *völkisch* political movement. In January 1933 Adolf Hitler came to power promising to carry through a 'national revolution', a complete reshaping of German state and society on *völkisch* lines.

When war broke out in August 1914 it was welcomed by the majority of the German people for various reasons.[2] The government and its supporters saw the war as, at worst, an opportunity to shelve internal political and social problems and, at best, a chance to give the prevailing order a huge injection of prestige. The war was a gamble which postponed the resolution of difficulties if it did nothing to solve them. Business interests saw it as an

[1]Basic works: I. Geiss (ed.), *July 1914, the Outbreak of the First World War: Selected Documents* (1967); L.C.F. Turner, *Origins of the First World War* (1970); M. Kitchen, *The Silent Dictatorship* (1976); J. Kocka, *Facing Total War. German Society 1914–1918* (Leamington Spa, 1985); G.D. Feldman, *German Imperialism 1914–1918* (New York, 1972).
[2]The peace movement in Germany was very weak: R. Chickering, *Imperial Germany and a World without War* (Princeton, 1975).

opportunity for economic imperialism. Many in the SPD saw the war as a chance to demonstrate their loyalty, to hasten the democratization of the *Reich* and to weaken the most despotic regime in Europe, Russia, and the leading international capitalist power, Britain, in the process making Germany the spearhead of European Socialism. For extreme German nationalists, the war was a means of demonstrating the superiority of German *Kultur* and of cementing the unity of the *Reich*. Many in the youth movement welcomed war as an escape from the boredom of the bourgeois world and a chance for action, heroism and comradeship. There was also a widespread conviction that the war would be over quickly.[3] Although this soon proved to be an illusion, the expectation of ultimate victory remained high in Germany until the last months of the war.

A great deal of attention has been given to the lavish war aims and expansion plans produced in Germany after August 1914 as part of an examination of Germany's responsibility for the outbreak of war.[4] Their value in that respect is limited but they are very useful in demonstrating developments in German nationalist thinking. As the war progressed a large number of groups, including business and industry, the armed forces, intellectuals and the nationalist pressure groups, jumped on the patriotic bandwagon, seeking to outbid one another in the grandeur of their conceptions for Europe after a German victory. Only a few Socialist and Liberal voices were raised against German expansionism but they were not heard. It appeared that many in the country were thinking in terms of a two-stage war aimed first at winning hegemony in Europe and secondly at making Germany a world power. There were plans for large territorial annexations to west and east to improve Germany's economic and strategic position. One scheme, known as *Mitteleuropa* (Central Europe), envisaged the creation of a great German-dominated customs union, capable of competing with the USA, Russia or the British Empire and including, in various conformations, Scandinavia, the Low Countries, the Balkans and German puppet states in Poland, Lithuania and the Ukraine. The popularity of this notion was increased by the publication in 1915 of Friedrich Naumann's pamphlet *Mitteleuropa*, though some German nationalists were unhappy about the large numbers of Slavs and Catholics to be included in Naumann's union and imperialists resented what they saw as the abandonment of *Weltpolitik* for an exclusively European strategy. During the war Germans began to take a much closer interest in Austria's internal affairs

[3]See L. Farrar, *The Short War Illusion* (Oxford, 1973).
[4]These are examined in detail in the works of F. Fischer: see chap. 6, n. 54.

and there was talk of a permanent close economic and political union between the two states after the war.[5] Austria was also encouraged to take measures to hold back the advance of its Slavs and to restore its Germans to a predominant position, vital if Austria was to act as a Germanic Eastern March (*Ostmark*).[6] The navy had plans for large-scale annexations in Africa in the event of a German victory to produce a huge Central African empire *Mittelafrika*, blocking British plans to dominate the continent. The German government, or the German army which was after 1916 effectively the government, seemed to be dragged along behind such expansionist dreams and the lack of coherent official war aims was reflected in the weakness of German propaganda during the war. While the Allies could claim to be fighting to protect the rights of small nations or to save Europe from Prussian despotism and militarism, Germany was fighting in defence of Germanness (*Deutschheit*) against its enemies.

Serious doubts about Germany's ability to win the war, and the first serious divisions in the nation, appeared in the spring months of 1917. In April the USA entered the war against Germany, which seriously reduced Germany's ability to win, even though it would take time for American resources to reach the fronts. The first major strike of the war took place. The Allies' blockade of Germany hit fuel and food supplies badly. The first food riots occurred in 1916 and an estimated 121,000 died of starvation and its consequences in that year, 260,000 in 1917 and 293,000 in 1918. War weariness was a growing problem. On 16 April 220,000 workers in Berlin and large numbers elsewhere protested in non-violent demonstrations against a reduction in the bread ration. In the Ruhr there was unrest because of unemployment in the coal industry caused by problems in transport and troops had to be called in to restore order. In general the unrest was not politically motivated and the troubles died away when the government announced an increase in the meat ration, raised wages and reduced the working week to 52 hours. The strikes in Leipzig did have a political element, however, as the demonstrators, in addition to demanding higher food and fuel rations, wanted a declaration that the government was ready to conclude a peace without territorial annexations. There was another wave of trouble in the early summer of 1917. In

[5]K.E. Silberstein, *The Troubled Alliance. German—Austrian Relations 1914—17* (Lexington, 1970); J. Koralka, 'Germany's attitude to the national disintegration of Cisleithania (April—October 1918)', *J.Cont.H.* 4/2 (1969), pp. 85—95.

[6]This was put forward in a memorandum given to the Austro-Hungarian foreign minister in Berlin in 1915. It is quoted by B. Sutter, 'Die politische und rechtliche Stellung der Deutschen in Österreich 1848—1918', in A. Wandruszka and P. Urbanitsch (eds.), *Die Habsburgermonarchie* III (Vienna, 1980), p. 324.

Berlin work only resumed in munitions factories when troops moved in and the strike leaders were threatened with imprisonment. In the Ruhr and Upper Silesia considerable coal production was lost and a distinct political note was visible in the demonstrations, with demands for peace and constitutional reforms.[7] The war was beginning to reveal the divisions in the nation. Until 1917 the German workers were remarkably docile and the government was successful in sustaining the war effort, in part by playing on the fears of the German people. Propaganda showing Allied 'plans' to repartition Germany into little states, returning it to the position before unification, was clearly believed to be an effective appeal to German national feeling.[8] Ludendorff's military administration after 1916 followed a pragmatic policy and was quite ready to negotiate with trade unions and grant increased wages if output was maintained. This was to have significant political effects. Inflation was high throughout the war and this hit the living standards of the lower middle classes, whose incomes, unlike those of skilled manual workers, did not keep up and who were more likely to be conscripted as less vital to the economy. This added to *Mittelstand* fears that the despised proletariat was overtaking them in material terms. The yield from investment was also falling. Many also patriotically invested in war loans, which were to become valueless. The impoverishment suffered during the war was to be prolonged after 1918. During the war the 'old' and 'new' *Mittelstand* began to drift apart, the 'old' towards capital and the 'new' towards organized labour to protect their interests. After 1918, however, they both drifted back to the Right.[9]

March saw the first Russian revolution of 1917. At first this was seen as beneficial to Germany's war effort and there were widespread hopes of a separate peace in Eastern Europe. In order to combat Allied attempts to keep Russia in the war, Ludendorff used Lenin and subsidized the Bolsheviks. The events in Russia encouraged opposition in Germany. In June 1917 anti-annexation groups began to coalesce and an interparty committee, drawn from the SPD, the Centre and the Progressive Party, was set up to press for constitutional reform and peace. The leadership of the SPD was increasingly worried by the emergence of a minority breakaway party, the USPD (Independent Social Democratic Party

[7]See John Williams, *The Home Fronts. Britain, France and Germany 1914–18* (1972).
[8]In the Second World War the government was helped to sustain resistance to the end by Allied demands for unconditional surrender and knowledge of the Morgenthau Plan to de-industrialize Germany.
[9]Kocka, *Facing Total War*, pp. 77–113.

of Germany), which seceded in January 1916.[10] The USPD adopted a peace policy and it was beginning to bite deeply into the Majority Socialists' working-class constituency. January 1916 also saw the publication of the first pamphlet of the Spartakus League, from which was to grow the German Communist Party. In June 1916 the SPD introduced a motion in the *Reichstag* rejecting *Mitteleuropa* and an imperialist Greater Germany and calling for the development of 'mutual political and economic relations between the nations, fostered by the extension of democracy, the abolition of secret diplomacy and the removal of customs barriers'. They denied that the common people of any country had willed the war and emphasized their fellow feeling with the sufferings of workers in all belligerent states. This return to the principles of Socialist internationalism was rejected by the *Reichstag* but by the summer of 1917 things were changing. The Centre Party was also beginning to abandon its support for the war. In July 1917 its leader, Matthias Erzberger, formerly a keen annexationist, came out in favour of peace. In a speech in the *Reichstag* on a motion calling for a peace without annexations he said that the Pan-Germans were lunatics and that it would be cheaper to build asylums to confine them than to go on fighting a war which they alone wanted. After the debate the house passed the peace motion with the votes of the SPD, Centre and Progressives, with the Conservatives and National Liberals voting against.

As the peace movement hardened, a distinct nationalist war party began to emerge, symbolizing the deep polarization again splitting the German nation. The pro-war forces came together in the *Vaterlandspartei* (Fatherland Party), headed by Admiral Tirpitz and Wolfgang Kapp, a civil servant. They campaigned for a 'Hindenburg Peace', a victorious peace with territorial gains, and the extension of the Prussian property franchise to *Reichstag* elections. The Fatherland Party never became a mass movement: at its greatest it had about one and a quarter million members, mainly in northeastern Germany and drawn from big business and the officer corps. It was never short of money and was able to set up an Organization for Patriotic Enlightenment, which spread propaganda in favour of the war and was even allowed access to army recruits. Organized business interests also kept up pressure on the government in favour of territorial annexations in Belgium, France and Russia.

Hopes of a German victory revived in late 1917. In October a joint Austrian–German army inflicted a massive defeat on the

---

[10]Another grouping, the Radical Left, containing German and Polish members, pressed for revolutionary action by the workers to end the war but with very little success.

Italians at Caporetto, which relieved pressure on the southern front. The Bolshevik *coup d'etat* led to negotiations for Russia's withdrawal from the war, which culminated in the peace of Brest-Litovsk in March 1918. Romania was also forced to come to terms by the peace of Bucharest. These two settlements have often been cited as evidence of the sweeping imperial ambitions of Germany. Russia in particular suffered massive territorial losses and preparations began for the creation of German satellite states in Poland, the Baltic states and the Ukraine. Certainly some German academics and businessmen had long seen Russia as an essentially artificial state, only held together by tsarist tyranny and ripe for dissolution and exploitation or colonization by Germany, but the old view that Brest-Litovsk was the realization of long-held German plans is questionable. The extension of German power and influence into large areas of Eastern Europe has the appearance of an improvised settlement, the result of opportunistic greed based on military and economic considerations arising out of a long period of full-scale war. Germany and, especially, Austria-Hungary needed Russian grain urgently. The military benefits expected from the peace did not materialize. The negotiations were long and large numbers of German troops had to remain in the east to preserve order. As a result Germany was not able to move sufficient forces to the Western Front to have a decisive effect before the arrival of the Americans.

Imperialist ambitions remained alive in Germany right until the end of the war. The ruling class persistently ignored the realities of the military situation and a widening gap opened between them and the mass of war-weary Germans. The winter of 1917–18 saw another wave of strikes and the political tone was much more visible than earlier. In January 1918 half a million men came out on strike calling for a peace without annexations. The collapse on the home front was preceded by military defeat. On 21 March the German army began its last great offensive on the Western Front, the so-called Emperor's Battle (*Kaiserschlacht*).[11] By June, after some 800,000 casualties had been suffered, the advance stopped. In July the Allied counter-attack began and the German front began to crumble. By November 1918 the German army was close to total collapse though it still occupied French and Belgian soil. Socialist propaganda was spreading among the troops and morale was beginning to break down. On 28 September Ludendorff informed the government that complete victory was still possible but that the breakdown of the home front and the spread of defeatism were letting down the army. On the 29th he informed them that

[11]M. Middlebrook, *The Kaiser's Battle* (1978).

the war was lost and advised immediate constitutional reform and an appeal to the Allies for a peace settlement on the basis of President Wilson's Fourteen Points.

Thereafter developments were rapid. On 3 October a new government under Crown Prince Max of Baden, a man with a Liberal reputation, was formed from the SPD, Centre Party and Progressive Party, which commanded a majority in the *Reichstag*. Germany had become a parliamentary democracy. A series of major constitutional reforms was carried through, including the subjection of the army to parliamentary control, the abolition of the three-class franchise in Prussia and a reduction in the powers of the federal states. Taken together, these amounted to a revolution from above. Armistice negotiations with the Allies began and there was a hope that they would treat the new democratic Germany more generously in the eventual settlement. Ludendorff and others in the Fatherland Party regarded the armistice negotiations as a useful breathing space for Germany and looked forward to a prompt resumption of the war. The knowledge that peace was near led to demonstrations, which eventually turned into the so-called revolution of November 1918.

The Revolution[12] is traditionally held to have begun with the naval mutiny in Kiel on 29 October, a rising sparked off by rumours that the officers were planning to rescue the honour of the German navy by a final sortie against the British fleet, the so-called Death Ride.[13] By 4 November the sailors and representatives of the Left, in the form of the Workers' and Sailors' Council, had taken over the city of Kiel after the authorities fled or went into hiding. Representatives spread the movement to other ports and then inland. At the same time soldiers' councils began to appear among the troops in barracks and behind the front line. The extreme Left, financed and encouraged by the new Soviet embassy in Berlin, was very active. Red flags appeared all over Germany. This, and the superficial similarity between the councils and the Russian soviets, produced the totally false impression that Communism was about to triumph in Germany. In fact, the extreme Left was vocal but very weak. The majority of the councils were dominated by the trade unions and democratic Socialists intent on the maintenance of order and fairness in a vacuum created by the collapse

[12]Basic works on the revolution of 1918: F.L. Carsten, *War against War. British and German Radical Movements in World War* (1982) and *Revolution in Central Europe 1918–1919* (1972); A.J. Ryder, *The German Revolution of 1918* (Cambridge, 1967); S. Haffner, *Failure of a Revolution: Germany 1918–19* (1973); R.M. Watt, *The Kings Depart. The German revolution and the Treaty of Versailles 1918–19* (1973); D.W. Morgan, *The Socialist Left and the German Revolution* (Ithaca, 1975).

[13]The fleet, the foundation of *Weltpolitik*, had played very little part in the war, spending most of the time in port. This added to the problems of maintaining discipline.

of the old order rather than a permanent takeover of political power or a social revolution. They mainly restricted their activities to the temporary supervision of government at the local level. Similarly, the soldiers' councils had no plan to make military decisions. Fear of the unreal threat from Communism affected the leadership of the SPD, who, throughout the revolution, were always more frightened of the Left than of the Right. In view of the mounting disorder in Germany, this is perhaps understandable.

By 9 November a growing conviction had spread that the Allies were refusing to come to terms with Germany while the *Kaiser* remained on the throne. On the morning of that day a general strike and mass demonstrations were organized in Berlin to enforce the removal of this last barrier to peace. Max of Baden announced the Emperor's abdication before it had in fact taken place. William II and his eldest son officially abdicated later in the day when his officers at the general headquarters in Spa told him that the troops could not be relied on to march back to Germany, with William at their head, to crush the risings. It is interesting how quickly the Emperor had faded into the background during the course of the war and been replaced by Field Marshal Hindenburg as the symbolic leader of the *Reich*. Before the abdication was officially announced Max of Baden's government had fallen after troops sent to quell demonstrators in Berlin disobeyed orders to fire on them and instead joined them in attacking officers. The leaders of the SPD demanded that Max hand over power to them as the last hope of maintaining order. Max agreed to this on a temporary basis until a regency was established and normal circumstances were restored. Similar events had taken place in other German cities more or less simultaneously. Almost everywhere power passed, in a virtually bloodless process, to democratic Socialists. On 10 November some representatives of the councils met in the Busch circus building in Berlin and, as a temporary measure, appointed a committee of six People's Delegates, three each from the SPD and the USPD under Ebert's chairmanship, to exercise power on behalf of the Berlin councils. This was a provisional measure until a full meeting of all the councils made definitive arrangements for Germany's future government. As a result, there was a distinct revolutionary potential in Germany: the country had two provisional governments, both headed by Ebert, one with some claim to legitimate succession to the last imperial government and the other deriving its power from a revolutionary situation. The accidental declaration of a republic by Ebert's deputy, Scheidemann, increased the revolutionary potential as, at a stroke, it demolished the legitimacy both of Ebert's chancellorship and of the delegation negotiating the armistice.

Eventually Germany pulled back from the revolution it nearly had. The old order was not destroyed in 1918. It stepped aside temporarily, reeling under the shock of defeat. The party which should have spearheaded change in Germany, the SPD, seemed paralysed throughout by fear of the extreme Left. There was no great transfer of property and no elimination of political opponents, except those on the extreme Left. No coherent attempt was made to take over administration either at the centre or in the localities. The leadership of the SPD seems to have been taken in by the myth of the efficiency of the civil service and the officer corps and feared that, without these experts, the whole administration of Germany would collapse in chaos, food supplies and transport services would seize up and thousands of German troops would fall into Allied captivity as demobilization ground to a halt.[14] The Social Democrats had made no preparations to take over power as the possibility had always seemed remote to them. Instead the party's energies had been devoted to ideological squabbles, internal reorganization and keeping its natural working-class constituency intact. When power fell into the leaders' laps, they had little idea what to do with it.

The SPD leadership's readiness to compromise with the old order was symbolized most clearly by a telephone conversation between Ebert and the army chief of staff Groener on 10 November. Groener agreed to make the army available to crush Bolshevism and in return Ebert undertook to keep politics out of the army. The soldiers' councils would be wound up and replaced with a system of trusties, which in effect meant the restoration of the officers' authority. The new government of Germany had immediately placed itself in a position of dependence on the army and had treated it as an equal rather than a servant of government. Building on this, Hindenburg in early December presented the government with an ultimatum demanding the disbandment of the soldiers' councils, elections for a national constituent assembly within a month and an end to council interference in government. This was a sign that the old regime was very quickly finding its feet again and reasserting itself in the army, judiciary and civil service. Collaboration between the provisional government and the army quickly deepened. The threat to German territory from a revived Poland and the apparent strength of German Communism led the government to ratify the creation of the free corps, units of carefully selected rightist officers and troops, which were to be the basis of a new

[14]Ebert's first manifesto to the German people on 9 November emphasized, above all, the vital importance of secure food supplies and contained the words: 'Fellow citizens, I urgently beg you all to leave the streets; preserve calm and order.' *Ruhe* was again *die erste Bürgerpflocht*.

German army being created in January 1919. Millions of German troops were still under arms in eastern Europe and orders were sent to certain units to weed out 'unreliable' soldiers and prepare for action inside Germany. After December 1918 the SPD leaders leaned even more heavily on the army after the USPD members left the government. From the same time the army, engaged in warfare against Polish irregulars in Silesia and against Bolsheviks in the Baltic states, began to arrest radical leaders inside Germany. Although the army command was ready to co-operate with the new order, however undesirable they found it, in order to avoid something worse, it was already conspiring to overthrow the Republic. In reality there was no need for the army to contemplate action. On 16 December a national congress of the councils met, dominated by moderate Social Democrats. It voted for elections to a constituent assembly to be held on 19 January 1919.

There is still dispute among historians as to whether there was a genuine revolution in November 1918.[15] In view of the fact that there was so little real change — the removal of the Kaiser and the other German monarchs was of symbolic rather than real significance — it is more accurate to talk of a potential revolution which ran away into the sand rather than the genuine article. The republic that eventually emerged contained at once too much and too little of the old Germany: powerful institutional centres of the old ruling class remained intact and were not subject to democratic control while many Germans saw the republic as originating in a revolution and therefore illegitimate. During the war the mass of Germans had remained politically apathetic and had supported the national war effort, though many political leaders of the Left were imprisoned and there was strict censorship. A mass opposition movement had only appeared in the last year of the war and had been motivated by war-weariness and material shortages rather than the vision of a new Germany. The Social Democrats had only stepped in to offer leadership to this movement when it seemed they risked losing support to more extreme parties of the Left. During the 'revolution' the SPD and the trade unions maintained discipline among the great majority of the workers. The extreme Left was noisy but weak and divided: it had impressive chiefs like Rosa Luxembourg but very few Indians. The German Communists attempted to seize power by a *coup* in January 1919, the Spartacist rising. This was quickly put down by force and succeeded only in strengthening counter-revolutionary forces and frightening those

---

[15]W.J. Mommsen, 'The German Revolution 1918–1920: Political Revolution and Social protest Movement', in R.J. Bessel and E.J. Feuchtwanger (eds.), *Social Change and Political Development in Weimar Germany* (1981).

who might otherwise have supported more radical change. The workers' councils were only rarely revolutionary in intention and few had any coherent plans for a new society. The majority disbanded themselves meekly when a new constituent assembly was elected. In only a handful was the extreme Left influential. The parliamentary system was never seriously threatened by a genuine revolutionary movement. If there was a revolution in Germany in 1918, it was the revolution from above of October, which created a parliamentary democracy. The events of November had a counter-revolutionary effect in that they prevented the changes of October bearing fruit: the moderate Left was so frightened of the extreme Left, too weak to bring about the revolution they wanted, that they turned their face against genuine radical change and rushed to co-operate with the old order, helping it to survive largely intact. Many members of the SPD and USPD did favour radical reform of the administrative system and the army, the elimination or serious weakening of the federal states, the nationalization or socialization of big enterprises, land reform and the creation of a people's militia but little was done. In the early days of the Weimar Republic the Wilhelmine social welfare system was extended, the eight-hour day was introduced (and later abolished) and the rights of the trade unions were recognized; but elements of continuity between the old and the new Germany were very strong. The leadership of the SPD seems to have harboured the naïve belief that social and economic reform would evolve as the inevitable result of political reform, that a democratic constitution would of itself produce a population of convinced democrats. In 1848 the Liberals, similarly, had naïvely expected a Liberal constitution to give birth to a Liberal Germany.

It could be argued that the Weimar Republic was much closer than the *Kaiserreich* to a genuine national state. It appeared to have arisen from the will of the people, was founded on the principle of popular sovereignty and contained no substantial non-German populations. Unfortunately, from the beginning of the Republic a substantial portion of German society was implacably hostile to it, seeing it as the work of jumped-up traitors from the gutters. Conservatives compared it unfavourably with the Hohenzollern state. The new state continued to call itself a *Reich* but for its conservative opponents it was an interim state (*Zwischenreich*). To them the real *Reich* symbolized everything which the Republic was not. Radical nationalists — the so-called New Right — saw it as totally alien, founded on un-German principles and devoted to the destruction of German values.

Both groups were further alienated when the terms of the Versailles peace settlement were revealed in May 1919. The terms of the treaty are well-known and do not need detailed rehearsal.[16] The whole negotiation was seriously mishandled by the German foreign minister von Brockdorff-Rantzau, who refused to be bound by the instructions of his government, thus effectively depriving Berlin of any say in the matter. The fact that the Republic's birth was accompanied by the loss of land long German, particularly to the Poles, made it appear in the eyes of many an incomplete state.[17] The war-guilt clause was psychologically damaging, as it appeared that the German dead had fallen for nothing and many Germans were convinced that their country had not lost the war. This, plus the naïve expectations Germans had entertained about Wilson's Fourteen Points, made the burden of Versailles very hard to bear. The attempt by the Allies to initiate general disarmament by limiting Germany's military strength left Germans with a sense of grievance. France was left militarily supreme on the Continent but the burden of preserving the settlement was beyond her capacity after Britain and the USA backed out of the permanent alliance with her agreed at Versailles. As an alternative, she sought to construct an alliance system among the small states of eastern Europe, which created chronic friction between Germany and her eastern neighbours and further stoked up nationalist emotion in Germany. Germany's strength was cut but her potential was still formidable. She was much stronger than her eastern neighbours and potentially stronger than France, whose demographic crisis had become much more serious as a result of the great bloodletting of the war.

A more serious criticism of the Paris peace settlement was that it led to the further balkanization of south-eastern Europe[18] and left 12 million Germans outside the *Reich*, many living under foreign rule in Poland, Czechoslavakia, Belgium, Hungary, Rumania and Italy. In reality the Allies were left with little option but to ratify what had already happened spontaneously during the final collapse of the Austro-Hungarian state in October 1918. The Polish, Yugoslav and Czechoslovak states were established before the peacemakers met at Paris. There had always been voices in the Allied camp in favour of the preservation of some sort of union or Danubian federation, if only to act as a barrier to Russian influence

[16]Watt, *The Kings Depart*, chap. 15.
[17]P. Nitsche, 'Der Reichstag und die Festlegung der deutsch-polnischen Grenze nach dem ersten Weltkrieg', *Historische Zeitschrift* 216 (1973), pp. 335–61.
[18]Works on E. Europe after 1918: L. Valiani, *The End of Austria-Hungary* (1973); C.A. Macartney and A. Palmer, *Independent Eastern Europe* (1962); H. Seton-Watson, *Eastern Europe between the Wars 1918–1941* (Cambridge, 1945; repr. New York, 1967); K.R. Stadler, 'The Disintegration of the Austrian Empire', *J.Cont.H.* 3/4 (1968), pp. 177–90; I.T. Berend and G. Ranki, 'Economic Problems of the Danube Region after the Break-up of the Austro-Hungarian Monarchy', *J.Cont.H.* 4/3 (1969), pp. 169–85.

and to preserve the economic benefits of Austria-Hungary, but this proved impossible. Eventually Austria-Hungary was replaced by a collection of small, weak, mutually hostile and mainly economically unviable states, all with national minorities and all with claims on one another's territory.

The destruction of the economic unit which Austria-Hungary had represented had damaging results: south-eastern Europe experienced chronic economic depression after 1918, with artificial borders separating suppliers from markets, high tariff walls and excessive military spending. The destruction of the Habsburg Monarchy did not solve the nationality problem but shared it out among the successor states, many of whom regarded the national minorities within their borders as a blot on their national sovereignty and subjected them to a variety of pressures often involving persecution. Attempts by the League of Nations to solve the problem by means of minority treaties met considerable resistance. The new Czechoslovak state, for example, was reluctant to treat the Sudeten German minority as a distinct unit, arguing that all the citizens of Czechoslovakia, regardless of nationality, enjoyed the same rights under the constitution. The position of the Austrian Germans was very difficult. On 21 October 1918 German-speaking members of the *Reichsrat*, including those from Bohemia, met in Vienna and declared themselves the provisional national assembly of German-Austria (*Deutschösterreich*), the first official name of the new state. Among the first acts of the assembly was a declaration of dependence: the overwhelming majority of the delegates, of all parties, were convinced that their state was not viable and that it must be united with Germany without delay. They were united on little else. In Germany there was a brief revival of *grossdeutsch* feeling in 1918−19 on the basis of the principle of national self-determination, which was supposed to be the foundation of the whole peace settlement, and a belief that the union of Germany and Austria would compensate Germany for her territorial losses − but that was vetoed by the Allies, who were fearful of strengthening Germany. This left a weak Austrian republic prey to serious internal divisions, which made the survival of democracy there very difficult.[19]

These factors were eventually to facilitate German economic and political penetration of the area, a policy begun under the Weimar Republic and pursued with greater vigour under the National Socialist government. The supposed sufferings of the German

[19]Works on Austria after 1918: E. Barker, *Austria 1918−1972* (1973); K. von Klemperer, *Ignaz Seipel. Christian Statesman in a Time of Crisis* (Princeton, 1972); F.L. Carsten, *The First Austrian Republic 1918−38* (1986).

minorities in Czechoslovakia and Poland were to be employed by
the enemies of the Weimar system as ammunition against it and
later by Hitler to justify expansionist policies, ironically using the
principle of national self-determination which was supposed to be
the basis of the Paris settlement.

The Paris peace settlement was a disaster for the new Republic
but was not the reason for its failure, which, as will be shown, was
caused by the political mistakes of democratic politicians. All
Germans regarded the peace settlement as grossly unjust and desired
its revision[20] but this did not lead to greater German unity as after
1919 even anti-foreign nationalism had lost its power to unite the
nation. Germans saw other Germans as responsible for the disaster:
the Left blamed the Emperor, the generals and the Pan-German
imperialists and the Right blamed the Socialists who had stabbed
the army in the back and saddled Germany with a party state
based on alien principles. If the *Reich* of 1871 had been profoundly
disappointing to many Germans, the Republic of 1918 was even
worse. If the French Third Republic survived because it was the
system which divided Frenchmen least, the Weimar Republic lasted
as long as it did because there was no unity among Germans as to
what should replace it. The basic weakness of the Republic was
that it was nobody's child: every group in Germany saw it as an
interim system to be tolerated until something better came along,
the Conservatives a restoration of the monarchy, *völkisch* nationalists the *Volksgemeinschaft* and the Left a truly Socialist state. Deep
division over Germany's future persisted throughout the Weimer
Republic, a cold civil war arising from the incomplete revolution
of 1918.

[20]Visual evidence of the bitterness felt on all sides in Germany after the terms of the treaty
were revealed is provided in: W.A. Coupe (ed.), *German Political Satires*, part III 1918–1945
(vols. 5 and 6, New York, 1985).

9

The Cold Civil War: German Nationalism in the Weimar Republic[1]

From the outset a significant proportion of the German population regarded the Weimar Republic as a 'system', an un-German aberration foisted on the country by traitors and foreigners. It was during the brief life of the Republic that German nationalism reached its full flowering, in both traditional and new forms. In January 1933 Adolf Hitler became chancellor of Germany. His success marked the culmination of all the traditional variants of German nationalism in the mutant forms which had appeared before 1914. Liberal nationalism had become imperialism, Romantic nationalism had become racist *völkisch* nationalism and xenophobia had become a chauvinistic belief in German superiority.

Right-wing parties very quickly recovered from the paralysis of will caused by defeat and the end of the old *Reich*. In the elections to the constituent assembly in January 1919 the German National People's Party (*Deutschnationale Volkspartei*), the main party of the Right, won some 10 per cent of the vote and 44 seats. In its election appeal the party accepted the new parliamentary system and renounced any intention of bringing it down by violence. The adoption by the party of the name *Volkspartei* symbolized its appeal to the whole nation and its rejection of the notion of class basic to Marxist ideology. The old Conservative rallying cry of 'Throne and Altar' was obviously no longer appropriate. At this point the illusion that a democratic Germany would obtain better peace terms from the Allies was still intact. After May, when the peace terms were revealed, the party grew rapidly and became the repository of nationalist views. For the first time a party to articulate nationalism was needed; there had been no such need before 1914.[2]

The DNVP was a coalition of divergent forces and it could have developed in a number of different directions. At its core were the

[1]General works on the Weimar period: A. Rosenberg, *A History of the German Republic* (1936); J.W. Hiden, *The Weimar Republic* (1973) and *Germany and Europe 1919–39* (1977); J.R.P. McKenzie *Weimar Germany* (1971); D. Felix, *Walther Rathenau and the Weimar Republic. The Politics of Reparations* (1971); F.L. Carsten, *The Reichswehr and Politics 1918–33* (1966); E.J. Feuchtwanger (ed.), *Upheaval and Continuity. A Century of German History* (1973); R.J. Bessel and E.J. Feuchtwanger (eds.), *Social Change and Political Development in Weimar Germany* (1981).

various components of the war-time Fatherland Party, reactionary conservative monarchists and anti-democrats looking back to the good old days of the *Kaiserreich*. It enjoyed support from some parts of industry, large-scale farmers, teachers, officials and white-collar workers. It also contained a significant *völkisch* anti-Semitic element and many local branches of the party refused membership to Jews. It also inherited much of the membership and support of the Pan-German League, an element which combined extreme nationalism with a belief in the innate superiority of the Germans. The German Conservative movement therefore contained radical elements from the beginning.

For most of the life of the Weimar Republic, the traditional Conservative nationalists, with their essentially restorative ideas and vision of the Wilhelmine Empire as the ideal Germany, were the most important anti-republican force. The early days of Weimar also saw attempts to bring the New, Radical or *völkisch* Right together into a single movement. In the immediate aftermath of the events of 1918 the extreme nationalists were in disarray. The Winter of 1918—19 saw a wave of anti-Semitic propaganda, blaming the Jews for Germany's defeat and the establishment of the Republic, labelled the 'Jew Republic' (*Judenrepublik*). In some ways the Republic was an easy target for such attacks as Jews were prominent in the parties of the Left, the Social Democrats (SPD), Communists (KPD) and the German Democratic Party (DDP), the pre-1918 Progressive Party under a new name, though the great majority were middle-class and conservative, ardent German patriots wanting only to be assimilated and accepted in German society.[3] The notion of an international Jewish anti-German conspiracy, using Marxism and capitalism as its weapons, was also freely circulating. In February 1919 leaders of various extreme nationalist and racist movements met in Bamberg and established the German League of Defence and Defiance (*Deutscher Schutz- und Trutzbund*) as an umbrella organization. The membership of the League grew quickly from about 25,000 in December 1919 to over 100,000 in October 1920. Its national headquarters were set up in Hamburg. But this first attempt to unify the radical nationalist Right failed: the League was banned in 1922 as part of the government's campaign to eliminate extremists of both Left and Right, after which

[2]D.P. Walker, 'The German Nationalist People's Party. The Conservative Dilemma in the Weimar Republic', *J.Cont.H.* 14 (1979), pp. 627—47; A. Chanady, 'The Disintegration of the German National People's Party 1924—30', *JMH* 39 (1967), pp. 65—91; H.—J. Puhle, 'Conservatism in Modern German History', *J.Cont.H.* 13 (1978), pp. 689—720; K. von Klemperer, *Germany's New Conservatism. Its History and Dilemma in the Twentieth Century* (Princeton, 1957); J.G. Williamson, *Karl Helfferich 1872—1924. Economist. Financier. Politician* (Princeton, 1971).
[3]D.L. Niewyk, *The Jews in Weimar Germany* (Manchester, 1980).

most of its supporters gravitated back into established parties, including the DNVP. They were never really at home there, however, as leadership of the party remained in the hands of traditional groups, large landowners, representatives of big business and former imperial civil servants, prepared to support social progress and reconciliation.

Alternative centres for the Radical Right also existed in the state of Bavaria and the Free Corps movement. As the Republic's government began to find its feet in the winter of 1921—2, it took tough measures against extremists, including special powers to defend the constitution. Right-wing extremists, under pressure in other parts of Germany, began to gravitate to Bavaria, which became a refuge for hundreds of small movements. The state elections in June 1920 saw the SPD lose 60 per cent of its support in a massive swing to the Right. The new state government was reactionary, combining monarchism, Bavarian separatism, clericalism and peasant conservatism, and was prepared to offer umbrella protection to the extreme Right. At the same time the Bavarian People's Party (*Bayerische Volkspartei*) broke away from the national Centre Party on the grounds that it was too left-wing.[4] Munich, in particular, became the home of a weird mixture of idealists, ex-officers, aristocrats, intellectuals, students, misfits, criminals and refugees from the Baltic and Sudeten areas, all deeply hostile to the Weimar Republic. Among the various fringe parties was the German Workers' Party (*Deutsche Arbeiterpartei*), set up in January 1919 by a railway fitter Anton Drexler and a few associates. This sought to win over workers for German or *völkisch* rather than international Socialism and had close links with other movements. It received money from more upper-class circles through Dietrich Eckart, publisher of the *völkisch* newspaper *Auf Gut Deutsch*. In the autumn of 1919 Adolf Hitler, employed as a political education officer by the Bavarian army, investigated the DAP. He joined it, quickly established a strong position in it and changed its name to the National Socialist German Workers' Party (NSDAP). It had close links with the army and the Bavarian government and became involved in plans to use Bavaria as the base for a military *coup* to take over the whole of Germany.[5]

The Free Corps movement was also involved in these plans. They often functioned as centres of political education, instilling anti-republican ideas in their members. Although they were brought under control in the winter of 1921—2, they contributed to the

[4] C. Landauer, 'The Bavarian Problem in the Weimar Republic', *JMH* 16 (1944), pp. 93—115 and 205—23.
[5] H. Gordon, *Hitler and the Beer Hall Putsch* (Princeton, 1972).

militarization of political life, which was such a prominent feature of the Weimar Republic. Most of the political parties acquired paramilitary organizations to defend their activities, including the Nationalist Socialist SA, the Socialist *Reichsbanner Schwarz-Rot-Gold*, the *Stahlhelm* veterans' movement associated with the DNVP and the Communist Red Hundreds. Perhaps the roots of this lay in the militarization and polarization of pre-1914 Germany but it was reinforced by the experience of the front-soldiers in the war and the events of November 1918. Even after the restoration of political stability in 1924 the paramilitaries continued to act as radical pressure groups within the parties. They continued to attract younger party activists and represented a repository of extreme attitudes and the politics of confrontation during the so-called quiet years of Weimar from 1924 to 1929.[6]

The period of chronic instability before 1924 provided extremists of all kinds with plenty of opportunities. The first general election under the Weimar constitution in June 1920 produced a major victory for the Right. DNVP representation in the *Reichstag* rose from 44 to 71 seats and the Weimar coalition, of the SPD, Centre Party and Democratic Party, which in the elections to the constituent assembly in January 1919 had won 76 per cent of the votes, gained only 43 per cent. The election of January 1919 had been held in an atmosphere of false optimism about the peace settlement; that of June 1920 gave a more accurate picture of the German people's attitudes. The result gave the traditional conservative nationalists in the DNVP new confidence and the party leadership no longer saw itself as dependent on the Radical Right for electoral support and political weight. This was to prove an illusion. Under the influence of able leaders like the former imperial finance minister Karl Helfferich, killed prematurely in a rail accident in April 1924, the party moved closer to the powerful economic pressure groups, which had quickly emerged and now sought to achieve their ends by direct links to political parties. The groups provided financial support in return for the defence of their interests in the *Reichstag*. The activities of political extremists, including outbreaks of violence and a series of political murders of which prominent figures like the Centre leader Erzberger and the foreign minister Rathenau were victims, caused a further distancing of the more respectable nationalists from the lunatic fringe. Anti-Semitism was played down by the DNVP leadership, for whom it had always been only an expedient political device.[7] For radical nationalists, anti-Semitism

[6]R.G.L. Waite, *Vanguard of Nazism: the Free Corps Movement in Postwar Germany 1918–23* (Cambridge, Mass., 1952).
[7]See chap. 6 of D. Calleo, *The German Problem Reconsidered* (Cambridge, 1978).

was perhaps the only part of the DNVP's policy with which they could readily identify. The party congresses between 1920 and 1923 saw a series of violent disputes and secessions of radical groups and the formation of new parties, such as the German Social Party (1921) and the German *völkisch* Freedom Party (1922).

The domination of the leadership of the DNVP by traditional conservatives increased as hopes for a speedy restoration of the monarchy faded in the absence of a suitable candidate for the imperial title. The Republic also showed itself capable of dealing with threats to it. The conviction grew that there was little likelihood of replacing it with something more desirable for some time and that it would, at least, have to be tolerated. Crises caused by the Franco-Belgian occupation of the Ruhr, the hyperinflation of 1923, a French-backed separatist movement in the Rhineland, Polish incursions into Silesia, Communist risings in Prussia, the Ruhr and Hamburg and the refusal of the Bavarian government and Communist/Socialist coalitions in Saxony and Thuringia to obey the central government were all weathered and the government in July 1922 obtained support for alterations to the constitution to equip itself with a much tougher law against political extremists. Using this law, the government in October 1923 banned the NSDAP newspaper, the *Völkischer Beobachter*. When the Bavarian government refused to enforce the ban, the army was ordered to march on Munich but refused. This participated the long-planned *coup* attempt, which Hitler seized control of on 8 November 1923 when his Conservative partners lost their nerve. The *putsch* was crushed by the Munich police on 9 November. It was clear that, even in Bavaria, the traditional nationalists were not yet ready to commit themselves to the revolutionary road to power. The hopes of the radical nationalists were again disappointed.

The restoration of a stable currency in early 1924 initiated a period of political and economic calm which lasted until the Wall Street Crash in 1929. Elections were held in May and December 1924 and again the DNVP achieved large gains, becoming the biggest party in the *Reichstag*. The movement in the party towards reconciliation with the Republic increased as many of its leaders convinced themselves that it was not very different from the old imperial constitution. The election of the imperial field marshal Hindenburg as president after Ebert's death in 1925 made the Republic even more palatable, as he was seen by some as a substitute Emperor (*Ersatzkaiser*), though many of the Radical Right saw him as guarantor and perpetuator of the Republic. American loans made possible impressive economic growth, which helped to win over many of the DNVP's paymasters in the economic pressure groups to support reconciliation, especially as many of the gains made by organized labour in the first years of the Republic were subsequently withdrawn. During these years the DNVP was willing to join governments or tolerate them. This left the radical nationalists floating, looking for a congenial political home.[8]

In considering the role of German nationalism in the Weimar Republic it is again necessary to draw a distinction between active and passive nationalism. Mass passive nationalism, as had developed during the Wilhelmine period, continued during the Republic. All Germans were nationalists but there was no unity within the nation. On the Right nationalism was fuelled by the ceremonial of war memorials, the funerals of generals and similar events, which provided opportunities for politicians to attack the Versailles settlement and the loss of German lands, to bewail the military weakness of Germany, to call for Germany's rebirth and to indulge in nostalgia for the old Germany. These divisions were reflected in different views of the German past. During the First World War, as William II had lost his charisma, the figure of Frederick the Great had been revived and had become an important symbol for the Right. Under Weimar Frederick was frequently used by opponents of the Republic as a symbol of the lost Germany. The Left and the Catholics retained their own ceremonials and the polarization of association life, seen under the Wilhelmine *Reich*, continued. All parties, including the Socialists, condemned the Versailles settlement and its consequences. Versailles opened old wounds, reviving memories of Germany's centuries-long weakness and humiliation. The strength born out of national unity appeared to have been temporary and jealous foreigners had again conspired to destroy Germany. Socialists were as vociferous as anyone in condemning the stealing of German land in Upper Silesia by 'Polish bandits' and they too subscribed to the myths of the stab in the back and Germany's lack of responsibility for the war. All believed Germany was being denied the place of importance in the world she deserved. All rejected as hypocrisy claims that the Paris peace settlement was the beginning of a new era of international political and economic co-operation based on national self-determination. The Allies' refusal to permit the union of Austria and Germany was condemned by all parties and there was a wave of *grossdeutsch* sentiment in 1919–20.[9] All governments after 1918 blocked the disclosure of the facts of Germany's role in the

[8]See L.E. Jones, 'The Dissolution of the Bourgeois Party System in the Weimar Republic', in Bessel, *Social Change*, pp. 268–88 and 'The Dying Middle: Weimar Germany and the Fragmentation of Bourgeois Politics', *Cent.Eur.H.* 5 (1972), pp. 23–54; A. Chanady, 'The Dissolution of the German Democratic Party in 1930', *Am.H.R.* 73 (1968), pp. 1433–53.
[9]S. Suval, 'Overcoming *Kleindeutschland*. The Politics of Historical Mythmaking in the Weimar Republic', *Cent.Eur.H.* 2 (1969), pp. 312–30.

outbreak of war in August 1914. The line taken by the Foreign Office in November 1918 was never abandoned and no serious attempt was made to investigate the question of German war-guilt. Former imperial officals were not willing to have embarrassing revelations about their past made public. The SPD government in 1918 felt itself dependent on such people and it refused to allow the total disavowal of the *Kaiserreich* which some Socialists wanted. It became part of the defence of German 'national interests' to challenge the accusation of German war-guilt. The SPD also connived at clandestine rearmament contrary to the terms of Versailles and supported the 'national' foreign policy of Stresemann, which aimed at undoing the Paris peace settlement and not at creating a genuine lasting peace in Europe. As a result the SPD aided those who drew unfavourable comparisons between the Republic and the old Empire.

All parties regarded the Weimar Republic as inadequate and imperfect, and by extension this helped to undermine the Republic and to demean it in the eyes of the German people. It was lack of unity of purpose among the Republic's enemies, rather than its inherent strengths, that enabled it to survive for as long as it did. The Republic was seen a having been born in Germany's defeat and as symbolizing its impotence. Active nationalists, of whom the *völkisch* were the most dynamic, went further and rejected the whole political and social system of Weimar and yearned even more fiercely for a completely new community based on national unity, a Utopian combination of socialism and nationalism summed up in the mystical concept of the *Volksgemeinschaft*. Although on the surface Germany appeared to have settled into a stable democratic system after 1924, important political changes were taking place at the lower levels of politics, especially the further development of an articulate lower-middle-class movement (*Mittelstandsbewegung*) and the growth of a widening gulf between the leadership of the DNVP and the mass of middle-class voters. Many Germans saw the whole Republic not only as failing to cater for their needs but as a machine devoted to their destruction without even the trappings of German power which had enabled the pre-1914 *Reich* to keep their support.

The years after 1924 saw the final emergence of the *Mittelstand* as a coherent political force, as common grievances and aspirations overcame the major differences between the various elements of which it was composed. After 1924 they began to desert the DNVP and move to support a number of small parties. This had the effect of diffusing their political weight but after 1929 they began increasingly to gravitate to the NSDAP, which took over the quasi-religious element in *völkisch* nationalism, gave people the chance to participate in a mass movement, to find spiritual fulfilment and to achieve the *Volksgemeinschaft* under a charismatic leader emerging from the body of the *Volk*. The National Socialists promised a 'national revolution', a short period of violence opening the door to a perfect world. It would destroy the Germany of the Weimar Republic, not in order to restore the pre-1914 state but to create a totally new society free of artificial divisions and purged of alien elements, in which status would derive from a man's value to the *Volk*, not from birth or wealth, a wonderful opportunity for upward mobility. This vision of the new Germany was becoming increasingly appealing to a substantial section of German society; it is estimated that in 1925 there were more than five million small enterprises in agriculture, retailing, transport and manufacturing. The 'little men' wanted concrete steps taken in defence of their interests, the restoration of guild restrictions, import limitation, provision of cheap credit and a ban on trade unions, departmental stores and co-operative shops, the end of the 'Americanization' of the German economy. They were reinforced by the large groups calling for a revalorization of debts repaid in worthless currency during the period of hyperinflation.[10] In 1923–4 there were massive sackings of civil servants and cuts in the pay of those who retained their posts as part of the general financial retrenchment. It is estimated that by 1924 the real incomes of lower civil servants and salaried employees were some 50 per cent lower than in 1914. Small farmers suffered badly throughout the Weimar period and began to break away from the tight control previously exercised by the Farmers' league (*Bund der Landwirte*). These various components of the *Mittelstand* were highly organized in sectional organizations and pressure groups, such as ratepayers' and revalorization groups, white-collar unions and small-farmers' leagues, which early became a vehicle of National Socialist influence, especially in Protestant rural areas like Lower Saxony, Mecklenburg, Schleswig-Holstein and E. Prussia. It is an error to see German

[10]M. Hughes, 'Economic Interest, Social Attitudes and Creditor Ideology. Popular Responses to Inflation', in G.D. Feldmann (ed.), *Die Deutsche Inflation: eine Zwischenbilanz* (Berlin, 1982), pp. 385–408; L.E. Jones, 'Inflation, Revaluation and the Crisis of Middle Class Politics', in *Cent.Eur.H.* 12 (1979), pp. 143–68.

[11]This has been shown in detailed regional studies of the growth of National Socialism, for example J. Noakes, *The Nazi Party in Lower Saxony 1921–33* (Oxford, 1971); G. Pridham, *Hitler's Rise to Power: the Nazi Movement in Bavaria 1923–33* (St Albans, 1973); T.A. Tilton, *Nazism, Neo-Nazism and the Peasantry* (Bloomington, 1975) (a study of Schleswig-Holstein); L.E. Jones, 'Crisis and Realignment: Agrarian Splinter Parties in the Late Weimar Republic 1928–33', in R.G. Moeller (ed.), *Peasants and Lords in Modern Germany* (1986), pp. 198–232, T. Childers, *The Social Foundations of Fascism in Germany. The Nazi Voters 1924–32* (Chapel Hill, 1983).

national politics, that is the *Reichstag*, as the only significant politics in Germany. Important developments went on at lower levels
and there was a time-lag before these made themselves felt in
politics at the top. Long before they were making a significant
impact in national politics, the NSDAP was building a strong
power base among such organizations.[11]

This development coincided with a serious split in the DNVP.
After the party's successes in the 1924 elections there was growing
pressure from the grass-roots against collaboration with the Republic. This led some party leaders to the conclusion that the only
alternative to a serious loss of electoral support was to cash in on
völkisch nationalism. The split between 'realists' and 'absolutists'
was symbolized in two men, Count Kuno Westarp and Alfred
Hugenberg, who had radically different views of the future of the
DNVP. Westarp was a traditional monarchist conservative; Hugenberg, in the words of one biographer, was 'a warped product of a
warped society'.[12] He was a former imperial civil servant, a co-
founder of the Pan-German League, a director of Krupps and the
owner of newspapers and UFA, the largest German film production
company. He had a very modern grasp of the power of the mass
media. He wanted to create a firm bloc out of the loose coalition of
the DNVP on the basis of rigid opposition to Weimar and its
pluralism and dreamed of a 'closed nation' purged of un-German
elements and under authoritarian leadership.[13] He led a movement
within the DNVP away from co-operation with the Republic and
towards an alliance with the National Socialists, who were emerging as the leading *völkisch* party, thanks to the charisma of Hitler
and the infiltration of *Mittelstand* organizations. Hugenberg's in-
flexible opposition to the Republic fragmented the non-Nazi Right
and left the National Socialists to inherit much of the support.
Westarp left the DNVP, with a minority of its *Reichstag* deputies,
to form the Conservative People's Party, a traditional monarchist
party.

The dissolution of the non-National Socialist Right was completed
by the Wall Street Crash in October 1929. This did not burst on a
country enjoying great and universal prosperity. Small-scale agriculture had been suffering severe depression since the end of the
war and during the severe Winter of 1928–9 2.4 million were
unemployed. The Crash had a disastrous effect on the German
economy and precipitated a period of intense political crisis.

[12]J.A. Leopold, *Alfred Hugenberg. A Radical Nationalist Campaign against the Weimar Republic*
(New Haven, 1977).
[13]K.R. Holmes, 'The Forsaken Past: Agrarian Conservatism and National Socialism in
Germany', *J.Cont.H.* 17 (1982), pp. 671–88.

It is necessary now to look at the final crisis of the Weimar Republic and the triumph of the NSDAP. It would be wrong to see the period 1930–3 as a step-by-step deterioration with the triumph of National Socialism as the inevitable outcome: there were many alternatives to the Weimar Republic. There was an unmistakable drift away from democracy and the emergence of fascist or authoritarian attitudes in parties other than the NSDAP. This was symbolized by the emergence of the Action Circle (*Tatkreis*) of intellectuals, who searched for an alternative to democracy in a 'total state' and glorified action and violence. The *Tatkreis* was a small group of writers with no basis in any politically or economically important groups and its journal *Die Tat* (*Action*) had a circulation of only about 30,000. It owed its significance solely to the extraordinary circumstances of the times. Under the influence of Oswald Spengler, Arthur Moeller van den Bruck and others there was a general intellectual rejection of democracy, characterized as 'rule by the inferior', and an espousal of corporatist ideas on the Italian model. The leaders of this movement also sought to revive Prussian traditions, Spengler in *Prussianism and Socialism* and Moeller in *The Prussian Style*.[14] To them, the greatest freedom was to obey and the greatest equality the subordination of the individual to the greater whole. They also revived the 'War against the West'. Ernst Niekisch, a leading spokesman of the National Bolshevik movement,[15] in *Entscheidung* (*Decision*) (1930) wrote: 'The West is Germany's death; salvation demands that she frees herself from everything from the West. ... With ruthless harshness, Germany must exterminate in herself everything connected with the West.' Part of the DNVP seceded from Westarp's rump party to form the Young Conservative Movement, which entertained distinctly fascist ideas. The Young Conservatives and others called for 'renewal', the defeat of Marxism and individualism, the creation of a new state and a new society under a restored monarch, a combination of

[14]Spengler's *The Decline of the West* (2 vols., 1926–8) earned him a major reputation as a philosopher of history. A translation of A. Moeller van den Bruck, *Germany's Third Empire*, was published in London in 1934. On the Action Circle; W. Struve, *Elites against Democracy. Leadership Ideals in Bourgeois Political Thought in Germany 1890–1933* (Princeton, 1973); G.D. Stark, *Entrepreneurs of Ideology. Neo-Conservatism Publishers in Germany 1890–1933* (Chapel Hill, 1981); J.P. Faye, *Langages totalitaires* (Paris, 1972).

[15]The National Bolshevik movement attracted a strangely mixed membership, including intellectuals and aristocrats. Its supporters believed that a Russian alliance was vital to Germany's future and that Germany should adapt its political and social system to Russia's. Some saw Stalin as genuine National Socialist. It had some followers in the NSDAP. See R.A. Pois, *Friedrich Meinecke and German Politics in the Twentieth Century* (Berkeley, 1972); Faye, *Langages totalitaires*; R. Kuehnemund, 'German Prophets of Doom and Hope', *J.Hist.Id.* 3 (1942), pp. 443–57.

nationalism and a specifically German Socialism. The Young Conservatives rejected the National Socialists as a vulgar gang tainted with left-wing views. Niekisch later spoke out strongly against the Nazis and many backed General Schleicher's attempt to set up a National *Volksfront* against Nazis and Communists but they helped to create an atmosphere in which Nazism could thrive. Similar pressures were building up in other parties. For example in the Centre Party Prelate Kaas, a clerical fascist like Dolfuss in Austria, became increasingly influential. The German Democratic Party, a progressive Liberal party which had suffered a massive loss of support since 1920, joined the fascistic Young German Order to form the new German State Party (*Deutsche Staatspartei*) in a desperate attempt to win back its lost voters. After Stresemann's death the *Deutsche Volkspartei*, the heir of the pre-war National Liberal Party, also moved to the right and took up contacts with the DNVP and the NSDAP.

The whole situation in these years was very fluid and complex and it is sometimes difficult to discern any clear intentions behind the actions of the leading participants.[16] The passivity of the democratic Left, the SPD, which seemed paralysed throughout the final crisis of Weimar, was striking. The summer of 1932 saw growing political violence as Nazis and Communists fought for control of the streets. In July the chancellor Papen took over the government of the Prussian state, dominated since 1919 by a Socialist/Centre Party coalition. Prussia was the citadel of the Republic, with its police and civil service influenced by Socialist ideas. Papen saw his action as an anti-Nazi measure: the NSDAP had done well in the state elections in April in which the former coalition had lost its majority. The coalition had remained in power as a minority government but it was very vulnerable to the extreme parties and Papen was afraid the National Socialists would take over the largest German state. This assault on the bastion of German Socialism passed without reaction. Some trade unions and Socialist party branches called for a general strike but the party leadership, afraid that there would be no support from the working class when there were six million unemployed and deep divisions between the SPD

[16]Basic works on the decline of Weimar and the rise of Hitler to power: A.J. Nicholls (ed.), *Weimar and the Rise of Hitler* (2nd ed., 1979); H. Holborn, *Republic to Reich. The Making of the Nazi Revolution* (New York, 1973); T. Eschenburg et al., *The Road to Dictatorship. Germany 1918–33* (1970); G.L. Mosse, *Masses and Man: Nationalist and Fascist Perceptions of Reality* (New York, 1980); K.D. Bracher, 'Democracy and the Power Vacuum'. The Problem of the Party State during the Disintegration of the Weimar Republic', in V.R. Berghahn and M. Kitchen (eds.), *Germany in the Age of Total War* (1981), pp. 189–202.

and the KPD, refused to call one. This was a severe blow to Socialist morale.

The main actors in the final crisis were representatives of the traditional nationalist Right. Hitler came into power as their sup- posed tool in a coalition government which represented an alliance between conservative and *völkisch* nationalism. All the Conser- vatives involved believed they were acting in the best interests of the nation but this was open to an enormous variety of interpret- ations. Certainly after 1929 the National Socialist party for the first time acquired mass electoral support, overwhelmingly from the *Mittelstand*.[17] The crisis of 1929 was the last straw for the *Mittelstand* and finally broke their grip on political reality. The Utopian and irrational solutions offered by Hitler, who admitted that his pol- itical strength lay in his ability to be 'the great simplifier', became increasingly attractive to them in their despair when the conven- tional parties no longer had anything to offer.

In March 1930 the government headed by Hermann Müller fell after losing its majority in the *Reichstag*. He was succeeded as chancellor by the Centre Party's Heinrich Brüning, who initiated a deflationary policy to deal with the economic crisis. He was un- able to win a parliamentary majority for his measures and had to rely on the president to issue them as emergency decrees with a limited validity under article 48 of the constitution. Hindenburg was anxious to find a government which could command a major- ity and agreed to call elections for September 1930 in the hope that the parties of the Right would make gains. The main gainers in the elections were the National Socialists, whose seats rose from 12 to 107, and the Communists. In addition to this visible move- ment to the extremes, the traditional right-wing parties lost votes to a range of small fringe parties, including farmers' and ratepayers' groups, which were temporarily enjoying the support of the *Mit- telstand*. The *Reichstag* became increasingly irrelevant to the German political process. Decision-making became concentrated in the hands of a small group of men around the aged president. A section of the army officer corps began to engage in active politics in the person of General Schleicher, who dreamed of heading a populist authoritarian state with the army as its backbone. The traditional ruling élites were beginning to lose their cohesion as deep divisions appeared among the economic interest groups representing large-scale agriculture, different branches of manu- facturing and commerce over the policies to be adopted by the

---

[17]H. Speier, *German White-Collar Workers and the Rise of Hitler* (New Haven, 1986), pp. 103–17; H.A. Winkler, 'From Social Protectionism to National Socialism: The German Small-Business Movement in Comparative Perspective, *JMH* 48 (1976), pp. 1–18.

government to deal with the economic crisis. There were loud demands for 'a new conservative order' but no unity on what it meant.

On 11 October 1931 the National Socialists, Hugenberg's DNVP and the *Stahlhelm* formed the Harzburg Front, an agreement to cooperate in the *Reichstag*, for concerted attacks on Brüning's government and to put up Hitler as a common candidate for the presidency. Its motto was 'National Renewal and Authoritarian Leadership'. It promised an end of party government and appealed for support to the army, the Churches and the civil service. Presidential elections were held in 1932 and Hitler won 11.3 million votes but Hindenburg was elected on a second ballot with the support of the SPD. This gave the government confidence to take firm action against political violence and the Nazi paramilitary groups, the SA and the SS, were banned. This made Brüning unpopular with the Right as the Socialist *Reichsbanner* was not simultaneously banned. Brüning seemed close to producing a balanced budget, though at the cost of painful austerity, and abroad Germany's position seemed to be improving with negotiations to end the payment of reparations nearing success. Brüning was also moving to a policy of state intervention in the economy on a scale not seen since the end of the war. These optimistic dev~lopments were ended when on 30 May 1932 Hindenburg dismissed Brüning as a result of an intrigue around the president involving the aristocratic Centre politician von Papen and General Schleicher. Schleicher was already negotiating with the National Socialists offering to have the ban on the party's paramilitaries lifted if Hitler agreed to support an authoritarian government under a traditional leader.

The fall of Brüning meant the end of presidential government tolerated by the *Reichstag* and the beginning of pure presidential government. Papen was appointed chancellor at the suggestion of Schleicher, who hoped to use him as a front man. He installed a cabinet of non-politicians, known as the Cabinet of Barons (11 out of the 13 members had titles). Papen was hostile to the National Socialists but was aware of the threat they represented. He sought to combat them by a move to the Right, by becoming more nationalist than the National Socialists. He also considered 'taming' them by allowing them a minor share in government. He lifted the ban on the Nazi paramilitaries. Under pressure from Hindenburg he called elections in July 1932 in the hope of securing a majority for the traditional Right. The National Socialist vote rose to 13.5 million and, with 230 seats, they became the biggest party in the *Reichstag*. The heavy losses by the traditional parties of the Right destroyed any possibility of creating a coalition large enough to outvote the Nazis and Communists, whose vote also increased. Hitler rejected all offers of a coalition with the DNVP and held out for the chancellorship. This caused serious splits in the NSDAP, as many believed Hitler had allowed the chance of power to slip out his fingers.

In September the *Reichstag* rejected Papen's emergency decrees under article 48, when they came up for compulsory ratification. Papen persuaded Hindenburg to dissolve the parliament in the continuing hope that elections would produce a majority for moderate parties. There was a movement back to the traditional Right and the National Socialists lost two million votes and 34 seats. The movement of votes from the SPD to the Communists continued and there was still no prospect of a firm majority without the extremist parties. At this point Schleicher began to take initiatives. He wished to abolish parliamentary government and establish an authoritarian regime but not with Papen as dictator. He dreamed of basing his rule on a populist alliance of the trade unions, the Socialist paramilitary force, the *Reichsbanner*, and the SA, each to be detached from its political party. He believed that the 'socialist' wing of the NSDAP, under Gregor Strasser and Goebbels, would be willing to secede from the party and back him. Like Bismarck, he had a rather naïve faith in the loyalty of the masses.[18] Political violence revived after the November elections and there was mounting fear of civil war in Germany between Nazis and Communists. Schleicher assured Hindenburg that the police and the *Reichswehr* would be able to deal with this, a general strike and a simultaneous Polish invasion to seize German lands in the east. Earlier, during Papen's chancellorship, when faced with the same question he had given the opposite answer. Hindenburg seems to have been deceived by Schleicher's assurances that he would be able to construct a popular basis for his government and on 2 December appointed him chancellor in place of Papen.

At this point the intrigue around Hindenburg reached its climax, culminating in the appointment of Hitler as chancellor on 30 January 1933. Hitler was probably very lucky to be admitted to power when he was. Serious divisions began to appear in his party during 1932 and many concluded that he had made a mistake in not accepting the vice-chancellorship after the first elections of that year, a view apparently confirmed by the sharp fall in the party's vote in the November poll. The NSDAP was not monolithic, in spite of Hitler's charisma. There were deep divisions on policy

[18]R. Breitman, 'German Social Democrats and General Schleicher', *Cent.Eur.H.* 9 (1976), pp. 352–78.

and tactics, which was one of the main reasons for the party's vague election appeals. Hitler was moving towards an alliance with the traditional Nationalists while the 'left wing' of the party, strongly represented in the growing SA, desired a genuine social and economic revolution.[19] A serious division threatened in December with the dismissal of Gregor Strasser from his party offices. The government's prestige also seemed to be recovering. The economic situation appeared to be improving during the year as the government's measures began to show results, though un-employment rose again during the winter of 1932–3. What eventu-ally gave Hitler power in Germany was the decision of von Papen deliberately to seek an alliance with him as a means of defeating Schleicher. Papen was responsible for arranging a series of meet-ings between Hitler and representatives of business interests de-signed to convince them that the NSDAP could be relied on to foster capitalism and fight Marxism. It has been said that all revol-utions are preceded by a split in the existing ruling class and the Nazi 'revolution' was certainly helped by deepening divisons with-in the business community between groups representing heavy and light manufactures, agriculture and commerce over govern-ment policies to restore the economy.[20] Papen and Hugenberg, representing heavy industry and large-scale farming, saw in Hitler an ideal partner in the task of defending their patrons' interests, stopping Schleicher, destroying the Republic and controlling the parties of the Left. They were able to convince Hindenburg that a coalition of the Nationalists and the NSDAP, with Hitler as chan-cellor but with his party in a distinct minority, would be able to solve Germany's problems and would enjoy majority support in the *Reichstag*. Their efforts to convince the reluctant president were helped when they won over Hindenburg's son Oskar to their cause.

It must be remembered that circumstances were not normal. The president may have been increasingly senile and unable to under-stand fully what was going on. Also there was a mounting atmo-sphere of panic reminiscent of November 1918. There was real fear of civil war. On 15 January the NSDAP won an absolute majority in the state elections in the tiny state of Lippe after a massive election campaign. This seemed to confirm that they enjoyed the support of the German people. On the 26th Hindenburg assured representatives of the army that he would never appoint Hitler

[19]J.L. Nyomarkay, *Charisma and Factionalism in the Nazi Party* (Minneapolis, 1967).
[20]For example, there were deep divisions on the question of Free Trade versus Protectionism: see D. Abraham, *The Collapse of the Weimar Republic* (Princeton, 1981).

chancellor but on 28th Schleicher resigned as his populist schemes had come to nothing. On 30 January Hindenburg appointed Hitler head of a coalition Government of National Regeneration or Concentration, believed to be the *Sammlung* or coalition which had eluded the German Right since 1918. In the elections held on 5 March 1933 this coalition of Nazis and Nationalists won 51.9 per cent of the votes, a bare majority but apparent confirmation that they had 'the nation' behind them.

A great deal of learned ink has been expended in explaining why the National Socialists came to power in Germany and in hypothesizing about how their victory might have been prevented. It is sometimes claimed that co-operation between the Social Democrats and Communists could have stopped the Nazis[21] but this would have been as likely to win more support for the NSDAP as the only barrier standing between Germany and the victory of Marxism. The actions of the intriguers around Hindenburg were important but are only a partial explanation. The twin causes of the Nazi victory were the political skill of the party and its leader and the decay of the democratic system of the Weimar Republic. Democratic institutions and democratic morale were collapsing in Germany as no important group saw democracy as an answer to the German nation's problems. The Nazi takeover was remarkably easy and rapid in the absence of effective opposition. It is clear that by 1932 the National Socialists had a firm hold on the minds of large numbers of Germans, many of whom voted for the NSDAP as an act of faith or despair not as a rational political decision. Even among the party's opponents there was a growing conviction that there was no alternative to National Socialism and that a Hitler government, even if short-lived, was inevitable. This attitude was symbolized clearly in the *Frankfurter Allgemeine Zeitung*, since 1856 the leading vehicle for reforming Liberalism in Germany.[22] It had opposed Bismarck and William II and had pressed for social reform and democratic government before the First World War. After 1918 it backed the progressive Democratic Party and favoured substantial reforms. In 1929 the large chemical combine I.G. Farben began to buy into the paper, which moved towards 'political realism'. In July 1930 it supported the formation of the *Deutsche Staatspartei* and came out in support of Brüning's authoritarian

[21]This is the basis of the SED, an alliance of Communists and Social Democrats, the ruling party in the German Democratic Republic.
[22]M. Eksteins, *The Limits of Reason. The German Democratic Press and the Collapse of the Weimar Republic* (1975) and 'The *Frankfurter Zeitung*: Mirror of Weimar Democracy', *J.Cont.H.* 6 (1971), pp. 3–28.

democracy as essential in view of the irresponsibility of the political parties and the need for a strong national leadership. In the weeks before Hitler's appointment as chancellor the paper's leaders expressed the view that the National Socialists had to be admitted into government in the interests of the nation.

10

National Socialism: The Apotheosis of Nationalism?[1]

Historians examining the Third *Reich* are faced immediately with a number of problems. It has been described as the most intensively studied 12 years in History: the literature on the period is vast and growing all the time. National Socialism was also deeply contradictory and ambivalent, being at one and the same time modern and anti-modern, traditional and revolutionary, unoriginal and innovative, ideological and flexible, devoted to the concept of a single all-powerful leader and in practice allowing power to be shared by a large number of different bodies. When in government, it quickly developed into a very complex and changeable phenomenon. Like nationalism itself it cannot be reduced to simple formulae. The massive impact of National Socialism on Germany and the world has inevitably produced deep divisions of opinion among historians on basic aspects of the regime, divisions often expressed with an asperity and public displays of bad temper unusual among academics. There are deep divisions on the nature of the phenomenon and whether what the National Socialist regime did or attempted to do was fundamentally different, except in style and intensity, from what had gone before. Much of this centres on the questions of inevitability, whether a national totalitarian state was the logical culmination of nationalism, and continuity, that is, the extent to which the roots of Nazism and the conditions which allowed it to succeed must be sought in Germany's history before 1914.[2] The National Socialists were themselves partly responsible for this. Through its excellent propaganda machine, the National Socialist government deliberately portrayed itself as the natural culmination of centuries of German progress and the heir of the work of great Germans of the past like the Hohenstaufens, the

[1]Basic works on the National Socialist period: G. Pridham and J. Noakes (eds.), *Nazism 1919–45. A Documentary Reader* (2 vols., Exeter, 1983–4); F.L. Carsten, *The Rise of Fascism* (1967); K.D. Bracher, *The German Dictatorship* (1971); G.L. Mosse, *Nazism* (Oxford, 1978); M. Broszat, *The Hitler State* (1981); E. Jäckel, *Hitler's Weltanschauung. A Blueprint for Power* (Middletown, 1972); J.C. Fest. *The Face of the Third Reich* (1970) and *Hitler* (1974); W. Carr, *Hitler. A Study in Personality and Politics* (1986); K. Hildebrand, *The Third Reich* (1984); P. Aycoberry, *The Nazi Question* (1981); J. Hiden and J. Farquharson, *Explaining Hitler's Germany* (Totowa, N.J., 1983); P.M.H. Bell, *The Origins of the Second World War in Europe* (1986), chap. 6.
[2]I. Kershaw, *The Nazi Dictatorship* (1985), as an introduction to the controversies.

colonizers of the eastern lands, the Hansa, Luther, Frederick the Great and Bismarck. Not surprisingly, such views were used by foreign enemies of Germany as proof that the German nation as a whole had proved throughout its history to be innately susceptible to authoritarianism, racism, militarism and extreme imperialist nationalism. Works published in Britain, France and the USA during and after the Second World War sought to prove that the germs of Nazism had been growing for centuries.[3] At its most extreme, this view found evidence of proto-Nazism among the Germanic tribes described by Tacitus. In self-defence some German historians after the war put forward the view that the whole phenomenon was a product of Germany's defeat in 1918 and subsequent troubles plus the 'daemonic' character of Hitler. The debate continues.

Arising from this, it can be argued that National Socialism was the culmination of developments in German nationalism since the beginning of the nineteenth century, including the *völkisch* movement and social imperialism. It very skilfully employed a political style already familiar in Germany; its rallies brought the *Volksfeste* of the late nineteenth century to their highest development. Its enthronement of race or 'blood' as the main criterion for membership of the nation was perhaps the ultimate form of national exclusivity;[4] other criteria of membership of a nation, for example language, culture, religion or acceptance or a political system, are open in the sense that they can be adopted at will. In reality, nationality has rarely been determined by a single factor but by a mixture of different criteria involving those listed above and others in different combinations. The same was true of the Nazi concept of Germanness; if 'blood' was central, other factors, including attitudes, were also important. This illustrates how complex the supposed 'great simplifier', fascism, was in its main German manifestation.

The new German government which took power in January 1933, the Government of National Concentration, placed great emphasis on its 'national' character in contrast to its political enemies, whom it accused of sacrificing German interests for narrow sectional gain. It had plans for Germany which involved not only the destruction of the existing political system but also the creation of a new kind of state and society. The social, it was said, would be found through the national. It was devoted to the revival of the country, the elimination of 'alien' elements and the assertion of

[3]For example, R.d'O, Butler, *The Roots of National Socialism 1783–1933* (1942); W.M. MacGovern, *A History of Fascist-Nazi Philosophy* (Boston, 1941).
[4]M. Hauner, 'A German Racial Revolution', *J.Cont.H.* 19 (1984), pp. 669–87.

German power in Europe. Initially the new government contained representatives of two streams of German nationalism, the traditional Wilhelmine imperialist and the *völkisch* variants. The 'left wing' of the NSDAP, strongly represented in the rapidly expanding SA, looked forward to a genuine social, economic and spiritual National Revolution, which Hitler had apparently promised, leading to the emergence of the *Volksgemeinschaft*. Continuity of personnel and attitudes in the army, civil service and economic élites was marked. There was considerable overlapping between the aspirations of each group; both wanted the destruction of the 'shackles of Versailles', German rearmament and the resumption by Germany of a place of influence and power in the world which her size and resources were seen as making hers by right.[5] When it suited them the National Socialists were happy to appeal to Prussian traditions. In the Prussian state elections in April 1932 they promised to return Prussia to its true traditions of discipline, duty, service, honour, simplicity and frugality. The traditional Right also borrowed *völkisch* language, seen for example in the army before January 1933.[6] The blending of old and new was symbolized most clearly in the State Act of 21 March 1933 in the Potsdam garrison church, the formal opening of the *Reichstag* elected on 5 March. Hitler and Hindenburg appeared as partners in front of an empty throne, with the Kaiser's eldest son standing behind it, and the tomb of Frederick the Great. The SPD and KPD were conspicuously not invited. The traditional nationalists and the Nazis believed they were using one another for their own ends. The triumph of Hitler could, therefore, be regarded as the culmination of the policy of employing nationalism as an instrument of distraction pioneered by Bismarck.

Although Hitler, while rebuilding his party after the failed *putsch* of 1923 and when in power, showed himself a pragmatic and flexible politician, he seems to have adhered firmly to a system of ideas or a *Weltanschauung* made up of a few basic points, a fanatical anti-Semitism and anti-Marxism, a conviction that the Germans were innately superior and a belief in Darwinian concepts of eternal struggle and selection of the strongest. In *Mein Kampf*[7] (especially volume 2, chapter 2) he portrayed himself as a *völkisch* nationalist politician devoted to the creation of the *Volksgemeinschaft*. There is considerable dispute as to how far *Mein Kampf*

---

[5]W.D. Smith, *The Ideological Origins of Nazi Imperialism* (Oxford, 1986); J.H. Jarausch, 'From Second to Third *Reich*. The Problem of Continuity in German Foreign Policy', *Cent.Eur.H.* 12 (1979), pp. 68–82.

[6]M. Messerschmidt, 'The *Wehrmacht* and the *Volksgemeinschaft*', *J.Cont.H.* 18 (1983), pp. 719–44.

[7]An English edition of *Mein Kampf* was published in London in 1969 with an introduction by D.C. Watt. See also W. Maser, *Hitler's Mein Kampf. An Analysis* (1970).

reflects faithfully Hitler's views and how far it formed the basis of his actions when in power.[8] Some historians reject it as irrelevant and see it as no more than empty day dreams. It seems to have caused some embarrassment to its author: according to Albert Speer's memoirs, Hitler in 1938 said he regretted having committed himself to definite statements so early in his career and that it no longer had much validity.[9] It is interesting that foreign governments scoured the book in an attempt to find clues to Hitler's likely behaviour after he came into power.[10] It would certainly be wrong to see *Mein Kampf* or Hitler's so-called *Second Book*,[11] a work largely devoted to foreign policy written in 1928 but never published, as in any sense the 'bible' of National Socialism or the repository of its ideology. Indeed, there must be doubt if the term 'ideology' can accurately be applied to what was in reality a collection of vague ideas and attitudes held together by a matrix of resentment.[12] It could be argued that Nazi ideology consisted of what Hitler happened to be saying at any given time. In addition, *Mein Kampf* itself is long, repetitive and badly written, reflecting the fact that Hitler dictated it chapter by chapter; a highly distorted autobiography and descriptions of historical events are mixed up with statements of principle in an apparently unsystematic and undigested manner. In fact there is a rudimentary logic in the structure of *Mein Kampf*: Hitler was keen to demonstrate in the 'autobiographical' section that his ideas rose out of his personal experience of real events during his sojourn in Vienna and as a soldier during and after the war. In the second part he describes the manner in which his vision should be turned into reality in the future when certain events took place. Hitler outlines the basic principles on which he believed the state should be constructed, describes the development of the NSDAP as the divinely appointed instrument for the salvation of the German *Volk* and details the circumstances in which the party must try to carry out its mission in the face of determined opposition from its enemies.

The basic message of *Mein Kampf* can be summed up in a few propositions,[13] all of which were second-hand and 'borrowed' by

[8]Hans Staudinger, *The Inner Nazi* (Baton Rouge, La., 1981), an analysis of *Mein Kampf* by an emigré SPD politician, produced in the USA in the years 1941 to 1943; M. McGuire, 'Mythic Rhetoric in *Mein Kampf*: A Structuralist Critique', *Quarterly Journal of Speech* 63 (1977), pp. 1–13.

[9]A. Speer, *Inside the Third Reich* (1970), pp. 182–3.

[10]'The Story of *Mein Kampf*', *Wiener Library Bulletin* 6 (1952).

[11]T. Taylor (ed.), *Hitler's Secret Book* (New York, 1961).

[12]B.M. Lane and L.J. Rupp, *Nazi Ideology before 1933. A Documentation* (Manchester, 1978); B.M. Lane, 'Nazi Ideology: Some Unfinished Business', *Cent.Eur.H.* 7 (1974), pp. 3–30; R.A. Pois (ed.), *Alfred Rosenberg. Selected Writings* (1970) and *National Socialism and the Religion of Nature* (1986); R. Cecil, *The Myth of the Master Race: Alfred Rosenberg and Nazi Ideology* (1972); A. Bramwell, *Blood and Soil. Walther Darré and Hitler's 'Green Party'* (Kensal, 1986).

[13]Most of this can be found in chap. 9 of volume I, 'Nation and Race'.

Hitler from other sources, some of which have been discussed in earlier chapters. The argument starts from the premise that the essential element of the German nation is its racial character. Hitler argues that traditional concepts of right and morality, governing the internal and external behaviour of governments and individuals, are fundamentally false and foisted on nations by the Jews in order to weaken them. Any action must be judged according to a sole criterion, whether or not it benefited the nation and the race. ('Foreign policy is only a means to an end and that end is solely the promotion of our own nationality'.) Hitler argues that the German people, being of one blood, has to live together in a single *Reich*. Otherwise small pockets of Germans would so vitalize inferior peoples as to make them dangerous to Germany. In addition, the German nation is too large for the territory it inhabits and, because of this overpopulation, it is forced to maintain an un-German commercial/industrial economy to produce export goods with which to purchase food supplies. As a result it has fallen prey to alien ideas and practices and its national essence is being corroded. Hitler believed a large and strong peasantry was vital to the health of a state. Only the conquest and colonization of more living space (*Lebensraum*) in Eastern Europe ('If we speak today of new soil in Europe, we can only think of Russia and her vassal border states') would give Germany the secure food supplies which would allow her to maintain a healthy 'balanced' economy. Germany must resume where she had left off six centuries earlier, ending the eternal German movement to the south and west and returning to her true destiny in the east. Food shortages were a valuable historical factor giving one people the incentive to destroy weaker inferior peoples. The basic principles of all human organization must be the 'aristocratic principle of nature' and the 'principle of personality', that is that each species maintains its strength by breeding only with its own kind and that the strong will always subdue and dominate the weak. Democracy and Marxism both negate this principle and therefore produce national weakness. Man is a fighting animal and the nation a fighting unit. Any organism which ceases to struggle is doomed to destruction. Only constant struggle can allow the best to rise to the top. The fighting capacity of a nation depends on its purity. The Germans were, like all peoples, a mongrelized race but retained more pure Nordic blood than any other nation. Only the Nordic or Aryan race was capable of creating culture and of true idealism. All other races were inferior and could therefore be exploited by the Aryans. A biological renaissance, a programme of racial eugenics and the purging of all foreign impurities, would, over time, restore the lost

racial purity and the unity of the *Volk*. The first duty of a government was to nationalize the masses, that is to imbue them with
national enthusiasm. Hitler said that if Germany had an army of
six million physically fit young men consumed by a fanatical
patriotism, she could achieve all her desires. As an interim measure,
national unity would be restored by a revival of Prussian militarism. Hitler seems to have belived that the state of the Hohenzol-
lens represented the *Volksgemeinschaft* in miniature: 'The principle
which once made the Prussian army the most marvellous instrument of the German people has to be the principle of the construction of our whole state constitution.' The restoration of racial
purity by eugenics and 'education in Germanism' were vital steps
in the 'nationalization of the masses': 'Without the clearest knowledge of the racial problem and hence of the Jewish problem, there
will never be a resurrection of the German nation .... The crown
of the folkish state's entire work of education and training must
be to burn the racial sense and racial feeling into the instinct and
the intellect, the heart and brain of the youth entrusted to it ....
The highest purpose of the folkish state is concern for the preservation of those original racial elements which bestow culture and
create the beauty and dignity of a higher mankind .... Education
has to be directed at giving the young German the conviction of
being absolutely superior to others.'

The German nation, as closest to racial purity, had a mission to
save the world from a Jewish conspiracy to take it over. In order to
fulfil this task, Germany would have to dominate the world and
destroy the Jews. It was Hitler's stated aim to convert 'a decadent
nation of poets and thinkers into the most voracious beast of prey
the world has ever seen'.[14] Hitler and his followers believed firmly
that the Jews were conspiring to enslave the world. The Jews were
devoted to the destruction of the German nation by all means
possible, realizing that it represented the last remaining barrier to
their take-over of the world after their conquest of Russia by
Bolshevism, of Britain by capitalism and of France by miscegenation.
Hitler's strongest objection to the Jews was their lack of nationality, their internationalism, as a result of which they lived as para-
sites on other nations. The colours of the flag of the German
Republic — red, black and gold — symbolized these internationals
Marxism, clericalism and capitalism, the three prongs of the Jewish
assault on Germany.

To sum up: it was the stated intention of the Hitler movement
to pull down the system which existed and replace it with a

[14]Quoted in Hauner 'A German Racial Revolution', p. 676.

Utopian new and better world. The genuine idealism of many who supported National Socialism must not be forgotten: Hitler's emphasis on the idealism of the Nordic race was an echo of a concept present in German intellectual attitudes throughout the period we have been looking at, the notion that the German spirit or soul had survived throughout the time of Germany's political fragmentation and the belief that moral freedom was superior to political freedom and spiritual values higher than material values.[15] To Germans impoverished by inflation, cast down by defeat and the treaty of Versailles, living under a system of government seen as imposed by foreigners and producing only misery and national humiliation, surrounded by degenerate culture and with no hope for the future, the optimistic message was very appealing, especially as its ingredients were already familiar to them. Hitler planned to regain for Germany national freedom of action, to restore the *Reich* of 1914 and then to bring together all Germans in a single *Gross-deutschland*. The National Socialists used *germanisch* (Germanic) as well as *deutsch* with no clear and obvious distinction between them. In April 1940, on the German occupation of Norway and Denmark, Hitler was recorded as seeing this as the foundation of the *Grossgermanisches Reich*. This state would be purged of democracy, Marxism, Liberalism and all the other aspects of 'modernity', which had undermined the Germanness of Germany, and refounded on truly German principles to restore national unity. Internally it would be prepared for war: for Hitler the ultimate function of internal policy was the forging of a powerful sword. Germany would then expand eastwards to win living space. This would in turn fit her for a bid for world domination, which would enable the German nation to fulfil its historic mission, the elimination of the Jewish threat. Hitler emphasized the nation, *Volk*, rather than the state, *Staat*, but the nation was only a means to an end.[16] The victory of the master race would initiate a *pax Germanica*, a period of unbroken peace and unprecedented cultural perfection. Hitler dreamed of stopping all historical, cultural and biological development and creating a world of such perfection that it would last unchanged for a thousand years.[17] At the borders of the new *Reich* there would be a permanent war against the non-Aryan barbarians to enable each generation of Germans to harden itself by a blood

[15]See Hajo Holborn, 'German Idealism in the Light of Social History', in *Germany and Europe. Historical Essays* (New York, 1970) and H.S. Hughes, 'The German Idealist Tradition', in *Consciousness and Society* (repr. Brighton, 1979), pp. 183–91; D. Calleo, *The German Problem Reconsidered* (Cambridge, 1978), pp. 146–157.

[16]In the last days of the Third *Reich* Hitler, according to Albert Speer's memoirs (*Inside the Third Reich* p. 578ff.), was quite prepared to see the German nation totally destroyed as they had proved too weak for their mission. The future therefore belonged to the stronger nations of the east.

sacrifice and prevent a softening of the race. These aims were pursued with a flexibility of policy which led many contemporaries to conclude that Hitler was no more than an opportunistic politician in search of personal power, who employed high-flown rhetoric in order to win votes.

In addition to the above, there is an interesting statement of what the National Socialist regime saw itself as having achieved in a collection of 21 essays published in London in 1938 under the title *Germany Speaks*.[18] This contained papers on a wide range of topics by leading figures of the regime and, according to the foreword by the foreign minister von Ribbentrop, its stated aim was to foster understanding between Germany and Britain by giving a true picture of conditions in Germany and of the hopes and aspirations of the German people. Certain themes recur.

Before 1933 Germany was fatally weakened by the legacy of disunity and particularism left by the Thirty Years' War and persisting under the Second *Reich* and, even more, the Weimar Republic. Under the National Socialists Germany is for the first time in its history a truly united state and nation, constitutionally and spiritually: 'National Socialist Germany, however, is not merely a unitary state; it is also a unitary nation and its governance is based on the principle of leadership. The nation constitutes the concrete substance of the National Socialist movement and the State is merely the means for the realization of its political aims'. (Dr Frick, minister of the interior.)

'National Socialism looks upon the community of the nation as an organization which has its own rights and duties and whose interests come before those of the individual.' The German legal system has therefore been standardized for the whole *Reich*. The status of written law has been reduced and a new criterion for the definition of a crime created, any act which is detrimental to the interests of the national community. (Dr Franz Gürtner, minister of justice.)

The education system was a particularly valuable instrument for the revival of healthy national sentiment. The pre-1933 system was deficient in that it did not prevent people falling prey to Marxism and cosmopolitanism and 'tended to impair the healthy spirit of the nation and a sense of national solidarity.' Excessive individualism had led to the destruction of the natural community of the

---

[17]*Tausendjährige Reich* does not only signify a system which would last for a thousand years but also the Millenium, the perfect world. The transcendental nature of the movement, emphasized by Norman Cohn in *The Pursuit of the Millenium* (2nd ed., 1962) and J.M. Rhodes, *The Hitler Movement. A Modern Millenarian Revolution* (Stanford, 1980), was originated by the Nazis themselves.

[18]*Germany Speaks* (1938).

nation and replaced it with 'artificial and super-national sham communities'. (Bernard Rust, minister of education.)

The social policy of the new government has abolished class and party strife, 'as if by magic', created solidarity between employers and employees and given dignity to all working Germans. Before 1933 class divisions were so deep in Germany because of international Marxism's poisoning of the minds of nearly half the population that a civil war was likely to break out at any moment. Now envy and divisions have been banished and all 'national comrades' (*Volksgenossen*) make a contribution to the welfare of the nation in a system of national solidarity based on social justice. Peasants and craftsmen, in particular, are afforded the honour due to them because of their special value as custodians of true German values and traditions, which reside essentially in the countryside. 'National Socialists are firm believers in the "back-to-the-land" movement and hold that something must be done to stop the excessive congregation of human material in towns and industrial districts ... the new social order pays due regard to such specifically German character traits as a sense of honour, loyalty, comradeship, fairness, collaboration and a pronounced love of nature. All these characteristics were temporarily submerged owing to the soulless mechanization typical of some aspects of modern civilization.' A special programme of building homesteads, houses with large allotments attached, around towns will enable industrial workers to experience the benefits of a rural life-style. The Strength through Joy Movement, by giving workers cheap holidays, has allowed ordinary Germans for the first time to visit other parts of their country: 'ethically and morally too, the division into North and South has vanished'. (Robert Ley, head of the German Labour Front, on National Socialist social policy.)

Symbols of the new national unity are everywhere. The new motorways, in physically linking the various regions of Germany, symbolize 'the deeper and spiritual movement of the National Socialist revolution, which signifies a psychic and cultural renovation of the German citizen'. More, their careful blending into the landscape, a harmonious mixing of technology and Nature, shows how National Socialism is able to blend modernity with the traditional best in German life. (Dr Todt, inspector-general of the German motorways.)

The greatest success of the National Socialist regime was in its propaganda. Large numbers of Germans became convinced as a result of Goebbels's efforts that they did live in a genuine *Volksgemeinschaft*. This was increased by symbolic devices such as the cheap *Volkswagen* car and *Volksempfänger* radio receiver, putting what had previously been luxury goods within the reach of ordinary Germans, and party-encouraged mass participation in the Winter

Aid (*Winterhilfe*) social welfare scheme. The reality was very different. The promise of a 'national revolution', the creation of a classless Germany with equality of opportunity for all and new criteria of worth to the nation, was not fulfilled. Where new opportunities for upward mobility did materialize, as for example in the economy or the army, it was a result of their rapid expansion rather than deliberate social engineering. There were many chances to rise high and rapidly in the Nazi party but this was effectively excluded from real power. Any hope of genuine social and economic change came to an end with the purge of the radical wing of the NSDAP in the Night of the Long Knives, June–July 1934. There was no great movement of Nazis into positions of power; on the contrary, many existing office-holders joined the party in the early months of 1933 in order to retain their posts.[19]

The impression of a kind of compulsory national unity was achieved by institutions such as the Labour Service, eventually made obligatory for all young Germans, and the process known as 'standardization' (*Gleichschaltung*). Under this a large number of National Socialist organizations were given monopoly powers within their own field and commissioned to carry out a political educational role. As membership of such bodies was usually compulsory for people engaged in a given profession, as was involvement in organized activities, a spurious air of unity could be created. Like the *Volksgemeinschaft*, however, *Gleichschaltung* was more a propaganda slogan than a reality. Movements such as the Beauty of Work (*Schönheit der Arbeit*) and Strength through Joy (*Kraft durch Freude*) involved attempts to humanize the factory by improving its physical environment and to make the worker a full member of the national community by organizing cultural and recreational activities, but in reality the status of industrial workers did not improve. The enforced mixing of classes under the auspices of the Labour Service, the German Labour Front and other National Socialist organizations might have done something to break down barriers but were just as likely to reinforce them.

The *Mittelstand*, the great strength of the party in membership and electoral support and the supposed backbone of the nation, were, ironically, the real losers. Small farmers and businessmen, although flattered in the regime's propaganda, were happily sacrificed when the government's real interests, above all the need to achieve rapid rearmament, demanded it. Both groups declined more rapidly under the Third *Reich* than the Weimar Republic. No return to the rural idyll envisaged by the *völkisch* nationalists was achieved. Two new garden cities were created, one, Wolfsburg,

---

[19]Some in the party continued to dream of genuine economic and social reform but postponed until after a victorious war: A. Speer, *The Slave State* (1981), chap. 7 on economic thinking in the NSDAP.

the site of the factory to build the People's Car (*Volkswagen*), another example of National Socialist *Volksgemeinschaft* propaganda, but both urbanization and the flight from the land accelerated during the Third *Reich*.

The only aspect of *völkisch* nationalism which was realized was the elimination of the Jews, to which, as time passed, the regime applied more and more of its energies. This was reflected in the growing power of the SS, which was encouraged by Himmler to regard itself as the institutional custodian of the racial mission. The SS carried out the Final Solution of the Jewish 'problem' and also planned to bring together valuable Nordic bloodstock from other countries into the *Reich* by policies for which new German words were coined, such as 'Nordicizing Up' (*Aufnordung*) and 'de-Latinizing' (*Entwelschung*). It supervised other aspects of the racial obsession, the attempt to recreate a pure Nordic race by selective breeding and the notion of an anti-Bolshevik New Order in Europe, in which not only Germans but other racially acceptable Aryans would participate. The latter was symbolized in the recruitment of volunteers for the armed SS (*Waffen-SS*) from German-occupied Europe. In the last stages of the war large numbers of ethnic Germans (*Volksdeutsche*) were shipped to the *Reich* from eastern and south-eastern Europe.

Probably the high point of national unity during the Third *Reich* came in June 1940 at the moment of victory over France. This, the humiliation of hereditary enemy (*Erbfeind*), was seen as revenge for Versailles and it produced a wave of enthusiasm for Hitler. At the same time, to the horror of the regime, it produced a great desire for peace and reconciliation with the French.[20] The popularity of the government slumped with the outbreak of war against Russia. The war-effort was sustained until the end but it is hard to say how much this was due to a sense of national unity, fear of the government or fear of the revenge the Allies would wreak on Germany if they won the war.

In operation Nazism, like other fascist systems, was very dependent on the established order and the co-operation of the traditional élites was vital in putting the National Socialists into power. Until 1938 Hitler, an amateur politician, lacked confidence and felt dependent on the institutions of the traditional ruling class, the army, civil service and big business, in order to sustain his regime. The Old Germany was not destroyed; the Nazi government and the so-called Bismarckian élites collaborated but Hitler was never the puppet his political partners expected. At first Hitler

[20]H.K. Smith. *Last Train from Berlin* (1942), pp. 69–70; P. Krüger, 'Rückkehr zum internationalen Faustrecht', in K. Malettke (ed.), *Der Nationalsozialismus an der Macht* (Göttingen, 1984), pp. 166–91.

emphasized international peace and national reconstruction and was happy to permit the illusion that Hindenburg was the true ruler of Germany. Initially, the main aim of the government was to eliminate Marxism. The National Socialist takeover was gradual and insidious after the Enabling Act of 24 March 1933, which gave Hitler's government dictatorial powers. Rival parties were eliminated and the powers of the federal states removed. Germany became for the first time a unitary state. With the *Anschluss* with Austria and the acquisition of the Sudetenland it contained within its borders the great majority of the German nation.

The Nazi party did not take over Germany. Instead the old institutions survived alongside parallel party organizations and there was constant rivalry for power between them, with Hitler's personal authority the main beneficiary. In the process the old order was slowly dismantled, a process speeded up by the great mobilization of the economy and the war. By the late 1930s some traditional conservatives were becoming increasingly worried about Hitler's risky foreign policy and there was talk of installing a government of moderate Nazis and nationalists, perhaps under Göring, on the Italian model. Such worries became serious after the declaration of war on Russia and the first major reverses of the war, El Alamein and Stalingrad. The Conservative resistance, much haloized since 1945, had no new view of the nation.[21] They certainly envisaged no return to Weimar democracy and pluralism. In the Kreisau Circle there was talk of a 'new *Gemeinschaft*' involving a hierarchy of indirectly elected bodies to rule Germany and a kind of state Socialism to remove social and economic divisions. The Officers' Plot in July 1944 led to a major breach between the government and the old élites and Hitler was seriously considering the abolition of the traditional army and civil service. The war ended before this process could be completed.

Some commentators argue that an unplanned but genuine social revolution took place during the Nazi period, with the elimination of Bismarck's Germany and the élites which had run the country since unification.[22] This is questionable. It was rather the total defeat, occupation and division of Germany, the massive land losses in the east and the establishment of a soviet regime in the Russian zone of occupation which swept away the 'old Germany' and, in the process, shattered the German nation.

[21]H. Mommsen, 'Social Views and Constitutional Plans of the Resistance', in Mommsen *et al.* (eds.), *The German Resistance to Hitler* (1970), pp. 57–147; P. Hoffman, *The History of the German Resistance 1933–1945* (Cambridge, Mass., 1977); H. Rothfels, *The German Opposition to Hitler: an assessment* (1961).
[22]R. Dahrendorf, *Society and Democracy in Germany* (1967); D. Schoenbaum, *Hitler's Social Revolution: Class and Status in Nazi Germany 1933–9* (1967).

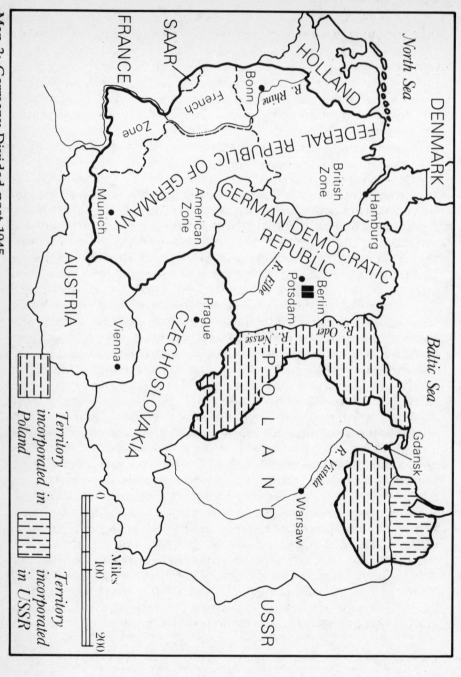

Map 3: Germany Divided post-1945

11
Nationalism in the Germanies since 1945

Germany's enemies did not fight the Second World War to extirpate Nazism but to destroy a powerful Germany, the existence of which was seen as an unacceptable threat to Europe, whatever the form of its government. This motivated the victorious Allies' treatment of Germany after its defeat in 1945. The defeat and the Allied occupation completed the dismantling of Bismarck's Germany and a reopening of the whole 'German question'.[1] Far more obviously than 1918, 1945 represented in many respects a deep caesura in German history. Germany's defeat was total and undeniable and there is no stab-in-the-back legend, though it is interesting that 1945 rather than 1933–45 is called 'the German catastrophe' (*die deutsche Katastrophe*). For Germans May 1945 was *Stunde Null* (zero hour), from which everything had a new beginning. It has been followed by profound changes. Substantial territories in the east, German for centuries, have been lost. This is now recognized on West German maps which no longer show the lost lands as 'under Polish and Russian administration'. Prussia no longer exists, having been abolished by the Allied Control Council in February 1947, an important symbolic break with the past. The *Junkers* , the core of the old ruling élites, were destroyed by the land reform in the Soviet occupation zone in 1945, which broke up their remaining estates. Denazification and re-education in the western zones, although ineffective and resented by the Germans,[2] at least symbolically purged the leaders of the old Germany and helped an infant German democracy on to its feet.

The 'German problem' still exists but now in a very different form. The German nation is divided into three states, East and

[1] M. Balfour, *West Germany. A Contemporary History* (1982); D. Childs, *Germany since 1918* (2nd edn, 1980); D. Childs and J. Johnson, *West Germany. Politics and Society* (1981); G.A. Craig, *The Germans* (1982), esp. chap. 13; K.D. Bracher, *The German Dilemma. The Relationship of State and Democracy* (New York, 1975) (collected essays); J. Ardagh, *Germany and the Germans* (1987); G. Smith (ed.), *Democracy in Western Germany* (2nd edn, 1982); S. Padgett and T. Burkett, *Political Parties and Elections in West Germany* (1986); L.J. Edinger, *West German Politics* (New York, 1985); G.W. Sandford, *From Hitler to Ulbricht. The Communist Reconstruction of E. Germany 1945–6* (Princeton, 1983); R. Dahrendorf, *Society and Democracy in Germany* (1967); M. McCauley, *The German Democratic Republic since 1945* (1983).
[2] T. Bower, *Blind Eye to Murder* (1981); J.F. Tent, *Mission on the Rhine* (Chicago, 1982).

West Germany and the Austrian Republic, with no realistic prospect of reunification between them. Germany as a nation state has ceased to exist except in the Utopian dream, maintained in the Basic Law or provisional constitution of the Federal Republic, that Germany within the borders of 31 December 1937 will one day be recreated following a final general European peace settlement. In none of the successor states of Hitler's Greater Germany does German nationalism play a large political role. Both the main German states are artificial in their borders and their internal political subdivisions, the West German *Länder* and the East German circles. Both states, especially the Federal Republic, acquired large new bodies of population in the form of refugees from the lost lands of the East, Silesia, E. Prussia, E. Pomerania and the Sudetenland, and German minorities from eastern and south-eastern Europe, who had no roots in the areas they settled in. It is estimated that about 12 million such people moved west after 1944, a brutal surgical solution to the nationality problem pioneered in south-eastern Europe and Asia Minor in the 1920s by the Turks, Greeks and Bulgarians. This enforced emigration created a kind of national unity in misfortune as all Germans, regardless of class, political affiliation or religion, were thrown out of Silesia, W. Prussia, the Sudetenland and so on. There are still German minorities in eastern Europe, including an estimated one million in Poland, but they seem to have little impact on their host countries.

In Austria a distinct Austrian national consciousness is firmly established, similar to that which developed earlier among the Swiss Germans, and there is no evidence of any desire for union with either of the German states. Localism is a more powerful political factor in Austria than in Germany: the Austrian federal states (*Länder*) have a more real historical existence than the German states. As early as the October 1943 Moscow Declaration the Allies decided to re-established a sovereign Austria. The State Treaty of 1955, which re-established Austrian independence, imposed neutrality and specifically precluded a union with Germany.

There are other signs that the German states are growing apart. Communication and personal as well as political contacts between the two Germanies are increasing but are still limited[3] and it could

---

[3]Economic links between the two states are growing but W. Germany still exports goods worth 50 per cent more to Switzerland than to the whole of Comecon. W. Germany uses its economic power to buy concessions for E. German citizens. West German television and radio can be received in the DDR. About 600,000 DDR citizens visited W. Germany on 'urgent family matters' in 1986, in addition to 1.6 million pensioners, who can go whenever they wish. In May 1986 new agreements were signed for a programme of youth and cultural exchanges and town twinnings. Statement by Chancellor Kohl, 13 January 1987: *Reports from the Federal Republic of Germany* (German Embassy, London).

be argued that they are beginning to develop distinct identities. There are interesting signs of linguistic divergence between the three states, though this can be exaggerated. Although all use High German, the Austrian version is very heavily accented and this may be deliberately emphasized, for example by television announcers, as a symbol of Austrian separateness. It is possible that spoken German in Austria could evolve into something like Swiss-German, which is incomprehensible to speakers of the high language. Even between the two Germanies there are audible differences. Official German in the DDR is purer than the increasingly Anglicized or Americanized language becoming common in West Germany.[4]

The building of the Berlin Wall in 1961, closing the last hole through which the citizens of the DDR could emigrate, stabilized the situation and made the partition of Germany permanent. The longer the partition lasts, the less it will mean and there must be doubts about the importance of the issue to future generations of Germans. Much will depend on how Germans are taught about the history of their countries. Both the German states are trying to create an identity for themselves and History has become a source of 'legitimacy ammunition' (*Legitimationsarsenal*). Both states claim to be the true heirs of Germany's past while, in reality, the only genuine historical tradition they have inherited is disunity. In the German Democratic Republic the cause of world Socialism is paramount. Since its foundation the East German regime has shown a desire to find roots for itself in Germany's past[5] and, apart from the obvious events like the Peasants' War of 1525, popular movements and German—Russian collaboration in the War of Liberation, the activities of Socialists and Radicals in 1848, the Spartacist Movement and Communist opposition to Hitler, in recent years it seems to have chosen Luther and the founders of the Prussian state as its forerunners. The regime even claims the Germanic chieftain Arminius/Hermann as the model for a freedom fighter against the alien American 'occupation' of West Germany. In its emphasis on the role of the state and the cultivation of old Prussia 'virtues' like obedience and duty, the DDR is probably closer to the traditional Germany than the increasingly Americanized Federal Republic, though both Socialism in the DDR and welfare capitalism in the Federal Republic have distinctly German characteristics.

Like the German Democratic Republic, West Germany searches German history selectively to try to find roots for a Liberal democratic system, of which there is as little trace in the country's past

---

[4]This is reflected in the publication of works like *Kleines Wörterbuch des DDR-Wortschatzes* (*A Little Dictionary of the E. German Vocabulary*) (Düsseldorf, 1980).
[5]A. Dorpalen, *German History in Marxist Perspective. The East German Approach* (1986).

as of Soviet-style Socialism. Much attention is paid to the Hansa, the 1848 revolutions, the foundations of democracy in 1918 and the non-Communist opposition to Hitler. It is ironic that both the major successor states are serving up to their people a version of German history as distorted, if for different motives, as that presented under Bismarck and Hitler. This rewriting of history is an echo of an earlier criterion of nationhood, the notion of shared experience. The claims of both to be the true heir of 'German national traditions' have produced a debate about the nature of German nationhood, which is still going on. The regime in the DDR has put forward the idea of 'two states, two nations' to justify the division of Germany, arguing that the DDR represents the Socialist German nation and the Federal Republic the capitalist German nation. The East Germans are taught that their state is the first truly liberated national Germany because the Federal Republic is still the victim of internal and foreign imperialism and that German unity will only be achieved when West Germany becomes a Socialist, that is Communist, state. The DDR ruling Popular Front Party, the SED (*Sozialistische Einheitspartei Deutschlands*, German Socialist Unity Party), sees patriotism as a very good thing. As defined in a party declaration of 3 March 1953, *Patriotismus* means dedication and loyalty to the DDR, Socialism, the SED and the friendship of the DDR and the Soviet Union. The creation of such patriotism is a high priority of national education. The same idea was contained in the new constitution of the DDR issued in 1968. The preamble spoke of the DDR's responsibility to the whole German nation to point the way to a future of peace and Socialism, in view of the historical fact that USA-led imperialism, in alliance with circles of West German monopoly capitalism, had divided Germany in order to make West Germany a base for imperialism. Therefore only Germans in the DDR enjoy genuine self-determination. Article I of the constitution states: 'The German Democratic Republic is a Socialist state of the German nation'.[6] This was changed when a new constitution was issued in October 1974. There is no mention in this of the German nation but the DDR is defined as a 'a Socialist state of workers and peasants' in perpetual alliance with the USSR. In the early 1980s DDR leaders issued statements to the effect that the DDR is a perfect Socialist nation state, which has nothing to do with West Germany. The old Marxist view of the nation as a product of the prevailing economic and social system now takes precedence over ethnic or cultural

[6]East German definitions of nationhood are clearly stated in the work of Alfred Kosing, for example *Nation in Geschichte und Gegenwart. Studie zur historisch-materialistischen Theorie der Nation* (E. Berlin, 1976).

criteria of nationality. Claims by the West German government to exclusive representation of the German nation, for example by the establishment in 1966 of a Department for All-German Affairs (*Staatssekretariat für gesamtdeutsche Fragen*), have provoked defensive assertions of distinct nationhood from the DDR, which are reminiscent of the *Deutschtümelei* of the nineteenth century. This has sometimes been mocked in the West in the form of cartoons showing street-scenes in which everything is labelled: DDR-dog, DDR-sky, DDR-door and so on. The DDR also makes frequent use of the word 'national' − national prizes, national championships − but this use refers exclusively to the DDR.

The West German government adheres to the notion of the unity of the German cultural nation but accepts its interim division into separate states. The preamble to the Basic Law in the BRD constitution, which contains the only specific reference to 'nation' in the whole document, commits the republic to the restoration of complete unity and freedom to the whole German people in free self-determination. This was confirmed in a Letter on German Unity sent in 1970 to various governments by the BRD government, reserving its position when it accepted the *de facto* existence of two German states within the borders of 1945. Symbolic of the problem is the West German government's choice of a national day. It is interesting that it rejected historical landmarks such as the promulgation of the constitution of 1849, the proclamation of the *Reich* in 1871 or the anniverary of the foundation of the Federal republic and chose instead as the Day of Unity 17 June, the anniversary of a popular rising against the government in East Germany in 1953. This is enjoyed by the population as a bank holiday but there is little sign that its real significance impinges much on popular consciousness. In West Germany, apart from pride in the country's remarkable achievements since the war (seen, for example, in headlines in the popular press to the effect that 'Germany is again Number One in Europe' in economic terms), Europeanism seems to enjoy more popular approval than nationalism. A commitment to this is written into the constitution: article 24 of the Basic Law states that the German nation desires to maintain its national unity but at the same time to contribute to the peace of the world as an equal member of a united Europe, if necessary at the cost of its sovereignty. This development was symbolized in the person of the first post-war chancellor Konrad Adenauer, a man from the Rhineland, an area which had long looked westwards. The major aims of his foreign policy were an historic reconciliation with France and a commitment to NATO and the alliance with the USA, motivated by fear of the Soviet Union. This is still at the basis of West German foreign policy. Chancellor

Kohl, in a statement to the *Bundestag* on disarmament on 4 June 1987, emphasized the fundamental importance of the EEC, NATO and Germany's special relationship with France.[7] The reunification of Germany and the recovery of the lost lands are a distant dream to which politicians pay lip-service, for example in an annual Report on the State of the Nation (*Bericht zur Lage der Nation*)[8] and in the existence of a Ministry for Inter-German Relations (*Bundesministerium für innerdeutsche Beziehungen*), but they are not important issues in West German politics. The two basic aims of West German foreign policy, the full integration of the state in western Europe and the reunification of Germany in peace and freedom, are incompatible. The DDR is a colony of the Soviet Union and is in a position of subordination to it unlike any other member of the Warsaw Pact because it is still regarded as part of the Germany defeated in 1945: the Russians refer to their troops in the country as 'Soviet forces in Germany'. The DDR's armed forces are under the control of Russian commanders. East Germany is strategically vital to the USSR not only as a border province but as a means of controlling other satellites like Poland and Czechoslovakia and as an advanced industrial economy. German reunification can only be achieved if it is in the interests of the USSR to renounce the Brezhnev doctrine that it has a 'revolutionary right' to dominate eastern Europe in perpetuity. West Germany can only seek to meet the requirements of the USSR if this does not damage her relations with the West.

The gradual acceptance of realities, the beginning of Eastern Policy (*Ostpolitik*), commenced in the 1960s under a Christian Democrat (CDU) government. The Hallstein doctrine, under which the Federal Republic refused diplomatic relations with any state recognizing the DDR, was abandoned and claims to an exclusive right to speak internationally for the whole German nation were watered down. The policy progressed rapidly under Brandt's SPD government, 1969–72, with acceptance of the Oder-Neisse frontier and virtual recognition of the DDR. In return the Soviet Union, by the Four-Power Agreement on Berlin of September 1971, accepted the constitutional link between West Berlin and West Germany. This agreement was welcome to the USSR because it implicitly recognized that, in international law, the whole of Germany is still subject to four-power control. *Ostpolitik* caused deep divisions in West Germany and threatened to bring down the government in

[7]*Report from the Federal Republic*, 5 June 1987.
[8]In a Report of 23 June 1983 Chancellor Kohl said: 'There are two states in Germany. But there is only one German nation. The German nation existed before the nation state and it has survived after the nation state. That is important for our future.' *Report from the Federal Republic*, 1 July 1983.

1972 but it ultimately won acceptance. The popularity of the policy with the voters was shown in their endorsement of the SPD in 1972. It culminated in the signing of a Basic Treaty (*Grundvertrag*) on relations between the two states on 21 December 1972, which was a *de facto* recognition of the existence of two Germanies.[9] The treaty involved a mutual recognition of sovereignty, territorial integrity and borders. The West German constitutional court accepted that it did not infringe the government's obligation under the constitution to work for a reunification of Germany as a carefully-worded clause stated that all existing agreements between the two signatories and third parties, including those between the BRD and western powers committing them to an eventual reunification, were not affected. Both sides hoped to gain something very different from it, the BRD that the easier contacts permitted by the agreement would strengthen all-German national feeling and the DDR that recognition of their sovereignty would produce a distinct East German national sentiment. The DDR government only agreed to it under pressure from the USSR, keen to reduce tension in Europe and ready to accept limited contact between East and West in the interests of stability in its satellite states. It is interesting that the DDR government ran campaigns after the agreement to persuade officials, students and young people to avoid all contacts with West Germans. DDR newspapers carried attacks on the SPD as German nationalists and instructed readers, especially young people, as to what they should do and say if, by some misfortune, they met a West German Social Democrat who talked about national unity. Groups of school children from West Germany visiting the DDR are received by well-briefed members of the FDJ, the Communist youth movement. There was some unfavourable comment in the West German press that the only mention of 'nation' was in the preamble to the treaty and then only to the effect that the two Germanies have very different concepts of it. In reply to criticism of it Brandt stated, realistically, 'We have given nothing away that was not anyway lost a long time ago.' In West Germany it roused expressions of sadness but a general acceptance that such a recognition of reality was inevitable. Perhaps this was due to vague hopes among the electorate that it might speed up reunification. It appears to have done nothing to foster organized nationalism.

There have been and are still some small right-wing nationalist parties in the Federal Republic but their following has been tiny and none has been able for some time to achieve the 5 per cent of votes cast needed to win a seat in the federal parliament, though

[9]The text of the treaty is in *Deutschland-Archiv* v (1972), pp. 1205–21.

they have won short-lived representation in some state parliaments. In Germany the Allies did not create a party specifically as a home for former National Socialists, unlike in Austria, where they set up the Freedom Party for them. The German nationalist parties are 'home-grown'. They enjoyed a slight increase in support, a 'national wave', in the early 1960s in reaction to the building of the Berlin wall in 1961, and in the late 1960s with the first faltering of the 'economic miracle' in the Federal Republic and the formation of the Grand Coalition government of the SPD and the CDU, seen by some as a sordid political bargain, but their anti-democratic tone and calls for a revision of the constitution to produce more unity and resolution had a very limited appeal. The National Democratic Party (NDP) gained 4.3 per cent of the votes in the 1969 election. The other main nationalist party, the Whole German Block/League of Refugees and Dispossessed (*Gesamtdeutscher Block. Bund der Heimatvertriebenen und Entrechteten*), drew its votes from refugees from the lost lands, a declining reservoir of support. The NPD, which had attacked *Ostpolitik*, collapsed in the 1972 election. In the late 1970s there were again signs of some unease among voters, caused by disillusionment over the lack of any tangible results from *Ostpolitik*, economic problems caused by the oil crisis and the rise of terrorism in Germany. This resulted in a movement back to the conservative CDU rather than to nationalist parties: the CDU has again established itself as a national party after showing signs in the late 1960s and early 1970s of becoming a regional and confessional party.[10]

Nationalist parties today have a tiny following among the electorate. The word *Nationalist* has had pejorative associations and all ideologies and movements (*Bewegungen*) have been suspect until the rise of the Green Movement, a mixture of ecology, anti-nuclear feeling and general non-conformity, the first real departure from very unadventurous voting behaviour based on class and religion in West Germany. Understandably, in the years after the catastrophe of 1945 nationalism was not a popular word in Germany. The Germans had rather more pressing concerns and the occupying powers did not initially allow much scope for political discussion. Many were convinced that, in Europe at least, the age of the nation-state was over. This produced what has been described as 'reverse nationalism', cultivation of the deliberate rejection of nationalism as a specifically German characteristic deriving from

[10]K.P. Tauber, *Beyond Eagle and Swastika: German Nationalism since 1945* (2 vols., Middletown, Conn., 1967); A. Ashkenasi, *Modern German Nationalism* (Cambridge, Mass., 1976); H. Pross, 'Reflections on German Nationalism 1866–1966, *Orbis* 10 (1967), pp. 1148–56; T.A. Tilton, *Nazism, Neo-Nazism and the Peasantry* (Bloomington, 1975), chap. 4 on the NPD in Schleswig-Holstein; R.E.M. Irving, *The Christian Democratic Parties in Western Europe* (1979).

the German experience. Perhaps the lessons of 1933–49 are fading but memories can still be revived in a spectacular and surprising way by events such as the screening of the American soap opera *Holocaust*, which produced a short period of intense and emotional public debate. The West German government has been very concerned with enabling its people to come to terms with their past, the process known as *Vergangenheitsbewältigung*, and the events of the Third *Reich* can provoke fierce debates, as for example recently on the questions of a statute of limitations for crimes committed under the Third *Reich* and whether the statement that Hitler's regime did not murder Jews should be a criminal offence.[11]

West Germany is a mass consumer society with no serious social anxieties and increasingly part of mid-Atlantic culture. All three major parties support NATO, the EEC, better relations with eastern Europe and the social market economy and all are 'peoples' parties' (*Volksparteien*), offering something for all classes and groups. The Liberal parliamentary system seems firmly established, in spite of attempts by certain elements in the student movement to question its legitimacy in the late 1960s. There is a lack of understanding among some Germans for some of the stranger manifestations of youth culture and some expressions of nostalgia for the order, discipline and conformity of the 'good old days' of the Third *Reich* but these are without political importance. There have been some expressions of nationalism in literature, including apologies for the Third *Reich*, accounts of Allied atrocities against the Germans and attacks on the materialism and degeneracy of West Germany, but their impact has been limited. There is also some nostalgia for the lost lands, the E. Prussian *Heimat* and so on, but no evidence that this affects politics.[12] At the same time there is strong awareness of Germany's economic power and efficiency and occasional statements of impatience that Germans should still have to live under the shadow of the Nazi period and not feel pride in their nationality. As part of this process some commentators

[11] It was declared a crime by the constitutional court in 1979.
[12] Typical are G. Krüger, *Das unzerstörbare Reich* (The Indestructible *Reich*) (Hamburg, 1952); E. Kern (ps.), *Verbrechen am deutschen Volk. Eine Dokumentation alliierter Grausamkeiten* (Crimes against the German People. A Documentation of Allied Atrocities) (Hanover, 1964); H. Härtle, *Die sexuelle Revolution. Genosse Porno regiert* (The Sexual Revolution. Comrade Porn Rules) (Hanover, 1971); and F.F. von Unruh, *Klage um Deutschland* (A Complaint about Germany) (Bodman, 1973). In 1978 Hellmut Diwald's *Geschichte der Deutschen* (Frankfurt) appeared, a popular nationalist 'history' of the Germans, which was panned by academic historians. Diwald subsequently appeared on public platforms calling for more 'national' history teaching in schools, which unleashed a heated debate. Typical of lost lands notalgia is: H. Bartsch, *Geschichte Schlesiens. Land unterm schwarzen Adler mit dem Silbermond. Seine Geschichte, sein Werden, Erbühen und Vergehen* (History of Silesia. The Land under the Black Eagle with the Silver Moon. Its History, Its Development, Blossoming and Passing Away) (Marburg, 1985).

have sought to relativize the crimes of the Third *Reich*, arguing that they were no different from Hiroshima or the mass murders under Stalin in Russia. Such views do enjoy support: many older Germans condemn the Third *Reich* as much for its total failure as for its crimes. The successes of the Federal Republic in producing stability and prosperity, plus the absence of a Hitler figure and of any substantial organized racism, make a revival of National Socialism a very remote possibility. Xenophobic hostility to *Gastarbeiter* (foreign workers) is present — groups like the Turks have not become assimilated to German life-styles — but there is little evidence that it is having a major influence on political life. There are small national minorities in the two German states, Danes in Schleswig-Holstein and Sorbs in Saxony. The former are protected under agreements with Denmark and the latter have received considerable encouragement to preserve their nationality since the foundation of the DDR after almost complete Germanization.[13] Neither is the object of national hostility. Tiny nationalist and neo-Nazi movements exist but seem to attract only weird enthusiasts and misfits.[14] The accusation of too close a relationship with National Socialism in the past is still enough to threaten political careers, even though the Allies' attempts to de-Nazify Germany after 1945 were a failure and all three German states have been served loyally by civil servants and others who served the Third *Reich* with equal loyalty.

There is more overt anti-Semitism and anti-Slav feeling in Austria but again this does not seem to have any substantial political impact outside the province of Carinthia, where there is a protected Slovene minority and where there have been some visible manifestation of old-style German nationalism in recent years.[15] There are also echoes of a more active German nationalism in the Italian province of Alto-Adige, the South Tyrol, an area with a German-speaking majority ceded to Italy after the First World War. Between the wars the Italian government tried to Italianize the area by encouraging immigration by Italians and persecution of the Germans. Under an agreement signed in September 1946 the ethnic

[13]D. Childs, *The GDR. Moscow's German Ally* (1983); McCauley, *German Democratic Republic*.
[14]Activities such as swastika-daubing and the sending of vicious anonymous letters to the Jewish mayor of Frankfurt have attracted disproportionate attention: 'Anti-Semitic undercurrents surface in secondary survey', *The Times Educational Supplement*, 12 December 1986.
[15]There is a German nationalist movement in Carinthia, the *Heimatdienst*. In the Austrian general election in November 1986 the Freedom Party, under its new leader, Jörg Haider, an outspoken German nationalist, increased its seats by 50 per cent. Arguably, support for Dr Kurt Waldheim as a presidential candidate in 1986 increased as a reaction against foreign criticism of his activities during the National Socialist period. This is Austrian rather than German nationalism: 'A lumbering pair, lumbered with each other', *The Economist*, 29 November 1986, pp. 59–60.

Germans are a protected minority and in February 1948 the area was given partial autonomy. Natural unforced Italianization continues, especially from the towns like Merano and Bolzano, and promises of full self-government have not been fulfilled, leading to outbreaks of sporadic violence from small German nationalist groups, which continue to this day.[16]

The so-called 'fatherland question' has surfaced regularly in West Germany, acutely for the first time with the introduction of conscription, which raised the question of what the conscripts were fighting for. General de Gaulle's idea of a Europe of nation-states promoted a mild revival of national sentiment in France, promoted also by a waning of fear of Soviet communism.[17] This found some echo in West Germany, where anti-Communism united the Socialist, Conservative and Liberal forces and made the early years of the Federal Republic tranquil. Eugen Gerstenmeier, lecturing at the CDU party conference in 1961 on the theme 'What is the German's fatherland?', concluded that it is the Germany of those 'committed to freedom' (*entschlossen zur Freiheit*).[18] In 1961 the federal chancellor and the retiring president of the federal supreme court complained publicly about a lack of national feeling among Germans. Some reacted by arguing that the whole issue was a hot potato better left alone but it led to the convening of conferences of academics, journalists and politicians to debate the whole issue. The SPD chancellor Helmut Schmidt's revival of Renan's thesis, that 'a nation depends solely on the will of those who wish to be nation. A nation is therefore a continuous plebiscite', 'the nation by will' (*Willensnation*), has not found wide support. Some concluded that it is possible to create a love of the fatherland without nationalism, a 'clean, normal or purified' national feeling. The Christian-Social Union, the Bavarian part of the CDU, has offered a combination of localism and the defence of Christian values, rather than nationalism. It looks to European union as a defence against communism and American trash and materialism.[19] In the 1987 election campaign, the leader of the CSU, Franz-Josef Strauss, came out vocally for a strong German national identity, saying that it was time Germans emerged from the shadow of the Third *Reich*.

[16] A.E. Alcock, *The History of the South Tyrol Question* (1970). 'South Tyrol separatists opt for bullet instead of ballot', *The Times*, 2 June 1987.
[17] De Gaulle's new constitution, significantly, removed a provision in the earlier constitution that France would accept limitations on its sovereignty in the cause of peace and European unity.
[18] Gerstenmeier frequently lectured on this issue. A collection of his talks was published in Stuttgart in 1965 under the title *Neuer Nationalismus*.
[19] Franz-Josef Strauss, *The Grand Design. A European Solution to German Reunification* (1965).

The debate continues. There is a huge literature but very few conclusions have been reached. Much of this debate is still conducted in terms of the German nation-state of 1871–1937 and its restoration and of the old categories of nationality: cultural/linguistic and subjective/objective. There are still very deep differences of opinion on the possibility of maintaining a common national consciousness in the populations of the two Germanies, especially as one important element of it, a common history, is being undermined. A leading academic supporter of the promotion of national awareness is the conservative political scientist Bernard Willms of the university of Bochum.[20] In a recent article he has written of a 'categorical national imperative' and argued passionately for a restoration of national feeling to give a sense of identity, vital for the spiritual health of a people: 'whoever attacks national identity attacks himself. ... A Socialist, who understands himself to be an internationalist and tries to operate politically in accordance with that, can objectively serve only the interests of the Soviet Union.'[21] An opposite view is taken by Professor H. Mommsen, also of the university of Bochum. In 1979 he published an article[22] as part of an exchange occasioned by a decision of the ministers of education and culture of the *Länder* that teachers of history and politics were to keep alive awareness of German unity among their pupils.[23] He questioned the assertions, made for example by expert witnesses in public sessions of the *Bundestag* committee on Inter-German Relations in 1978, that loss of national identity would lead to psychological damage and that a deracine youth, without a fatherland with which to identify, was especially dangerous. He also stressed the difficulties of teaching 'national' history without nationalism and expressed the suspicion that appeals for more 'national' history teaching were politically motivated. He sees particular danger in teaching about the lost lands and the notion that West Germans have a national duty to concern themselves about the internal affairs of the DDR.

In reality the situation has reverted to what it was in Germany before the 1860s: there is a great debate among politicians, journalists and academics but no evidence that the mass of the population are very interested in the issue. Conservative politicians are

[20]B. Willms, *Die Deutsche Nation* (Cologne, 1982). Serious contributions to the debate can also be found in G.–K. Kaltenbrunner, *Was ist deutsch? Die Unvermeidlichkeit eine Nation zu sein* (Freiburg, 1980) and E. Schultz, *Die deutsche Nation in Europa* (Bonn, 1982).
[21]B. Willms, 'Überlegungen zur Zukunft der Deutschen Nation', in Willms *et al.* (eds.) *Nation und Selbstbestimmung in Politik und Recht* (Berlin, 1984), pp 85–108.
[22]H. Mommsen, 'Zum Problem des deutschen Nationalbewusstseins in der Gegenwart', *Der Monat* 31/2 (1979), pp. 75–83.
[23]This originated in May 1978, when the CDU members of the North Rhine–Westphalian *Land* parliament passed a resolution calling for 'improvements' in history teaching, that is the introduction of a greater 'national' content.

reported to be making much more use than previously of the word *Vaterland* in their speeches. In the campaign preceding the January 1987 general election it was said that CDU politicians were using nationalist appeals as a vote-catcher, a process referred to as a 'raising of the taboo threshold'. In the manifestoes of the parties for the general election on 25 January 1987 only the Greens, in their statement on *Deutschlandpolitik*, came out for full recognition of the DDR and an end of 'the self-deception of an all-German identity'. Only the CDU/CSU mentioned 'nation' in its manifesto. In the election the CDU/CSU lost support, attributed by some to alarm among voters at the growing emphasis on nationalism. A policy statement of the new government in the *Bundestag* on 18 March 1987 stated an intention to preserve popular awareness of German history: 'We adhere to the unity of our nation .... We shall make every effort to keep alive the awareness of the unity of our nation'. The West German government has also revived claims to 'stand up for' *all* Germans, including those in the DDR and minorities in eastern Europe. An important statement of Bonn's policy on the German question was given in a speech by Dr Ottfried Hennig, parliamentary secretary of state in the Ministry of Inter-German Affairs, at the Royal Institute of International Affairs on 1 May 1987: 'People and nations have dreams. The Germans dream of a reunited fatherland with open and peaceful borders in a united Europe'. In spite of political divisions, the Germans are a 'community of fate' (*Schicksalsgemeinschaft*) and there can be no DDR nation because the Germans do not want it. Hennig denied that this is nationalism as unity is not placed above all other considerations: unity can only be achieved in freedom.

After the election it is likely that a revival of national awareness will continue to be a theme of the CDU. In the early summer of 1987 some commentators, reading between the lines of a speech by the Soviet leader Mr Gorbachev, claimed to hear hints of a reunification of Germany and recent opinion polls show that Mr Gorbachev has a higher popularity rating in Germany than Ronald Reagan.[24] An idea circulating in the early 1950s, before the two German states joined NATO and the Warsaw Pact, has recently reappeared and enjoys some support from the more radical Left, playing on anti-Americanism. This so-called Austrian solution posits that neutralism and a denuclearization of central Europe are the solution to Germany's problems. It suggests that both German states should withdraw from the ideological contest between East

[24]'As sparks fly upward', *The Economist*, 6 June 1987, pp. 60–3. For the 1986 manifestoes: *Prozeduren, Programme, Profile* (Bonn, Inter Nationes, 1986). For the policy statements: *Reports from the Federal Republic*, German Embassy, London.

and West and become the core of a united Europe, including eastern Europe, holding both super-powers at arm's length. By implication this would lead to a reopening of the question of the lost lands and the Sudetenland. Some politicians have suggested that the question of German reunification should be made an item in superpower disarmament discussions. This is quite unrealistic as it would involve the dismantling of the Soviet empire in eastern Europe. In July 1987 the president of West Germany, Richard Weizsäcker, visited Moscow but attempts to raise the question of reunification and representations on behalf of the German minority in the USSR met a very frosty response.

The tone of the debate has become sharper as a strange alliance of extreme Left and Right has tried to cash in on the national issue for political purposes, a ghostly echo of the National Bolshevism of the 1920s. The impact remains limited. In spite of the efforts of pressure groups like the *Kuratorium unteilbares Deutschland* (Curatorium Indivisible Germany) and the *Gesamtdeutsche Institut* (All-German Institute), there is no evidence of any great interest in the 'national' question or in the lives of 'brothers and sisters in the other part of Germany', as CDU politicians describe the citizens of the DDR, among the mass of West Germans. There is also no evidence of any problems arising from a deficient national identity. Suicides, crime rates, mental illness, alcoholism and broken marriages are not remarkably different in West Germany than in other similar industrial societies. Opinion polls show substantial support for the idea of the reunification of Germany but also substantial pessimism that it will be achieved in the foreseeable future. Events, in themselves trivial, can produce short-lived outbreaks of interest in the national question, but it is not an important issue in West German politics. In July 1986 a minor political squabble broke out in the state of Baden-Württemberg when a local school teacher taught children *all* the verses of the German national anthem, *Deutschland über alles*, when only one, verse three, is officially used. Parties of the Left condemned this while Conservatives came out in support of the teacher. There are faint echoes of the *völkisch* idea that Germanness is inherent in the landscape in the Green Movement's desire to protect German forests and rivers against destruction, especially when that destruction comes from foreign power stations or chemical works. Such environmental threats can, realistically, only be removed by international co-operation. The Greens also represent a reaction against materialism which has precedents in earlier nationalism. Awareness of the decline of knowledge of the German language abroad leads the West German government to devote considerable effort and money to promoting

German culture through bodies like Inter-Nationes and the Goethe Institutes.[25]

The Germans are still the largest nationality in Western Europe, totalling some 70 million. The place of West Germany in the 'Europe of ethnicities', which some politicians see as the future shape of the Continent with the dismantling of the 'power states' of the nineteenth century, is another problem.[26] It used to be accepted that, as a result of two world wars, Europe had finally evolved into a collection of nation-states but this has now been thrown into question again by the vogue of 'ethnicity' in certain circles. It is a kind of intellectual jig-saw puzzle in reverse, which envisages greater international unity, created by the EEC, NATO and the multinational company, being accompanied by the devolution of power downwards from the artificial constructs like France, Britain, Spain and so on to the Welsh, Occitans, Catalans, Flemings and so on, the ethnicities, the so-called basic building blocks of Europe. In its idealism and optimistic belief that this return to roots would solve the problems of modern man in an industrial society, the ethnic movement might be seen as a modern version of the Mazzinian vision of the 1830s. It is very hard to see how the Germans will be fitted into such a scheme. Germany was the last and the greatest construct of the nineteenth century but its inhabitants are of one ethnicity. Germany could only be dismantled by an artificial revival of some form of 'tribal' consciousness, as perhaps survives in the case of Bavaria. Of all the German *Länder* the 'Free State of Bavaria' retains the strongest sense of separatism, as has long been the case, but there are signs that other *Länder* are developing a consciousness and beginning to behave independently, for example in maintaining offices in Brussels to negotiate directly with the EEC Commission.[27] But what is a Lower Saxon or a North Rhenish Westphalian? Perhaps some Germans would prefer to be part of an ethnicity of 70 million.

It is possible that in future resentment of the division of Germany and of the fact that both Germanies are simply outposts of someone else's political system might develop, especially if the EEC fails. In the 1980s there have been some signs of impatience at the

---

[25]In 1986 the W. German government spent DM450 million (c£150m.) to encourage the spread of German abroad, an increase from DM320 m. in 1983. There is concern at a decline in the numbers studying the language at schools and universities in the USA and European countries and the closure of many university departments of German. German has also declined as an international scientific language and as a *lingua france* in E. Europe; information from the Goethe Institute.

[26]T. Nairn, *The Break-Up of Britain* (1981), chap. 8 'Supra-Nationalism and Europe'.

[27]'The coach that has eleven horses champing at their bits', *The Economist*, 12 July 1986, pp.53–4.

size of Germany's financial contributions to the EEC. There is no sign of mass opposition to Europeanism but serious questions are being asked about it.[28] It seems clear that European unity is a remote prospect and that nation-states will survive into the foreseeable future as there is no immediate prospect of viable institutions being created to take over their functions. Germans are realistically aware that answers to their predicament can no longer be found in national terms: the German problem can only be solved by foreigners. In Austria and West Germany at least, democracy has delivered the goods in material and psychological terms, which, it could be argued, no German government has done to the satisfaction of a majority of its subjects since 1789. Fear of a reunited Germany still exists among her neighbours. In 1984 the Italian foreign minister, Guido Andreotti, said in public: 'There are two German states and there should stay two German states'. Any change in the division of Germany will have to involve deep changes in the world as a whole and there is little that the Germans themselves can do about this. Helmut Schmidt has stated that the division of Germany is an essential element of the European balance of power which guarantees the peace of Europe.[29] It is now accepted that Austria is not part of Germany. Perhaps eventually, if satisfactory arrangements can be found to overcome the very real human misery caused by the division of families, which will not involve the DDR's population emigrating to the West, it will be accepted that there are two German states and that the division of Germany is a small price to pay for the peace of Europe.

---

[28]R. Dahrendorf, 'Europa als Ersatz für die Nation ist gescheitert' (Europe as a substitute for the nation has failed), *E.G. Magazin*, January 1982, p. 16.
[29]Craig, *The Germans*, p. 309.

Index

absolutism, 32ff.
Action Circle (*Tatkreis*), 198
Alsace-Lorraine, 127, 155–6
Alvensleben Convention (1863), 155
anti-Semitism, 147, 172, 190, 192–3, 211, 216
Arminius (Hermann), 152, 221
Arndt, E. M., 27, 43, 48, 81, 146, 151
Ausgleich (Austro-Hungarian Compromise) of 1867, 165–6
Austria, 32, 41, 58, 66, 102, 115, 118–20, 123–4, 220, 228; 1848 revolutions in, 84, 90f., 97; German nationalism in, chapter 7 *passim*; Austro-German Dual Alliance, 160–1, 170, 175, 177; Austrian Socialists and nationalism, 171–2; effects of the dissolution of (1918), 186f.

Baden, Crown Prince Max of, 181
Bauer, Otto, 172
Bismarck, Otto von, 7, 57; in revolution of 1848, 98, 104–5; basis of his policies, 101f., 114n.; as prime minister of Prussia, 108, 114–15; German policy, 118ff., 135, 208; as German chancellor, 153, 157, 160
Brest-Litovsk, treaty of (1918), 180
Brüning, Heinrich, 200–1

Carlsbad decrees (1819), 61, 69, 75, 78
Catholicism, Roman, 73–4; Catholic Centre Party (*Zentrum*), 153, 156, 199
Christian Democratic Union (CDU), 231
churches, 73–4, 96
Communist Party of Germany, 190

Confederation, German, of 1815 (*Bund*), 55ff., 85; North German (1866–71), 121
conservatism, 98–9, 122, 157, 189–90
culture struggle (*Kulturkampf*), 153, 156–7

Ebert, Friedrich, 182, 183
Enlightenment, 34–6
Empire, Holy Roman, 7, 21, 30–1, 40–2, 58, 128
Empire (*Reich*), German, of 1871, 128–9, chapter 6 *passim*
Erfurt, Union of (1850), 103f.
Erzberger, Matthias, 179, 192

Fatherland Party (*Vaterlandspartei*), 179, 190
Fichte, J.G., 25f.
Forster, George, 39
Frankfurt parliament (1848–9), 85, 88f.
fraternities, student (*Burschenschaften*), 77–8
Frederick III, German Emperor, 115, 134
Frederick William IV, king of Prussia, 81–3, 90, 95, 96–7
free corps (*Freikorps*) (1813–14), 43–4; in the Weimar Republic, 183, 191–2

German Democratic Republic (*Deutsche Demokratische Republik*), 220ff.
German Federal Republic (*Bundesrepublik Deutschland*), 220ff.
German National People's Party (*Deutschnationale Volkspartei*), 189f., 193, 197

Germany, definitions of, 7, 18, 88, 92
Gironde party, 38

Hambach meeting (1832), 74
Heine, Heinrich, 80
Herder, J.G. von, 24f.
Hindenburg, Paul von, 182, 183, 193, 200f.
Hitler, Adolf, 5, 171, 173, 175, 188, 191, 193, 200f., 208ff., 216f.
Hugenberg, Alfred, 197, 201

Jahn, Friedrich, 27, 44, 146, 151

Landwehr (Prussian militia), 96, 111
liberalism, 4, 22f., 35, 45, 54, 63–4, 69–77, 82–3, 99–100, 111–12, 121–2, 131–2, 158
Liberation, war of, (1813–14), 42–6
Ludendorff, Erich von, 178, 180–1
Lueger, Karl, 170–1

Mazzini, Guiseppe, 9
Marx, Karl, 10, 82, 95
Metternich, Klemens von, 43, 55, 58–9, 61, 85, 94
Mitteleuropa (Central Europe scheme), 161, 176
Mittelstand (lower middle class), 99, 147f., 178, 195–6, 200, 215

Napoleon I, 40–1; results of his policies in Germany, 50ff.
Napoleon III, 101–2, 115, 123
nationalism, general definitions of, 2ff., chapter 2 *passim*, 229f.; as a mass movement, 78–9, 86, 102, 115–16, 131, 194; conservative use of, 16, 80–1, 104, 133, 149f.; *völkisch*, 133, 139, 142ff., 170, 175, 190, 195, 215–16, 232; xenophobic, 28, 38, 119, 125; in West Germany, 225f.
National Bolshevism, 198, 232
'National Revolution', 175, 196, 208, 215
national socialism, 1, 130, 146, 175, chapter 10 *passim*; resistance to, 217

National Socialist German Workers' Party (NSDAP), 191, 195, 197, 201–4
National Society (*Nationalverein*), 116–17
Naumann, Friedrich, 160, 176
New Right, 185, 190

Olmütz, Humiliation of, (1850), 103

Pan-German League, 139–40
Papen, Franz von, 199, 201
Poles, German attitudes towards, 91, 154, 194
Prussia, 6, 31–2, 39, 58–60, 62, 107–8, 199; Prussian Reform Movement (1806–19), 46–50, 64; Prussian Army Crisis, 108ff.

radical movement (1847–9), 82–3, 86, 94–5
railways, 67
Renner, Karl, 172
revolution, German (1848), 83ff.; (1918), 175, 181ff.; French (1789), 4, 11, 21, 30, 33, 36ff., 51ff.; (1830), 74; (1848), 84–5; Russian (1917), 178
Rhine, League of the, (*Rheinbund*) (1806–14), 41–4
Romantic movement, 23f., 77–8

Sarajevo, assassinations at, (1914), 174
Schleicher, Kurt von, 199, 200, 202
Schleswig-Holstein, 87, 89, 91, 94, 119
Schönerer, Georg von, 169–71
Schwarzenberg, Prince Felix von, 102
Social Democratic Party of Germany (SPD), 159, 163, 190, 195, 199; in the 1918 revolution, 182f.
socialism, 95f., 113, 115, 138, 154, 158–9
Socialist Unity Party of Germany (SED), 204 n.21, 222
South Tyrol, 228–9

Spartakus League, 179, 184
Stein, Baron von, 44, 47–8
Stöcker, Adolf, 160

Taaffe, Edward, 167
teutomaniacs, 28, 79–80
Treitschke, Heinrich von, 1, 150
Trias (Third Germany), 58, 124

USPD (Independent Social
  Democratic Party of Germany),
  178–9, 182, 184

Versailles, treaty of, (1919), 185f.,
  189, 194

Wagner, Richard, 79, 144
Wartburg meeting (1817), 77–8
Weimar Republic, 175, 184, 185,
  188, chapter 9 *passim*
William I, king of Prussia and
  German Emperor, 110, 128, 152
William II, German Emperor, 5,
  134, 136, 151–3, 159, 161, 194;
  abdication, 182

Young Germany movement, 80

Zollverein (German Customs
  Union), 50, 65–6, 105ff., 121